James George

Thoughts and High Themes

Being a Collection of Sermons

James George

Thoughts and High Themes
Being a Collection of Sermons

ISBN/EAN: 9783337085940

Printed in Europe, USA, Canada, Australia, Japan

Cover: Foto ©Lupo / pixelio.de

More available books at **www.hansebooks.com**

THOUGHTS

ON

HIGH THEMES:

BEING

A COLLECTION OF SERMONS

FROM THE MSS. OF THE LATE

REV. JAMES GEORGE, D.D.,

MINISTER OF ST. ANDREW'S CHURCH, STRATFORD;

Formerly Professor of Mental and Moral Philosophy in Queen's University, Kingston, Ontario.

TORONTO:
JAMES CAMPBELL & SON.
MDCCCLXXIV.

PRINTERS, TORONTO.

PREFACE.

IN compliance with the expressed wishes of many to whom the author ministered in his lifetime, this series of Discourses is now published. Only two of those embraced in the volume, namely, "The Good Old Way" and "The Duties of Subjects to their Rulers," enjoyed the advantage of being brought through the press under the supervision of the Rev. Dr. George himself. These two being preached on special occasions, were published by request immediately after their delivery. The other sermons which go to compose the volume, were never intended for publication, and have consequently not had the benefit of receiving a revisal at the hands of the author. The discourses here presented are to be taken as average specimens of Dr. George's powers as a preacher, rather than as the highest efforts of which he was capable. The principle upon which the selection was made was that of securing variety in the matter of the publication; so that the topics discussed determined what discourses should be chosen, rather than the superior excellence of the discourses themselves. Many sermons of great beauty and power have been excluded, because the subjects they discussed ran in lines parallel to

PREFACE.

one or other of the topics elucidated in this volume. In the arrangement of the discourses, regard has been had to the natural order in which the subjects grouped themselves, more than to the relative merit of the sermons themselves. It will be observed that, in the discussion of doctrine, the author manifests no sympathy with the modern school of subjective theology. In both his teaching and preaching, Dr. George kept in the "Good Old Way," which he has so eloquently commended in Sermon VI. But it would be a mistake to suppose that, because he discountenanced what are known as new views in theology, his discourses are a mere repetition of commonplace utterances on the topics he discusses. So luxuriant is his imagination, so wide is his grasp of thought, and so full of splendour are his illustrations, that he invests the most familiar subject with a charm and freshness that cannot fail to interest the reader. But powerful as is much of the writing contained in this volume, no one who did not hear the author speak with the living voice can from them gather an adequate estimate of his effectiveness as a preacher. The man's very presence was so manly and noble that it set off his magnificent thoughts to advantage. And, then, his preparations were so carefully and conscientiously made, in order to be able to speak his discourses without the aid of the manuscript, that his subject had full possession of his whole being, when he ascended the pulpit; and this subjective identification of himself with the matter of his discourse imparted an intense realism to all that he said.

His utterance, too, was impassioned, sometimes soft and low, and at other times loud and vehement—the whole force of his mental and moral nature being concentrated, as it were, in the topic under discussion—so that the hearer's attention was compelled to the subject, his mind was flooded with light, and his heart stirred with emotion. Some may object to the length of these discourses. And if length was determined merely by the number of pages covered by them, respectively, there would, perhaps, be some ground for the remark. But length is a relative not an absolute term, in such a connection. Some discourses spread over *ten* pages would to a discriminating reader be longer than others extending to even *thirty* pages. No one listening to Dr. George as he preached ever thought his sermons long, in the sense of being tedious; and so, no one who prizes superior thought, clothed in a perspicuous Saxon style, will grow weary over these pages, or complain of the length of the sermons. The eloquent Preacher and Professor being dead, yet speaketh by these discourses; and they will no doubt be heartily welcomed, not only by his many friends and admirers but also by all lovers of sound thought and evangelical truth to whom the author may have been an entire stranger.

CONTENTS.

CHAPTER I.
GOD'S TENDER PLEADINGS WITH SINNERS.

PAGE

"How shall I give thee up, Ephraim? how shall I deliver thee, Israel? how shall I make thee as Admah? how shall I set thee as Zeboim? mine heart is turned within me, my repentings are kindled together."—Hosea xi. 8.   1

CHAPTER II.
THE BEARINGS OF CHRIST'S INCARNATION AND DEATH UPON GOD'S UNIVERSAL DOMINION.

"The Lamb which is in the midst of the throne."—Rev. vii. 17.   20

CHAPTER III.
THE INTEREST FELT BY ANGELS IN THE WORK OF REDEMPTION.

"Which things the angels desire to look into."—I. Peter i. 12.   34

CHAPTER IV.
THE TESTIMONY THAT DEVILS GAVE TO JESUS.

"They cried out, saying, What have we to do with thee, Jesus, thou Son of God?"—Matt. viii. 29......................   54

CHAPTER V.
THE TESTIMONY THAT DEVILS GAVE TO JESUS.—*Continued*.

"They cried out, saying, What have we to do with thee, Jesus, thou Son of God?"—Matt. viii. 29...............   64

CONTENTS.

CHAPTER VI.

THE GOOD OLD WAY.

"'Thus saith the Lord, Stand ye in the ways, and see, and ask for the old paths, where is the good way, and walk therein, and ye shall find rest for your souls."—Jerem. vi. 16 ...... **74**

PAGE

CHAPTER VII.

THE RIGHTEOUSNESS OF THE SCRIBES AND PHARISEES.

"'For I say unto you, that except your righteousness shall exceed the righteousness of the Scribes and Pharisees, ye shall in no case enter into the kingdom of heaven."—Matt. v. 20 ...... **104**

CHAPTER VIII.

WHAT IS IMPLIED IN NAMING CHRIST.

"'Let every one that nameth the name of Christ depart from iniquity."—II. Tim. ii. 19 ...... **115**

CHAPTER IX.

THE PURIFYING INFLUENCE OF CHRISTIAN HOPE.

"'And every man that hath this hope in him purifieth himself."—I. John iii. 3 ...... **127**

CHAPTER X.

THE OCCUPATION OF THE SAINTS IN HEAVEN.

"'Him that overcometh will I make a pillar in the temple of my God, and he shall go no more out; and I will write upon him the name of my God, and the name of the city of my God, which is New Jerusalem, which cometh down out of heaven from my God; and I will write upon him my new name."—Rev. iii. 12.. ...... **142**

CONTENTS.

CHAPTER XI.

BACKSLIDERS CALLED TO REPENTANCE.

PAGE

"Repent; or else I will come unto thee quickly, and will fight against them with the sword of my mouth."—Rev. ii. 16. 155

CHAPTER XII.

WITHDRAWING ABUSED MERCIES, THE RULE OF GOD'S GOVERNMENT.

"Whosoever hath not, from him shall be taken away even that he hath."—Matt. xiii. 12...................... 168

CHAPTER XIII.

DARK DISPENSATIONS OF PROVIDENCE.

"But it shall be one day which shall be known to the Lord, not day, nor night: but it shall come to pass, that at evening time it shall be light."—Zech. xiv. 7....................... 181

CHAPTER XIV.

THE DUTIES OF SUBJECTS TO THEIR RULERS.

"Let every soul be subject unto the higher powers."—Rom. xiii. 1.............................. 193

CHAPTER XV.

THE SOLEMNITY PROPER TO THE HOUSE OF GOD.

"How dreadful is this place! this is none other but the Aouse of God."—Gen. xxviii. 17....... 231

CHAPTER XVI.

THE TERCENTARY OF THE REFORMATION IN SCOTLAND.

"And Moses said unto the people, remember this day."—Ex. xiii. 3... 246

Thoughts on High Themes.

CHAPTER I.

GOD'S TENDER PLEADINGS WITH SINNERS.

"How shall I give thee up, Ephraim? how shall I deliver thee, Israel? how shall I make thee as Admah? how shall I set thee as Zeboim? Mine heart is turned within me, my repentings are kindled together."—Hosea, xi. 8.

THE Admah and Zeboim, spoken of in the text, were two of the cities that perished when God overthrew Sodom and Gomorrah. As a loathsome, universal corruption of morals prevailed in those cities, God, in justice, at length brought upon them terrible vengeance. He rained fire and brimstone upon them, and the earth opened her mouth and swallowed them up. Yet this was but the beginning of the misery of these wicked men; for an inspired writer tells us that the fiery tempest with which they were swept away was but the commencement of that eternal suffering which God has prepared, not only for them, but also for all that die impenitent. When God, therefore, threatens a punishment similar to that referred to in the text, He threatens, not merely temporal, but eternal, vengeance.

The expression, Ephraim and Israel, is merely an emphatic way of designating the whole kingdom of the ten tribes; as Ephraim was the largest and most influential of these. As the two tribes that remained attached to the house of David were called the kingdom of Judah, so the others were known as the people of Israel. As their revolt under Jeroboam deprived them of many spiritual advantages, so it led to many ill consequences. Their kings were wicked men, while the political, as well as the moral history of Israel, was to the last degree dark and repulsive. Yet God bore long with them. And we find that He sent some of His most gifted and zealous prophets—as Elijah, Elisha, and Hosea—to instruct, warn and reclaim them. For, although the ten tribes had withdrawn from the house of David, and but little frequented the service of the temple, they were still a part of the ancient church. Hence God dealt with them long in a way of mercy before He gave them over to final destruction. But as they were now ripening fast for destruction, the appeals of God by His prophets became at once more terrible and more tender. The Book from which the text is taken is full of illustrations of this. How astonishing are the words we have read!—" How shall I give thee up, Ephraim? how shall I deliver thee, Israel? how shall I make thee as Admah? how shall I set thee as Zeboim? Mine heart is turned within me, my repentings are kindled together."

Surely this language, uttered by the great God, is every way remarkable. To pass it over slightly were not well, for assuredly it is one of the most awful displays of what justice is in the Divine mind, and, at the same time, one of the grandest bursts of Divine tenderness to be found in the Bible. Yet it were not wise to explain this language with a rigorous analogy to the sentiments and emotions of the human mind. The expressions, " My heart is turned within me," " My repentings are kindled together," if employed to unfold the state of the human bosom, would give an expression of affection in the deepest agony. It would manifest all the tenderest and most powerful passions in terrible conflict with some insuperable difficulty—whether to give up, or to hold on, whether to smite or to spare, whether to try or cease to try any more, the affectionate and afflicted bosom knows not. As if an affectionate physician were in painful suspense whether to give up his patient as hopeless or make a further attempt; or, as if those in a lifeboat, who had again and again been buffeted back from the wrecked vessel, should say,— what can we do more? shall we make another attempt yet, or shall we leave them to perish? shall we give them up? Or, as if an affectionate parent were in a sore strait with a wayward child, betwixt the claims of pity on the one hand and the claims of justice on the other. Shall he, then, just give him up to destruction, or make even yet another effort to save him? How shall I give him up? how shall I leave him? My heart is turned within me, my repentings are kindled together. In man, this is affection in great strength, in sore conflict with difficulties, and it may be with the greatest of all difficulties, the claims of justice. Than this battle with sorely mastering difficulties, the human bosom has nothing to show that is more grand, solemn, tender and interesting. Yet it were not wise to liken this conflict, that affection may have in the breast of man, with the emotions of the Divine mind. It is true the human mind was at first an image of the Divine. It could then see truth clearly, and could be moved aright by the sight. These true emotions were then true passions. But sin, that hath spoiled so much, hath spoiled the human passions. The understanding is now darkened; hence our emotions are often not truthful. They neither spring from what is true, nor are regulated by the true. But our emotions, whether joyous or sorrowful, are no further right than they are true. All feeling that is holy and wise is founded on truth, while all passion not founded on truth is but madness and sin, and must end in misery. And, as even the best are to some extent under the influence of sin, and do not see truth perfectly, their emotions, with much that may be beautiful and tender in them, are not perfectly right. There is defect or extravagancy, perturbation or despondency.

Now, there can be nothing of all this in the Divine mind. God is true—sees all truth at once, and sees it perfectly. Hence, the Divine emotions must be all in the highest sense perfect. It were a daring presumption to attempt any metaphysical analysis of the Divine mind. Suffice it to say that, MERCY IN GOD IS BUT THE TRUTHFULNESS OF HIS GOODNESS TO THE UNWORTHY; *justice in God is but God true to Himself, true to His government, true to His creatures.* My brethren, what makes the mercy, as well as the justice of God so awful, is this—that both are truthful.

Now, you will perceive that our best emotions can give but a feeble, and even confused, reflection of the Divine emotions. Yet it is so needful that we should know something of the Divine emotions, that God has been pleased, as one may say, to translate the language of His own mind, into the language of the human bosom. In language entirely suitable to the mind of God, we possibly could understand but little of the Divine emotions thus expressed. You are not to think that the language of the text implies defect, pain, or perturbation. It is spoken after the manner of men, yet spoken with a truly heavenly accent. It shows us mercy coming forth in all its truthfulness, justice also coming forth in all its truthfulness: justice demanding that guilty Israel shall be punished, as Admah and Zeboim were; mercy willing to pardon, ready to bless; but mercy at the last point—cannot go a step further—cannot wait longer. Just and right is He, yet oh! the height and depth of His mercy when He says, "How shall I give thee up, Ephraim? how shall I give thee up, Israel?"

I shall throw the great truth which the text contains, into the shape of a question: HOW IS IT THAT THE GOD OF MERCY THUS STRIVES TO SAVE SINNERS? The answer to this question will illustrate the text.

I.—*Because it is a great thing that is to be saved or lost.* It is the immortal soul! Man was made at first but a little lower than the angels. His body, although material, is fearfully and wonderfully made. Yet the body with its wonderful senses and other powers, is nothing more than the covering of the man, or the instrument with which he works. That creature of reason, of conscience, memory, passions, and of moral excellence,—that creature capable of living eternally with God in the highest bliss, or of sharing with devils the terrible miseries of hell, — is man. Not the wealth, the honours, or even the body, but the mysterious, rational, conscious self, constitutes the creature, man. It is this that gives such peculiar value to his nature. A creature with such capacities for intellectual and moral actions, happiness and misery, as man possesses, must be intrinsically and relatively a creature of great value in the universe. We know but imperfectly the various works which God has created; yet assuredly, when we think of the capacities of the human soul, we cannot but regard it as a very wonderful work of God. The Saviour's declaration, "what is a man profited, if he shall gain the whole world, and lose his own soul?" plainly indicates its great value. It is possibly no exaggeration to affirm, that one human soul may be a greater work of God than the whole material universe. These great globes and shining suns are but masses of matter, but the human soul is immaterial. It came directly from God, has wonderful intellectual capacities, and can bear a likeness to the moral perfections of Jehovah. It is the highest honour and happiness of any creature to resemble the Creator in His moral perfections, and to voluntarily do His will, and be eternally happy in His friendship. All this may be affirmed of man : hence his greatness. And yet, does not his greatness appear in the fact that he can be damned? Brute beasts cannot. They have not the greatness, metaphysically or morally, to fit them either for heaven or hell. The moral conscience with which man is endowed, not to speak of other qualities, gives to his nature a wonderful greatness, and strange interest. In comparison with the infinite God, he is but a worm of the dust; in comparison with angels, when glorified in heaven, he will be in many respects on a par with them; and, if lost in hell, he will be in many respects there, in the greatness of his accountability and misery, on a par with fallen angels.

To boast, as some have done, of the dignity of human nature—forgetful of human depravity—is very foolish: bad theology, and bad metaphysics. But there is a folly on the other side, against which we need to guard. Let us not speak absurdly, when we speak of man as a degraded creature. Yes, he is, indeed, base and utterly vile, just because he is a sinner. But, then, the fact that he *could* sin, is a proof of a certain greatness—a proof that he could be a subject of moral government—was made capable of eternal rewards and punishments, and was fitted to be influenced by motives drawn thence. The creature of whom all this can be affirmed, is a creature around whom there hang momentous interests. But man is that creature, and it is with man that mercy and justice have to do; for, if he be not the object of the former, he becomes through all eternity, the victim of the latter. Although no created mind can estimate the worth of the soul, yet He that made it, and sees its destiny, knows this fully. Now, God loves not to destroy the works of His hands, and assuredly not this noble work— the immortal soul. Some astronomers think that one of the great planets in our system has at some period been shivered to atoms, and the fragments scattered through space. Without stopping to speculate on the probability of this, or daring to guess what may have been the causes of it, we may affirm that, if intelligent beings, angels or others, beheld this wreck of a world, they witnessed a very terrible spectacle of ruin; yet, if it was nothing more than the up-breaking and ruin of a material world, we speak soberly, when we say, that the same intelligent minds, beholding an immortal soul perish, witness a sight more terrible, than if a planet were smitten into ruins by the hand of Omnipotency. But to dismiss this illustration, we remark that, as One who sees what a soul is, and ever shall be, its salvation cannot but be an object of deep interest to God, who is infinite in goodness as in wisdom. Oh! my brethren, a most noble thing perishes, when the soul perishes. Hence, the God of love says, "How shall I give thee up?"—how can I leave thee with thy intellect, memory, conscience, passions, and moral actions, to perish? "My heart is turned within me, my repentings are kindled together."

II.—But the God of mercy thus strives to save sinners, *because He knows fully what the whole outcome is to be: eternal life on the one hand, to the righteous; but on the other, eternal death to the wicked.*

Very clearly, we are now under a moral government of rewards and punishments. Every wilful sinner feels that the way of transgressors is hard; while every obedient child of God comes in the end to know that wisdom's ways are ways of pleasantness. Yet it cannot be denied, that this mighty truth on which so much depends is rather indicated than fully illustrated in the present life. Not seldom are the righteous greatly afflicted, while the wicked may have much outward prosperity. Whatever there may be in this to perplex reason, there is nothing in it dangerous to faith. The Christian believes that at present he is permitted only in part to know this matter; and, furthermore, he believes that the course of God's moral government is now only seen in its commencement. The full manifestation, when all apparent anomalies may be cleared away, is to be in a future life. When the soul enters on its course in eternity, then it shall be seen that with the righteous it shall forever be well—that with the wicked it shall forever be ill. You all believe that as men sow now they shall reap hereafter; that if they sow to the spirit, they shall of the spirit reap life everlasting; but if they sow to the flesh, they shall reap everlasting death. These are, indeed, the true sayings of God, and, when believed, yield precious lessons, alike for warning and consolation. Yet, my brethren, who can comprehend what everlasting life or everlasting death is? Angels and the spirits of the just made perfect, who have long shared in the friendship of God in heaven, know far more of the former than the holiest man on earth; while devils and the spirits of the lost know far more of the latter than the most miserable sinner in this world; and yet, on the whole, how imperfect must the knowledge of creatures be on either of these matters! If the happiness of the righteous and also the misery of the wicked are to go on increasing through eternity, how little can really be known of what the eternal joys of heaven are to be, even by those who have been there for thousands of years, or how little can be known by guilty spirits in hell of what the miseries of that place may grow to in eternity!

But God knows the whole, perfectly. He, by His power, wisdom and goodness, made heaven as the home of the righteous. Its skies of never-fading light, its tree of life, its river of life,—in a word, all its material glories, whatever they may be,—are the works of His hands. But its intellectual and moral glories—its high, angelic society—its holy, lofty and gratifying pursuits were appointed by Him, and are upheld as sources of the purest enjoyment to those souls that He has made capable of participating in them. Nor must it ever be forgotten that, as God Himself is the real fountain of all enjoyment to redeemed souls, He knows what His perfections can communicate of happiness to the redeemed through eternity.

On earth, the best can understand the joys of heaven but imperfectly. John, who saw much of heaven in a vision, exhausts the most splendid imagery in giving a few hints of its glory; and Paul tells us, after he was caught up into the third heaven, that its wonderfulness was such that no words could express it. Yet a little of the vast may be known, and enough of heaven is known, to awaken strong hopes and ardent desires. There you will meet with the highest and holiest of creatures, converse with them, join in service with them, and share with them in their joys, while you will dwell eternally in a society where all is truth, confidence and love. And there, weakness, pain and sin shall forever be unknown. Yet who can comprehend the rich and varied happiness of the heavenly state? God only can fully comprehend that happiness, for He is the Author of it, and hath made the soul in its powers and desires capable of largely partaking of it. At His right hand there are fulness of joy and pleasures for evermore. The Omniscient God knows perfectly what this fulness of joy will be to His children, millions of ages hence.

But then, by sin we have forfeited that heaven, and, alas! man blinded by sin knows not what he has lost. But God knows it—knows what a boundless treasure heaven will be to the soul, and therefore in mercy He comes forth, not only offering heaven, but oh, marvellous! He pleads with men that they would accept of it—pleads with them that they would be eternally happy, and not destroy their own mercies by slighting His mercy; and hence He says to this one and to the other, how can I give thee up? how can I leave thee out of that heaven which I have prepared? all its sources of joy are full, will be lasting, and are ready for thee. All My saints will welcome thee, all My angels will rejoice over thee—how then can I give thee up? For if I give thee up, thou wilt not only lose this heaven, but be eternally miserable. "My heart is turned within me, My repentings are kindled together." "How shall I give thee up?"

And this leads me next, my brethren, to speak a little of God's knowledge of the misery that awaits those that are given up. He knows perfectly what this misery will be. On earth there is somewhat of the misery of sin felt when the sinner drinks even a few drops from the cup of punishment. What is said in the Bible of future punishment, gives a fearful expansion to the truth which experience teaches. Hell is utter darkness—a lake of fire and brimstone—a fire prepared for the devil and his angels—the worm that never dies. Admit that this language is, to a great extent, figurative, yet how terrible are the truths that these figures teach! Alas! the imagery, so far from being hyperbolical, must fail to unfold the truth; for is not hell the eternal abode of malice, falsehood, pride, and despair, in unchecked operation in powerful minds? No man who has felt the punishment of sin in himself, or has seen it in others, can be wholly ignorant of what hell is, while he who believes God's word on this subject has considerable knowledge of what future punishment is; and, were this knowledge pondered as it ought, in the moment of temptation, the soul might well be appalled when allured to sin. Yes, my brethren, hell is a place—a fact, a very terrible fact, in the universe. It is the place where justice clothes itself with vengeance, and reckons with those who have died in rebellion against God. Can that be other than a place of unutterable torment? Ah! and so it is. For who can dwell with unchecked malice and ungrateful pride? Who can dwell where there is no confidence, no truth, no love? Who can dwell where there is no hope, but despair, and despair ever? In a word, who can dwell with those everlasting burnings, kindled by eternal justice and kept alive by the omnipotency of God?

This is hell. These awful intimations are God's announcements. Yet, on the whole, how little can we really know of the prison-house of heaven's justice. No man can understand it fully. The human mind can at present but feebly realize the truth of these announcements. Nor must this be wondered at, for earth has no suitable image of hell. The anguish of remorse may be painful; but it is not the worm that never dies. The society of wicked men may now be painful; but wicked men are not on earth what they will become in hell, nor are they devils. On earth the rod of God may smite heavily, yet that is not like His wrath in hell; for amidst all our trials, reformatory or penal, here there is ever much to mitigate. But there, there shall not be one drop of water to quench the burning tongue. My brethren, we cannot understand what hell is. Oh! that we never may! But God knows what it is—to Him it has no covering. All its instruments of torture are known to Him, for He made them all. And then He knows what the soul, with its reason, memory, conscience, and passions, will have to endure when cut off for ever from His love, His help, and His friendship, and shut up with other depraved and malignant spirits in darkness, anarchy, and despair. To the eye of God all this is seen, while He sees that the sinner, dying without His mercy, must by divine justice be consigned to this place of misery as his portion. Now, the God of mercy, seeing all this, says, "How shall I give thee up?"—give thee up, immortal soul, to this eternal woe? How shall I deliver thee over to avenging justice in hell? "My heart is turned within me, my repentings are kindled together."

III.—But the God of mercy thus strives to save sinners, *because of what has been done for their salvation.*

The grand want of the sinner is pardon. But those who fancy it easy for the holy Ruler of the universe to pardon sin, have never thought deeply on the matter. Yet that has been done, which not only renders the pardon of sin possible, but the granting of it glorious to God, while the bestowment of it is every way beneficial to the pardoned, and indirectly the cause of an increase of good to all holy creatures. The Son of God did this. The Word was made flesh, that what was necessary for pardon might be done by Immanuel. "God so loved the world, that He gave His only begotten Son, that whosoever believeth in Him should not perish." God spared not His Son, but delivered him up to do and to suffer all that is necessary for the granting of pardon. "Herein is love, not that we loved God," or were worthy of His love, but that He so loved us, that He "sent His Son to be the propitiation for our sins." These are the terms in which the Bible speaks of what was done, that guilt might be removed, and man brought home to God. The Son of God did this work, and the work done is our redemption. Without faith, my brethren, you will see nothing in all this to awaken either your admiration or your love. And with such faith as many of us now have, we see but little of the greatness of this work. Yet, oh! how marvellous! how wondrous in design! how astonishing in execution! and how truly great in its benefits for sinners! You cannot look at the work of redemption in any aspect without exclaiming, What wisdom, what power, what condescension and love, are here! Without attempting anything like a full answer to the question, What was done that man might be saved? I would briefly remark that the incarnate Son of God did all, and suffered all that is necessary to vindicate the government of heaven from all appearance of weakness, vacillation, or inconsistency in granting a free pardon to the guilty, and in opening heaven for their admission to a full participation in the friendship of God. The decree which all holy creatures must have understood is this: Die, *man*, or *justice* must; but when the Saviour came forth and in man's room died, justice lived; and whosoever believeth in the Son may live eternally. Oh! yes, to Him it was death, the whole death. For, from the manger in Bethlehem to the cross on Calvary, it was death; for all this while He was a sin offering, and in His soul and body, sustained by His divinity, He met that awful death, by which He ransomed myriads of our race from eternal death. "And darkness was over all the land till the ninth hour," and Jesus cried with a loud voice, and then rocks were riven, and the veil of the temple was rent. Ah! my brethren, the mystery of godliness was then meeting its accomplishment—justice saved, and yet man saved. And so it was when He said, "It is finished;" the darkness vanished, for the mighty work was done. Hell was vanquished, man saved, heaven regained, and God glorified.

There is full provision, then, my brethren, in what the Saviour has done, not only for the pardon of the sinner, but for his full acceptance with God. The work of Christ is, for this, in every sense perfect. Nor is the merit of His sacrifice, or the efficiency of His Spirit less now, than when first applied for the salvation of souls. He is as able and as willing to save now, as when He ascended from Mount Olivet; and the heaven He purchased, has been long since prepared for His followers.

In a word, all things are ready. The atonement finished, the door of mercy opened, the spirit sent to strive and to sanctify; so that the invitation is "Ho! every one, come." Come, ye guilty, and get pardon; come, ye depraved, and get holiness; come home to your Heavenly Father's arms, oh! ye outcasts, for all that ye need can be granted with honour to God the Father, and with honour to God the Son, and with honour to God the Spirit, and with joy to all angels, and the souls of the redeemed in heaven, and with benefits abundant and lasting to yourselves.

Now, all things being thus, the God of Mercy speaks in the text, "How shall I give thee up" to ruin? How can I deliver thee to destruction after all this has been done? Well might God say, as He does by another prophet, "What more could I have done for my vineyard than I have done?" What more could He have done for thee, sinner, than he has done? He has given His Son to redeem thee, His Spirit to sanctify thee, His friendship to support and comfort thee in life, and He offers thee His heaven as thy home at death. And hence it is that, amidst all this fitness of things for thy salvation, the God of Mercy is heard saying, "How shall I give thee up? My heart is turned within me, my repentings are kindled together." But,

IV. God in mercy thus strives to save sinners, *because He knows, if He gives them up, they are in every sense lost.*

Those who believe in God as their Creator, believe in Him also as their Preserver. But the pious man as readily admits his dependence on God for all spiritual blessings and future enjoyments, as he does for his temporal support. On God we must depend for everything which we need, either as creatures or as believing Christians. No truth commends itself more readily to the reflecting mind than this—that, if God gives up any creature, it must either be to annihilation, or to an existence of misery. It is utterly impossible that any creature should be separated from God and continue in a holy state, or be at all in a condition to taste happiness. But there is reason for thinking that creatures endowed with a moral conscience are never to be annihilated. When devils were given up they were not annihilated, but left to be miserable. Creatures with a moral conscience, when they rebel against God, lose their holiness, and are given up by Him, must in every sense be wretched. The Word of God teaches this with terrible plainness. Hence, when God says, "they are joined to idols, let them alone," they are, in a fearful sense, given up to be lost. But in order to show more clearly what this giving up implies, I would notice two or three particulars.

And, first, *when the sinner is left to his own ways*, to gratify his own passions and appetites, and to live to himself and for himself, *he is given up*. Now, this is just what poor, infatuated mortals earnestly desire. But this is madness—and, if all madness is not sin, yet surely there is no madness like the madness of sin. Leave the sinner to his own way—to nurse his pride till it turn him into a selfish, arrogant fiend—to nurse his vanity until he is crazed by the most pitiable follies—to nurse his avarice till he is turned into an earth-worm, forgetful that there is a God to be feared, a heaven to be sought, or a hell to be dreaded—to nurse his sensualities till he is turned into a brutal idiot, with nothing but selfish and voracious appetites—to nurse his malice, till he is turned into a monster of insatiable revenge. Ah! my brethren, it is even so—to this it comes—for when God gives up a sinner, so that the infatuated man is left to choose his own ways, and to follow the devices of his own heart, and the allurement of passion and appetite, is not that man lost?

But, in order to see the danger of being given up of God, let us carry our enquiry a step further. 1. *Men when given up of God, become the helpless victims of Satan.* It is unnecessary in a discourse of this kind to inquire at large into the character and pursuits of devils. Suffice it to say that, from the malignity of their nature, they seek to dishonour God by destroying man, or rather by destroying the image of God in man.

It does not admit of doubt that an intelligent mind in alienation from God will, as temptation offers, become more and more wicked, and sink deeper and deeper into misery. But the human heart is not left to the spontaneous operations of its own depravity; devils are ready and powerful auxiliaries in expanding this depravity. We do not stop to inquire into the mode of Satanic influence. Experience, as well as the Bible, teaches that much of the wickedness of man springs from Satanic influence. Indeed, the sinner being given up to the power of Satan, then the course of depraved human nature is literally set on fire by hell. Then it is that the lascivious wish becomes the foul act—the malicious thought, the murderous deed—for, under Satanic influence, conscience is seared, shame lost, God defied, consequences disregarded, and all manner of sin committed with greediness. For then comes that dreadful infatuation when men "put darkness for light and light for darkness, and call good evil and evil good," going on from iniquity to iniquity as if they had made "a covenant with death and an agreement with hell." Yes, thus it is when God gives up the sinner to the unchecked dominion of Satan, to be tempted, deluded, tormented.

But lastly, on this.—2. *The sinner given up of mercy becomes the victim of avenging justice at the hand of God.* Assuredly there is fearful justice in giving up the sinner to his own depraved will, and the power of his spiritual enemies. Nor can it be questioned that much of the punishment of sin will consist in this. But God's fair creation is not to be made the battle field in which depraved dispositions, or the evil passions of different orders of creatures, are to fight out their penal and terrible results. Hell is the place prepared for this, and is indeed the place in which justice in its more comprehensive forms will take effect on those whom God has given up. But as I have already directed your attention somewhat to this subject, let it suffice at present to remark that the sentence once passed by the Judge, " Depart from me, ye cursed," and the gates of perdition then forever close—the soul is then forever given up. No place more for repentance. Mercy that goes so far cannot go there. Many a pardon has been vouchsafed just on this side the gate of hell, but no pardon has ever been granted to any within the prison walls of that place. When the justice of God consigns a soul to that place, all is lost. This prison door never shall be opened. The voice of mercy shall never sound more in the ears of those who despised it. For those who enter there are for ever given up—given up to all the effects of sin in their own passions—given up to the influence of malignant and despairing creatures—in a word, given up to all the punishments which a just God sees meet to inflict on the impenitent. My brethren, is it not most true that if God gives up the sinner, all is lost? Hence, the God of mercy, seeing all this, says, "How can I give thee up? how can I leave thee?" "My heart is turned within me, my repentings are kindled together."

So much for the illustration of the truth contained in the text. And now I conclude with one broad inference and a brief application.

Our inference is that if the sinner resist this Divine

tenderness, and treat with indifference all that this implies, he must be given up.

I have shewn that this tenderness is the mercy of God ardently seeking the salvation of sinners. It has been also shewn that this manifestation of Divine compassion is made through Christ. It was through His bleeding wounds and His breaking heart, that this mercy of God could come forth to lost sinners. God in Christ is all mercy to the believing penitent; nor does He offer mere acquittance of punishment, or mere impunity to the sinner—for this of itself would be little—but He offers also His own Fatherly love, with all that this implies; and He offers this most sincerely, urgently and tenderly. Now let me ask, how can he escape who neglects this? But some may be ready to exclaim, Why all this ado? If God is in earnest to save sinners, where is the difficulty? He is omnipotent, He surely can do it. This is a dangerous, although plausible delusion. Yes, God is omnipotent, and by His omnipotence He can do much; but mark it, it was not by a mere effort of omnipotence that sinners could be saved, else the Word incarnate had never lain in a manger, or been nailed to a cross. True, God can save sinners, but He can only do it as a just, holy, and wise Governor of the universe. God will save, but He will do it in His own way—in a way that is wise, just, and good; not according to the folly and caprice of men, for that would not be either for their good or His glory. The question then is not, Is God willing to pardon the most guilty for the merits of Christ? The whole Bible answers this in the affirmative; the text is a conclusive answer; but the question is, If ye treat the blood of the covenant as an unholy thing; if ye do despite to the spirit of grace pleading with you; if ye despise the mercy of God offered to you, tell me, then, for this is the question, How do you expect to get pardon? If ye will not accept the blood-bought pardon, offered with all the tenderness of Divine compassion, how can ye be saved?

Do not think of it, do not dream of it! God's omnipotency cannot save you to the dishonour of all His moral perfections.

Blessed be God! there is salvation; but it is in no other name than the name of Christ, and through no other way but through the mercy of God in Christ. But then, he who will not accept of pardon in this way, must be given up. What hardness of heart! What infatuation of soul! "Come, let us reason together," saith the Lord, "Although your sins be as scarlet, they shall be as wool!" No, says the sinner; except in my own way, and on my own terms. Wonder, oh heavens! and be astonished, oh earth! wonder at the all gracious Ruler of the universe, thus pleading with men, that they would not destroy their own mercies. And wonder at the madness of men, who by their unbelief are virtually saying to God, Leave us! Give us up! Yea, and such must and shall be given up, as thus neglect and despise the great salvation. I cannot tell you at what point, in this despised forbearance of God, the angels of heaven and the redeemed would rise and demand that those who thus despise God's mercy and Christ's blood should be given up. Yet doubt it not, if these beings rejoice over the sinner that is converted, they can also, with their ardent love of God, and high sense of justice, when they see the eternal throne insulted, exclaim, Let them be given up! Hallelujah, let the Lord reign! Yea, and methinks that the spirits in perdition will also at a certain point demand that despisers of mercy should be given up. There must be not a little of a strange sense of justice in hell. And might not those who have been justly condemned for their offences, rise up and exclaim, If they are to be saved that have thus despised such offers of mercy, how is it that we are damned? But the most terrible view of all is, that the justice of God will demand that such shall be given up. God will be true to Himself; and He has declared, that those who will not believe in the Son shall never see life. Gospel despisers, who can resist all this tenderness of the love of God, must be given up.

But in fine, my hearers, how can ye resist this? Is your heart harder than the nether millstone? Are you resolved to go to damnation, trampling on the cross? Are you resolved to go in amidst the wailings of perdition, with these accents of the God of mercy ringing in your ears?—" How shall I give thee up? how shall I deliver thee? Mine heart is turned within me, my repentings are kindled together." No, no; thou wilt not. Thou man, that hast never cried for mercy before, cry for it now. Go to thy closet this night, and cry earnestly to the Lord, Give me not up, leave not my soul to perish; but save me, thou God of mercy, save.

CHAPTER II.

THE BEARINGS OF CHRIST'S INCARNATION AND DEATH, UPON GOD'S UNIVERSAL DOMINION.

"The Lamb which is in the midst of the Throne." Rev. vii. 17.

EFORE proceeding to unfold the doctrine contained in these words, it is needful to fix the sense of the two terms, "Throne" and "Lamb." When taken literally, the term "throne" signifies the royal seat of a prince. But in its figurative sense, the word often represents the abstract notion of sovereign authority. Hence, in those passages in which we have the phrases, "The throne of God," or "The throne of judgment," it is the sovereign authority of God that is meant; and in a more especial manner does the term throne signify His moral sovereignty: Jeremiah, 14–21. It is not denied but there may be a literal sense attached to the phrase, "throne of God." The supposition is fair, and supported by some share of evidence, that there will be at the day of judgment a glorious something, on which the Judge shall appear in the air; and there is also ground for supposing that there is a place in heaven of surpassing glory, which is called the throne of God. But in the text, and in other passages, the term "throne" is to be taken in its figurative sense, as implying the sovereign dominion of God over His moral creatures.

To those who are acquainted with the phraseology of Scripture, it is at once apparent, that the term "Lamb" is applied to Christ as the sacrifice for sin. Under the Jewish dispensation, the lamb was not only offered frequently, but on such solemn occasions, as to mark it out as a chief type of Christ. Hence, when the Saviour made His first public appearance as Mediator, the Baptist pointed Him out, as "the Lamb of God which taketh away the sin of the world," or, in other words, as the true sacrifice for sin. To the same purpose is the declaration of Peter: "We are redeemed by the precious blood of Christ, as of a lamb without blemish and without spot;" while the song of the ransomed in heaven is, "Worthy is the Lamb, who died to redeem us from our sins." And John tells us, that one of the wonderful visions he had of heaven revealed to him "a lamb as it had been slain." These passages conclusively fix the sense of the term "Lamb," as applicable to Christ, as the true sacrifice for sin. It is therefore with a singular disregard of the plainest truth, when men have affirmed that the term "Lamb" is applied to Jesus because of His meekness and gentleness. That He possessed these qualities in the highest degree is not denied; but when He is called the "Lamb of God," it is clearly not His moral qualities that are designated, but His atoning sacrifice for the sins of men, with all that this implies, in accomplishing redemption.

Having thus fixed the sense of the two terms, it is easy to see, that the meaning of the whole phrase, "The Lamb in the midst of the Throne," implies that an atoning Saviour is the central object in the moral government of God, as seen in heaven. We may assume what there is abundance of evidence to prove, that the whole work of redemption is well known in heaven. Now, the doctrine we adduce from the text is this: that those of God's intelligent creatures in heaven, who would acquire the clearest and fullest views of the moral reign of Jehovah, will find these in the work of redemption by a crucified Saviour.

In illustrating this doctrine, I shall show:—

I. That the redemption of Christ unfolds, even in heaven, the highest view of the necessity of a government of moral law.—For "the Lamb is in the midst of the Throne."

By the necessity of the moral government of God, we mean that it is in the highest sense fit that He should rule over His creatures, and that, in the nature of things, it ought not and cannot be otherwise. Finite minds cannot rule for themselves. All sin is just the attempt to do this; and hence the anarchy and misery which sin produces. He only who created minds can rule them. But the reign of God over intelligent beings is far different from that which He exercises over material agents and irrational creatures. It is a reign by fixed principles, sustained by rewards and penalties, as creatures are obedient or disobedient. All nature obeys God; but intelligent minds can alone, by a loving volition, own Him as Supreme King. His omnipotency keeps other creatures in harmony, and makes them answer the end of their being; but it is His moral reign that keeps rational minds in harmony with each other, and in harmony with Himself, as the source of all wisdom, truth, and goodness. The rational soul not only feels the force of moral government and discerns its equity and its benefits, but can see the whole flowing from the Divine mind. This is the peculiar excellence of rational creatures, and in this lie their responsibilities, their means of high advancement, and their purest enjoyments. Hence, to deny the necessity of the moral reign of God is at once to dishonour Him, and to sink man down to a creature of mere instincts and physical influences. Thus it is that atheists, while they strip man of his moral responsibilities, always deny him every hope of a future existence. Whatever, therefore, weakens our notions of the moral reign of God is to the last degree pernicious. But it is not enough for the high ends of our being that His government is admitted—it must be clearly seen and felt; and just the more fully it is realized, the holier do intelligent creatures become, the higher do they rise in the scale of existence, and all the greater and purer is their happiness. The application of this must be equally true to all minds, in all places and at all times alike. Hence, the text teaches us that the highest lessons that can be learned of the moral government of God in heaven are learned from the redemption of Christ: For He is "the Lamb in the midst of the Throne."

In showing how Christ, as Mediator, unfolded the necessity of the reign of God, I remark:—

1. That He perfectly obeyed the Divine Law.

As a Divine person He was not subject to Law, but as Mediator He came fully under it. To all the laws of God, ceremonial as well as moral, He was entirely submissive. Hence His own declaration that it behoved Him to fulfil all righteousness. He came not to do His own will but the will of God. Indeed, all that He did and said was but practically carrying out the petition, "Thy will be done on earth as in heaven." Nor was this obedience less perfect in suffering than in doing the divine will. In the depths of His agony His language still was, "not my will, but thine, be done." But in His active obedience this was more fully brought out, as during the whole of His sojourn on earth, He acted the part of His Father's servant. Now, there must have been something of highest moment to be accomplished by this. The making of an atonement was a grand end of His incarnation, but not the sole end. The truth is, that while He was to atone for a broken law, He was also to magnify an unbroken law. He thus bore the penalty of the former, and likewise showed the glories of the latter; for in being the Father's servant in obeying, He showed how equitable, wise and good the law of God is. Hence, He not only taught with incomparable clearness and beauty what the law of piety is, and what the law of justice and charity is, but by His whole conduct He illustrated both branches of the Divine law. He did this in all the relations in which He stood to God and man. Thus it is that the life of Christ is the most perfect exemplification of what piety towards God, and justice and charity towards men, are. It is but little of Christ's excellence that unbelievers can see, yet a little has been seen and acknowledged even by infidels; for some of them have owned that the character of Jesus is the consummation of moral excellence. This is true to a far greater extent than they can comprehend it, but its truth lies simply in this, that He kept the Divine Law perfectly, for the beauty of Christ's moral character is but the beauty of the reign of God in a perfectly holy mind. It is not affirmed that nothing more of excellence was in Him than a perfect conformity to the Divine Law; but this perfect conformity and its results is the subject we have at present to do with.

Now, that the Son of God should as Mediator have been for three and thirty years perfectly obedient to the Divine law, is an amazing fact, and mighty ends must have been answered by it. Yes, and mighty ends were answered; for it proved that the law of God was perfectly just, wise, and good; it showed that there was a high necessity in the nature of things that the reign of God over His creatures should be sustained.

But, 2. Christ obeyed the law from love.

Much is done when the law is taught and illustrated, but, to the high ends of obedience, right motives must also be taught. The grand motive is love! Hence, says the apostle, "Love is the fulfilling of the law." Other motives may be auxiliary to this, but without this they become worthless. God will be feared, but it must be with a loving heart; His servants are to have rewards, but they must seek these under the influence of a supreme love to him. God will not be served because He is omnipotent, but because he is all excellence. He will reign, not by the mere terror of His arm, or by bribing creatures to submission, but because He only has the right to reign, and because obedience to Him, in confidence and love, is the only moral condition in creatures—honourable to Him and beneficial to them. Hence, He requires that His intelligent creatures shall serve Him from love.

This is grand, beautiful and simple; but this was fully illustrated by Christ. It was love to the Father that brought Him into the world; it was love to the Father that animated Him in all that He did and suffered. So that Christ, as Mediator, was not only entirely submissive to the Divine will, but all His obedience sprang from love. And thus He showed not only that obedience is right, but that love is its grand motive. Truly He magnified the law, made it honourable, showed it to be one of the grandest of God's works; for, in keeping it, He unfolded what the reign of God is in its principles, motives and results. What a grand development was this! The obedience of Christ gave it as it was never given before. He showed that for the servants of God to obey, is their place; is to answer the highest ends of their being; that in this way the reign of God, so necessary to His glory, and so essential to their happiness, is carried on. Yes, it is "The Lamb in the midst of the Throne!" For the redemption of Christ in His active obedience will proclaim through all eternity the necessity of the authority of God. Has not the whole universe thus got the most luminous exposition of that statement, "The Lord will reign?" Can creatures who know the work of redemption ever conclude that it is possible God should be indifferent as to His own reign, when they know that the Son of God, when He became Mediator and the Father's servant, was in all things perfectly obedient to the Divine will? And wherever this is known,—and I take it that it will be known throughout the whole universe,—it also will be known how unspeakably important the moral government of God is. Not all the eloquence of angels, not all the thunders of Sinai, could proclaim in such majesty the necessity of the reign of God, as was done by the three and thirty years of the obedience of the Son of God as Mediator.

Having thus shown how the obedience of Christ establishes, to all intelligent minds, the necessity of the moral government of God, I come now,

II. To show how the redemption of Christ unfolds the nature of the Divine reign.

1. It does this by showing that God's government is conducted by love.

It has already been stated that love in creatures is the grand motive to obedience; but we are now to prove that love is the grand principle in the mind of God in carrying on His government. It is a vicious logic that attempts to define a passion or emotion by a single term, as if the passion were a separate element of mind. Is not love rather a mood of the whole mind than a distinct element? Is it not just the mind delighting in excellence, and seeking rightly the diffusion of happiness? Suppose this to be correct as to the mind of creatures, it becomes us nevertheless to speak with great caution on moods of the Divine mind. Yet surely there is nothing rash in the supposition that Divine love is God's infinite delight in excellence, and desire to diffuse happiness. Now, whatever shows that His government is conducted on this principle must be of the last importance to all creatures under it. Redemption does this, as it shows,

1st. *That God delights in the excellence of His creatures.*

By sin man had lost all excellence—had become loathsome and degraded; but by redemption we are created anew. The redeemed are sanctified. Their souls are restored to a likeness to the moral excellence of God. Hence we see that God delights not only at first to communicate His excellence, but to restore it to creatures who have lost it. Among fallen men love is supposed to consist in gratifying the mere likings of others. But in the reign of God, as seen in redemption, the love of God seeks the happiness of its objects, by first making them excellent or holy. Hence there is in His love no weakness or caprice, but the most perfect wisdom; so that all its favours are unmingled benefits. The redemption of Christ fully shows this, but,

2nd. *It also shows somewhat of the depth or richness of Divine love in the reign of God.*

The angels of heaven and all holy creatures, from their high endowments and the rich and varied blessings they possess, cannot but know well that God is good. But redemption has unfolded such a depth of His love that they now know it to be boundless. If He hath given us His Son, will He not with him freely give us all things? So reasoned the apostle, so will all creatures reason in heaven. After this unspeakable gift creatures can never entertain a doubt that God's love will keep from them anything which His justice and wisdom can grant. In the gift of His son, He hath passed the finite; everything else lies short of this. It is not assumed, however, that even this can enable creatures fully to comprehend the love of God; for that is literally infinite. Yet, far as the intellectual vision of a creature can search, it never can reach a point beyond the gift of His Son. This in reality must have presented a new and grand view of the depth of the Divine love.

3rd. *But redemption shows at the same time that the love of God is not merited.*

It brings out this momentous truth, that creatures are not the *cause*, but the mere *recipients*, of His love. True, He may promise them rewards for obedience, still this is but a development of His own love. The arrangement sprung from it; the power to perform the condition was a result of it; the benefit, the fruit of it. But may it not be of the last consequence that this should be placed in the clearest light to all minds? Redemption has done this. For the gift of His Son, with all this implies, is so unspeakably great, that whatever may be thought on earth, be assured of it, intelligences in heaven see clearly that this never could have been merited. But as all this was conferred on sinners, who in no sense could have a claim of merit on it, may not this unfold the broad principle in the clearest light, that the reason why any order of creatures have happiness, is not to be traced to their merit, but to God's love? Assuredly the redeemed from among men will ever feel this with a profound and peculiar gratitude. Yet, may not the thing that was done specially for them, and which puts the thought of merit, when they taste their blessings, utterly out of the question, teach indirectly to all other creatures, that their blessings also are in a sense unmerited, and flow directly from the love of God? And thus the mode of His reign will be still further unfolded.

4th. *The love of God in redemption has been manifested in wondrous condescension.*

Betwixt God and the highest of His creatures the distance is infinite. So that intercourse with the highest, or favours bestowed on them, is condescension. But, when both of these things are done to a low order of creatures, the condescension then becomes the more apparent. This is vividly seen in redemption. The angels that had sinned were far nobler creatures than man, yet no mediator was provided for them. Christ took not their nature on Him, but the nature of man. It was, therefore, in behalf of an order of creatures low in the scale of being that the highest manifestation of Divine love was given. But this condescension of God's love is not seen, unless there be a clear perception of what the second person of the Trinity condescended to do. It was He that became man, that was born in a stable, that lived a life of poverty, that submitted to the malice of men and devils, and at last died a shameful and painful death. To redeem men, it was needful that all this should be done, and the Son of God did it. Say it was His human body that was spit on, buffeted, nailed to the cross; that it was His human soul that was in an agony. Yes, and yet was not His human nature all the while united to His Divine? It was Immanuel, personally, that passed through all this. Oh! what condescension of love! Comparisons, in other matters so useful, are out of place here. For what were it should the mightiest monarch descend from his throne to toil in a ditch to aid the meanest family—to this? What were it should the mightiest angel descend to earth, and take on him the position of the most loathsome beggar—to this? This was not the love of a pure, but distant, sympathy, that stands on high and scatters benefits down on sufferers far below. It was love that came down and took on itself all the wretchedness of the low and degraded sufferers. For, although in the form of God, and thinking it no robbery to be equal with God, yet He humbled Himself and became obedient unto death, even the death of the cross. Oh! what love! Oh! what condescension of Divine love!

But let us see how this applies to the reign of God; for, says our text, "the Lamb" was "in the midst of the Throne." God can rule the universe, because He is love. Now, we have shown that redemption unfolds His love to all intelligent minds in the clearest, grandest and most tender forms. For in this His love is seen to be the highest delight in excellence, and is seen to be a love so vast that having done this, it can do aught that is possible; and in this His love is seen to be unmerited, so that all the happiness of creatures springs from Him. And in redemption His love is seen in amazing condescension. Now, what a view must all this give of God as a ruler! What confidence must this view of His love inspire in His reign! Shall not intelligent creatures, seeing in redemption what the love of God is, rejoice to obey Him who reigns by such a love?

2. But, next, redemption shows to all creatures that the reign of God is the reign of justice.

It is a simple and comprehensive definition of justice to say that it is the preserving of rights, holding sacred what, in the nature of things, belongs to God, so that all things are properly rights of His. As Creator, all creatures belong to Him as His rights. As the source of moral order, all law essentially belongs to Him as a right; and, as the Supreme Governor of the Universe, its peace, happiness, and moral beauty are His rights. When men, therefore, talk, and oftener think than express it, how easy it is for God to pardon sin unconditionally, they little understand what they say. Yes, it were easy for God to grant unconditional pardon, if it were easy for Him to give up His rights as Creator, Lawgiver, and Judge of the Universe. For, be it remembered, that sin is a direct assault on all these rights of God. To permit these rights to perish were at once to resign all that is essential to Him as God; were to give up His universe to anarchy, and to allow the caprice and will of creatures to take the place of His sovereign authority. This is what unconditional pardon must lead to.

But in subordination to, and in connection with the rights of God, creatures also have rights. The obedient have the rights of happiness, the disobedient the right of punishment. We deny that this is an arbitrary arrangement. It is in the nature of things essentially the product of consummate wisdom. With reverence be it spoken, God would be unjust if he punished for obedience, but equally unjust if He did not punish sin. For, if the right of obedience be happiness, the right of sin is punishment. But, say they, He may punish or not as He chooses. Yes, if He can choose to give up all His rights as Creator, Lawgiver, and Sovereign Ruler—cease to act by fixed principles, and act arbitrarily and leave all rights to be supplanted by wrongs. Such is the foolish and impious conclusion to which we are led, the moment we assume it possible that pardon can be granted, short of the condition that all rights are sustained.

But there is pardon for sin through the redemption of Christ, just because that redemption has in it a condition that sustains all rights. The condition in redemption secures all the rights of God as Creator and Supreme Ruler. It secures also all the rights of holy creatures, and, we may add, the rights also of the guilty and impenitent. Had God left guilty men, as He did rebellious angels, to that punishment which is the right of sin, He had done them no wrong. But pardon was to be extended to man—myriads of our race were to be saved, and this was to be done, not by God giving up any right, but by laying the punishment of our sins on Christ. Hence these declarations, "The Lord hath laid on Him the iniquity of us all," and "His own self bare our sins in His own body on the tree." No creature could bear this, nor was any creature dragged out as a victim on whom this vicarious punishment was laid. The Son of God had the right voluntarily to offer Himself. He said, "Lo, I come," and He did come, and, by the assumption of our nature and our cause, made Himself a sin offering. In dealing with this momentous matter, we are not called upon to solve the question, whether the Saviour endured as much suffering as His people would have had to endure throughout all eternity. It is enough for us to know that His sufferings amounted to what in the fullest sense sustained the rights of God, as Creator, as Lawgiver, as Judge of the universe. This is what is meant by that mighty, but much misunderstood phrase, the righteousness of Christ. Yes, my brethren, your Saviour was perfectly holy, but you will mark it, it was not His holiness that made out a righteousness for God to act by in granting pardon, nor a righteousness for sinners to stand up under in receiving pardon; but it was what He did as Mediator, and especially what He *suffered*, that made it right in a holy God to grant pardon to those who believe in Jesus. God might, as we have said, put all to rights by simply punishing the sinner; but in that case the sinner would have perished. But when the Son of God bore the punishment due to sin, then it became all right in God to show mercy to the believer in Jesus, inasmuch as the substitute met the right of sin, which was punishment. The imputation, then, of man's sin to Christ, was simply Christ bearing what was man's right to bear— the punishment; while the imputation of Christ's righteousness to man, is simply the mercy of God extended to man, for what the Saviour did and suffered in sustaining rights. We know that Christ did this in the fullest sense. "Father," said He, "if it be possible, let this cup pass from me; yet not my will, but Thine, be done." And the Divine will was done. For there was no abatement of the Divine claims, and just because God could give up none of His rights, and yet would give pardon to sinners. Is it asked, where is mercy then? Mercy, my brethren, is seen in this matter everywhere; but is seen nowhere amidst the ruined rights of God. For the mercy of God is not the destruction of order, that anarchy may prevail; is not the destruction of law, that the lawless may live; is not the subversion of rights, that wrongs may be established. Ah! no. This were not mercy. The mercy of God is His goodness to the unworthy; but in granting it no worth must perish, and hence Christ had to merit it by bearing the penalty of sin. Now, this is the mighty lesson which redemption unfolds to the whole universe, that the reign of God, even when He is showing mercy, is a reign of the most perfect justice, by which all rights are gloriously sustained. Pardon could not otherwise be possible. Pardon is certain, for the Son of God could do that mighty thing. Hence, the redemption of Christ has given the most awfully grand view of the reign of God as just. No creature that knows what the Son of God had to suffer before pardon could be granted, can ever think that God will give up any of His rights. "Father, if it be possible," said He. It was not possible. And if it was not possible in His case, when He had taken up the right of sinners, which was punishment, shall it be possible in their own case to escape that punishment which is their right? To all angels, to all men, to all devils, the redemption of Christ hath settled this question.

3. By the Lamb in the midst of the Throne may be meant not only a new view of the reign of God, but *a new visibility of the Divine Ruler.*

Immanuel is God. Every creature that sees Him sees a present God in a way that all nature cannot show. But on this I do not enter.

In conclusion, then, what a work of God is redemption! God manifest in the flesh! This thing is altogether extraordinary! Infinite wisdom must have intended to elicit from it the mightiest results. The salvation of man is to us its direct result, and will ever be its most interesting aspect. But its direct benefits in the salvation of man, although the most wondrous, may not be its greatest or its most widely diffused benefits. To us the Lamb of God *on the cross* is the all in all; but the Lamb of God *in the midst of the throne* may be to the whole universe the all in all as to the reign of God. Not that the worlds of holy creatures could know nothing of His reign except from this. Assuredly, from many a source they could learn much as to what He is, and how He reigns. Nevertheless, it seems plain that when the highest of creatures in heaven, or creatures in any other part of the universe, wish to learn the most profound, the most cheering and the most awful lessons, they must turn and seek their information from redemption. It is in this that the reign of God is seen in ineffable splendours. For in this the principles of His government are seen to be for ever immutable, and His reign is seen to be a reign of perfect love and of perfect justice. Hence, the angels desire to look into Christ's work; hence, the Saviour has thus gathered into one all things that are in heaven and things that are on earth; and hence, thrones, dominions, principalities and powers are subject unto Him. For in Him dwelleth all the fulness of the Godhead bodily. He is the image of the invisible God. For "the Lamb which is in the midst of the throne" is the grand development of the reign of God.

CHAPTER III.

THE INTEREST FELT BY ANGELS IN THE WORK OF REDEMPTION.

" Which things the angels desire to look into." I. Peter, i. 12.

THE things into which the angels desire to look are the essential and peculiar parts of the Work of Redemption. The context clearly shows this. The words employed by the Apostle are the strongest compound terms which the Greek language furnished. It were out of place to enlarge on the force and beauty of the original. Suffice it to say, that the sense which it conveys is that angels contemplate the work of Christ with intensity of mind, and that, not merely as high intellectual observers, but with emotions of the most ardent love.

The Bible does not profess to give a circumstantial account of the attributes or pursuits of angels. This is not a defect. Revelation is not, in the proper sense, a history of the universe, but a history of man, and of man's redemption. Nevertheless, from many hints, incidental it is true, yet sufficiently clear, a careful reader of the Bible may gather the following facts :—that angels were the first creatures that God made; that they are the highest creatures, are perfectly holy, possessed of great powers, are capable of great improvement, are constantly engaged in the service of God, and take the deepest interest in whatever displays the Divine glory.

Such creatures must feel a pleasure in studying even the least of God's works, and from the contemplation of the least must derive some advantage. The least production of the Divine mind reflects some rays of the glory of that mind. With what interest and advantage then must angels have contemplated the work of redemption, a work in which every attribute of Jehovah shines with full splendour, and every person of the Trinity is so peculiarly employed. Shall this chief work of Jehovah yield to angels no new information, nor enlarge their previous views, nor open up for them any new sources of happiness? Such a supposition were contrary to all sound theology, as it were dishonourable to the work of redemption. We do not mean that angels received from the work of Christ, salvation, or their first stock of enjoyment. Pardon, regeneration, and a title to the Divine favour, which are the direct benefits of redemption, are benefits in which sinners—sinners of our race—alone can share. Christ "took not on Him the nature of angels."

But, among the many things peculiar and remarkable in the works of God, this is not the least, that, while there is one main and direct result, one class of creatures which the work is intended specially to benefit, the indirect results may be numerous and great, and extend not to one but to many orders of creatures. Now, if this principle holds in the work of redemption, and doubtless it does, then angels may share largely in its indirect benefits. From this, it is true, their happiness has not sprung. We have rason to believe that angels were and would have remained happy though the Son of God had never appeared as a Redeemer; yet, who will say that this work of God has not tended to increase their happiness, improve their intellectual dignity, and enlarge their sphere of labour in the Kingdom of God? Accurate notions of redemption and of the character of angels will lead to the supposition the reverse of this. In my own mind there is not a doubt that angels acquired information at the cross of Christ, as well as new elements of feeling, which must have given additional dignity to their character, and furnished them with many new enjoyments. This is not mere surmise.

The proof for it stands prominently out in our text. Nor do we need to rest the proof upon one isolated passage. If we examine the Book of Revelation, in which we have many hints as to the spiritual economy, we find that angels are represented as adoring and praising Messiah for what *He has done.* If they cannot join with the redeemed in singing salvation through His blood, yet how ardent is their song! Admiration, love and gratitude breathe in every note! They adore Him for having opened the seals of the Book which none else could open —they adore Him as the Lamb slain. A careful analysis of this portion of Sacred Writ would, I am convinced, throw great light on this interesting subject. But this we cannot attempt. Let us, however, take one quotation from Paul—Ephesians, iii. 10.—" To the intent that now unto the principalities and powers in heavenly places might be known by the Church the manifold wisdom of God." Here is decisive proof how much angels are indebted to the work of Christ for some of their choicest advantages. But let us endeavour somewhat fully to show what these benefits are, and how they have resulted from the work of redemption. I remark :—I. That the work of redemption must have benefited angels greatly *by presenting before them more accurate and enlarged views of the moral perfections of God.*

Angels must know much, very much, of God. Creatures who are endowed with such great powers, who traverse the universe with such rapidity of motion, who survey the scenery of a world or a sun at a glance, who can look, it may be, at a system of planets in motion, as *we* may at a piece of machinery, must possess wonderfully clear notions of the omnipotency and omnipresence of God. The works of God thus beheld furnish, to creatures of high intelligence, not so much the materials for induction, as evidence which compels an instant assent to the eternal power and Godhead thus seen. The demonstration is, indeed, seen as soon as the data. It is worthy of notice that the knowledge of the eternal power and Godhead lies the first in order for creatures to learn, is rapidly acquired, and is on the instant complete as to proof. The reason for this is plain. Such knowledge of God is indispensable as a first element of piety. Hence, the notions of the being of God, and of His omnipotency and omnipresence are acquired from creation with very great distinctness. And is there not the same abundant and clear evidence for the moral perfections? Unquestionably; yet, to the mind of man or angel, as far as we know, neither is this sort of knowledge presented in the same mode, nor does it rest on the same kind of evidence. Making allowance for the original impress on the soul, we apprehend that all knowledge of the moral perfections of God must be acquired from an observation of His dealings with accountable creatures. But, in order that this treatment shall be seen, and the lessons which it is fitted to teach learned, time and circumstances, both common and peculiar, under which creatures are placed are requisite.

A knowledge of the moral perfections of God must be to all creatures of the greatest consequence. It was probably some capital mistake on this very matter that led to the first outbreaking of sin. A defect on this point stamps any rational creature with degradation, while gross ignorance of the moral attributes must lead to misery. On the other hand, just in proportion as the purity, love, justice and truth of God are seen, and loved, and revered, so will the minds thus instructed and moved rise to higher dignity and be fitted for more enlarged enjoyments. This, we presume, is an universal truth, and is applied to angels just as much as to men. Nor ought it to alter this conviction when we admit the great excellence of angels: yet, from a fallacy of imagination rather than of judgment, we are apt to suppose that the angelic mind, from its original qualities, as well as from its capacious adornments, has hardly any room left for making advances. This is to forget that, how great soever the distance may be betwixt them and us, the distance betwixt them and Jehovah is still not less than infinite. An archangel has still boundless room for improvement, and shall not the very excellence of such creatures prompt them to seize every opportunity by which their knowledge of God may be enlarged, and their feelings still further elevated and purified?

Now, we affirm that, of all the works of God which are known to us, the work of redemption is best calculated to teach a full knowledge of His moral perfections. In it all the moral attributes are as clearly displayed as is His omnipotency in the greatest works of creation. The three attributes, wisdom, justice and goodness, so essential to a perfect moral governor, are in redemption brought fully into view. We do not say that angels were ignorant of these attributes until they saw them in redemption. Far from it. We believe that from the moment of their creation they had a knowledge of them, and this impression must have been deepened by every part of the Divine treatment towards creatures, which they ever beheld. Still we think it may be shown on good grounds that, much as angels knew of these perfections, their knowledge was far from possessing completeness until they saw them manifested in redemption. And next, we think it may be shown that in the work of redemption there was given to them, as well as to all the intelligent universe, the most perfect demonstration of the moral perfections.

It derogates not from the honour of God to affirm that until redemption was finished, His perfections of wisdom, goodness and justice appeared often to conflict, or rather one or other of these was seen but imperfectly, even by the wisest creatures. He knows best when and how to reveal Himself to His creatures. Let us examine this for a moment. His goodness would be perfectly seen in the happiness which He had diffused among creatures. His justice would be evidenced in the punishment which He brought on the violators of His authority, while perfect wisdom would, no doubt, be seen in both this goodness and justice. This for all would be plain. But, may we not suppose that in the case of our world there would arise a mysterious peculiarity? Man had sinned, had offended the same God that devils had offended. He is driven from Eden; but not into hell. He is forbidden to taste the tree of life; yet he dies not as a malefactor dies. For him a grand design of mercy is revealed. Did angels not rejoice in this, and yet was there not, along with their joy, much perplexity? Had they not seen God punish their guilty compeers? This was just. But had they not heard the threatening, " In the day that thou eatest thereof thou shalt surely die?" Yet man lives. Is God partial, unjust? Shall His threatenings fail—shall His truth perish? Far from such minds be the impious thought. Never for a moment did their faith and loyalty swerve from their Eternal King. Yet, well may we suppose that darkness rests on the scene, and the highest minds are perplexed, and must wait for light.

It is the glory of God to conceal a matter. Say not there was no concealment, that in the first promise, and subsequent announcements, the ministers of the eternal throne saw not only the design of mercy to man, but also the mode by which mercy and justice were to be equally honoured. Readily do I grant that the typical economy, especially when illuminated by the vision of prophecy, taught much of Him that was to come. To us, all is clear. But before the event happened, it might be far otherwise to the wisest observers. My brethren, there is something so amazing, so peculiar, in the fact that the second person of the Godhead should assume human nature and die in the room of sinners, that it must have become matter, not of prophecy and of figures, but of history, ere it could be clearly understood. But it must not be forgotten that the mode of redemption was the very hinge on which the moral government of God may be said to have revolved. It was in the *mode* that the intelligent universe was to find the solution of every difficulty. But, was the mode clearly seen from the first, and if not, may we not suppose it was often whispered in heaven, not with suspicion and fear, but with anxiety and wonder, if man is to be saved how is God to be just? Before the throne was there a seraph that could answer this question?

Was the angelic mind, then, held in suspense for four thousand years? And did these high spirits feel themselves compelled to recede from many a lofty conjecture and speculation, and seek repose in the simple faith that the Judge of the universe will do right? This is more than probable. Nor would this keeping in abeyance of high powers produce waste of power. The angelic mind thus held under check would acquire vigour from the effort to move forward, and learn a profound resignation from the impossibility of advancing. It may be highly necessary that the wisest creatures shall at times reach a point where created wisdom utterly fails, and then be compelled to pause, till God shall say, "Let there be light." Thus shall they learn that the source of their being is the source of all wisdom.

Possibly the mind of the universe has its grand periods or revolutions. If so, may we not suppose that the breaking out of sin in heaven was the commencement of one of those eras, and that the words "It is finished," uttered on the cross, closed it? At all events, great lessons were learned during this period. Circumstances had occurred which had evolved the moral perfections of Jehovah on a grand scale. The fall of Satan, the fall of man and its consequences, had shewn much, both of justice and mercy. True justice, mercy and wisdom were seen from heaven, were felt in earth. There was light, but it was light shining in darkness, or, like the wheels in the vision of the prophet, the light was terrible and the shining glorious, but the motion was complex and mysterious. It was in redemption that angels beheld the moral government of God, as simple in apparatus as it was grand in its parts—as perfect in justice as in benevolence.

For in this work each perfection was seen in individual glory, as all were seen in mutual triumph.

But, now, let us enquire more fully how the work of Christ furnishes such perfect instruction on the moral perfections, and, of course, on the moral government of God. I remark :—

First. That in this work the *justice* of God shines forth in awful majesty. No conception can be more terrible than that of a Being of omnipotency without perfect justice. And, the more clear the notions of creatures are of the omnipotency of God, the more need is there that they have equally clear conceptions of His justice. We have shown that angels must have had from the first grand conceptions of the power of God. Now, any work of His that would give them equally grand and full notions of His justice would not only tend to enlarge their sentiments but greatly to increase their happiness. Proofs of justice they had had in the punishment of guilty creatures ; but a grander proof remained to be given in the punishment of imputed guilt in the Son of God. Angels had heard the curse denounced on man, yet they had seen many of our race saved. They knew far too much of the Divine Government to suppose that the sacrifices under the law, or the imperfect repentance of man, could take away sin. They would see that justice must be satisfied. If the atonement was to be vicarious, still there must be satisfaction to justice. It was vicarious. Justice was satisfied, and though no creature could have devised, or, if he had, could have ventured to propose the substitution of the Son of God in the room of sinners ; yet, when this *was* done, and when the atonement was made, angels would clearly discern in the awful transaction the most awfully grand display of justice.

I shall take for granted that many of these creatures were in attendance on the Saviour, and watched with deepest interest every incident in the closing scene. And saw they not, think you, the justice of God as they never saw it before? Did they see the Son of God in an agony, when His soul was sick unto death? Did they hear that prayer: "Father, if it be possible, let this cup pass from me!" Did they hear that bitter complaint on the cross: "My God, why hast thou forsaken me?" Did they know that the Father loved the Son, as no creature can be loved by Him, and yet did they see that Son, when He stood the substitute for sinners, left in darkness that fell just short of despair? Oh! yes, they knew that there was love in the Father's bosom for the Son, yea, infinite love. But with Him there was also justice, and that justice must do its perfect work; the curse was then in being borne, man was to be saved and God was to be true—and true He was, for the dart threatened fell on the Son. Oh! most plainly did these high intelligences see the justice of God in every drop of blood, and in every tear which the Saviour shed, and they heard its awful demands in the groans and cries which He uttered. Did they not at that hour exclaim with astonishment, this is justice, this is the justice of God? If the eternal King, the Father of mercies, must not abate one iota of the law's demand, when His own Son is the sufferer, who shall harden himself against the Almighty and prosper? Fall what may, come what will, perish who shall, justice shall never fall, dishonour on His authority shall never come, and His truth shall never perish. Be assured of it, my brethren, that never, never, was the conviction of all this so deeply felt by angels as when they saw the sword of Jehovah awake and smite the Shepherd of His people.

But, further, the *wisdom* of the Divine mind was no less clearly displayed in redemption than was justice. On this I shall only make a few observations. Looking at the scheme of redemption as a whole, we hazard nothing when we affirm that no work of God with which we are acquainted gives such displays of wisdom. How utterly amazing the means, how wonderful the adaptation of the means to the end, and how great the end! How glorious in wisdom is the whole—the union of the Divine and human natures—wonder of wonders! Thus the curse literally fell on the nature that sinned, for it was the human nature of Christ that suffered; yet, inasmuch as no creature could bear that suffering, omnipotency is exerted in this union, so that the Divine sufferer is enabled to bear the penalty. And then, when we think of the union of believers to Christ, and the work of the Holy Ghost, the change by which a sinner becomes a child of God, an heir of glory, is of itself a wonder, to which no change or matter can bear any comparison. These are but a few points in this scheme, and the more it is seen, the more we are impressed with the conviction that the whole is a grand display of infinite wisdom. But before we can form any just conception of this wonderful work of God, our dull apprehension must be greatly sharpened, and we must know a great deal more regarding our own nature, and our eternal destiny, and a great deal more of the perfections of God. But to the angelic mind, which saw all this with wonderful clearness, we cannot doubt but in the work of redemption they then saw the most perfect proofs of Divine wisdom—and of Divine wisdom displayed in moral government.

But the *mercy* of God was most conspicuously displayed in redemption. When the inspired writers speak of God giving His Son to die for sinners, they seem utterly lost in admiration of His love. Words are wanting, and language fails even these eloquent men, and they utter the glorious sentiment in broken sentences and ecstatic hints. "Herein is love," says one, as if no manifestation of Divine love was worthy of being compared to this. Amidst all the acts of Divine benevolence, it is ever spoken of as standing alone, peculiar. And no wonder that these gifted minds, fired with intense conceptions, were overpowered with the glory of this love. We see it, alas! but as a distant star is seen, bright, but small. Inspired men, and holy angels, must have seen this love, as that same star is seen by those who stand near it, and behold in it all the splendours of a sun. Angels had seen much of God's love in heaven, and often must they have exclaimed, Great is His benevolence; but when they saw the love of the Father in sending His Son to suffer for sinners, they must have exclaimed, Oh! the height, the depth, the breadth, the length of this display—it passeth knowledge. Had God sent His Son to our earth to utter words of wisdom, and to reveal some design of mercy, it had been great kindness; but to send Him to assume our nature, and to be a man of sorrows, for three and thirty years, and at last to die, that rebels might live, what goodness, what benevolence, what wonderful mercy! But oh! my brethren, I want enlargement of intellect, and I have not the burning zeal necessary to speak aright on this sublimest theme; nor do I think it will be until we see hell close on the damned, until we stand at the foot of the Throne, until we know much, very much, of what the love of the Father is to the Son, until we see Jesus face to face, until we see the hands that were pierced holding the sceptre of the universe, until we see the head that was crowned with thorns crowned with glory, that we shall be able to form anything like just conceptions of the love of God in redemption. The intellect, the love, the zeal of angels, and the place where they dwell, fit them for taking grand views of this love, and think you they have not been moved by the sight? Have they learned nothing new from it? Has it given to them no new enjoyments? The reverse we must suppose to have been the case. If there ever was a manifestation of Jehovah that struck all heaven with mute astonishment, when silent amazement was the only praise, when the seraph found his harp unfit for the song, it was when the hosts of heaven beheld this manifestation of Divine love. For aught that we know, angels may yet witness far greater displays of God's powers in creation, and greater proofs of wisdom in the organization of matter and mind; but the greatest display of love hath been given, with reverence be it spoken, that God can give, and great as the acts of His love may be, never in eternity shall any creature be able to say: Here is love greater than was seen in the gift of His Son. To the love of God in redemption, angels and men shall ever revert, when they wish to think and to feel how great is the love of God.

And, hence, from what has been stated, it must appear plain that angels would acquire a vast enlargement of knowledge on the *moral perfections* of God from what they saw of these in the work of Christ. In this they beheld justice as it was never seen before, and in the incarnation of the Son of God, and in bringing greatest good out of direst evil, they must have seen great wisdom, and in this they saw mercy so magnificent, that for a time it seemed, if I may so speak, to impoverish heaven that it might enrich eternity, and cover the sceptre of God with new glories, and fill the crown with new gems. Say, then, is not redemption a great work, and have not angels gained much from looking into it? Oh! my brethren, it is not fancy to suppose that during those hours when darkness hung over the earth, and the veil of the temple was rent, the whole angelic mind was moving forward to higher ground, from which these noble creatures were to view Him that sitteth on the Throne under a new, and more awful and interesting light, and at that time opening up emotions purer and higher, than even the angelic mind had yet felt? Amazing crisis! Thrones, principalities and powers were then entering upon a grander cycle of knowledge and happiness. But I remark,

II.—That angels, from the work of redemption, *would obtain more distinct notions of the evil of sin.*

It were easy to shew that accurate notions of sin must furnish to angels most essential wisdom, and many lessons of highest utility. Sin has not only presented created minds in a new and terrible aspect; it has also given occasion for peculiar displays of the Divine mind. This of itself would be sufficient to lead angels to seek an accurate knowledge of the nature of sin. But, further, we apprehend that in proportion as they see the evil of sin, so will they discover the beauty of holiness, the nature of happiness, the worth of moral government, the source and dependence of all virtue, the justice of God in punishing sin, its eternal incompatibility with Divine holiness, the degradation from which they had been preserved, and the misery from which they had escaped—these are high and practical lessons which would be learned from clear views of sin. And, possibly, these lessons are not less, but even more needed, the higher creatures stand in the scale of being.

It is true, angels saw much of the evil of sin before they saw it in redemption. They saw it first in heaven. We cannot conjecture how pure spirits felt when they saw, for the first time, God dishonoured, and His authority opposed—opposed at the foot of the Throne. Great must have been their horror when they saw their compeers cast down their harps in scorn, and exclaim, "Let us break their bands asunder:" "who is Lord over us?" The change on such creatures, in such a place, the change from benevolence to malignity, from truth to falsehood, from purity to pollution—in a word, their mad hatred and impious rebellion against their Maker and benevolent King—must have given on the instant an appalling view of the nature of sin.

We know not how long it was after this before our race was seduced. But, when this happened, the nature of sin would be still more clearly understood. It would be seen that those who were once benevolent spirits had become the disseminators of misery; that the mischief, dreadful thought, might be spread through other orders of intelligent creatures. But not in Eden only—in the awful consequences, in the violence, falsehood, dishonesty, pollution, the utter degradation of souls on earth, and the eternal ruin of these souls in hell—would angels find plain enough proofs what sin can accomplish on moral natures. It was, however, in the life and death of the Saviour that they saw the evil of sin most fully. The nature of sin was displayed under a very awful light, in the treatment which the Saviour met with from men and devils, and especially from the suffering which He had to endure, when His Father dealt with Him as under imputed guilt. A few remarks on each of these points will show how clearly the nature of sin was brought out in the work of redemption.

We cannot doubt but the appearance of the Son of God on earth gave rise to joyous anticipations among angels. They knew this Divine personage, they knew His benevolence, they knew the glory He had with the Father, for they had seen Him adored and served in heaven, and the song which they sung at His advent evidenced their joy and their anticipation—the anticipation that the reign of peace and happiness was to commence on earth under Messiah. Was it not natural for such creatures to expect that so soon as His majesty and benevolence shone forth, that as soon as His wisdom was heard and His love displayed, every human heart would be filled with reverence and love, and every mouth filled with praise? They had seen the greatest of God's messengers abused, yea, some of their own order insulted; but surely man will reverence the Son. This we suppose was a universal opinion in heaven when Christ appeared on earth. What, then, must their astonishment have been when they saw His majesty and benevolence treated with indifferency or contempt, when they saw His benevolence met with cruelty, His love with hatred, His condescension with slander, His wisdom with insolent folly, and His omnipotency blasphemed as Satanic power! Man made in the image of God is roused to fierce malice when that image in its glory is displayed before Him by the incarnate Son. He showed man the Father, and they hated Him. He did before them the works of the Father, and their malice knew no bounds. Practical demonstration this, of the nature of sin.

It was, however, at the closing scene that all the virulence of sin broke out. "Away with Him, away with Him, crucify Him, crucify Him," cried those who had seen His miracles and shared in His benefits. Had He not healed their sick, given feet to the lame, bread to the hungry; had He not instructed the ignorant, and given joy to the desponding, and had He not shed tears of compassion at the sight of their approaching ruin? Yet, with one voice, they cry out, "Crucify Him, crucify Him." This was sin in its fruit, and that fruit in perfection. Did not such outbreakings of pride, malice, ingratitude and mortal hatred, as angels witnessed against the Son of God in the palace of the High Priest and in the Judgment Hall, and on Calvary, show to them, with terrific certainty, what sin is?

But there was another and more painful aspect in which the same thing was to be seen. All His disciples forsook Him and fled. If in His enemies there was supreme malice, in His followers, oh! what treachery! One of them betrays Him for thirty pieces of silver, and he that saw Him on the Mount of Transfiguration denies that he knew Him! Sad sight! Yet in the oaths, and falsehood, and treachery of Peter, the evil of sin was clearly seen, and not the less so that he who thus acted was, upon the whole, a great and good man. Angels were possibly not more struck with the mercy that spared and pardoned the fallen Apostle than with what sin could accomplish in such a nature. In this way they learned what it is, not in a devil, but in a saint.

But in this dreadful scene there were other actors than mortals. That night hell was moved, and the subtlest spirits of the pit rushed to share in a conflict which was to decide the empire of Satan. Devils appear from the first to have had dim yet dreadful forebodings regarding Messiah and His work, and now had come the time when these forebodings were to be realized, and hell gain a temporary triumph—expectation or fear sufficient to arouse Satan to desperate deeds.

Is there a recognition of persons and feelings among spirits? If so, then angels can see devils and in some measure discover the temper of their mind. Saw they the temptation in the wilderness, in it they must have seen much of the nature of sin. But surely the last temptation was emphatically "the hour and power of darkness," the grand effort of Satanic wrath. It was the struggle of despair for falling empire. Now, may we not suppose that angels saw approaching these fiends of darkness, saw their voice more hell-like from the boundless malice, mysterious terrors and wild anticipations, which filled their minds at this time? Do they see these beings thus fierce and mad gather around the Son of God, assail Him with all the loathsomeness and malignity of hell? All this they might see. And now say, was there not something in this near and bold assault of devils on such a personage that must have presented sin in a more audacious light than when the same beings made war in heaven? This was, with reverence be it spoken, hell encountering divinity. This was a conflict not so much with the authority as with the very person of Deity. But here the foot trembles and the tongue falters, and we hasten back—yet we cannot quit the scene. Did angels see the leer of triumph on many a demon's cheek, when the crown of thorns was placed on the head of the Son of God? Did something like joy, a frantic lurid flash, light up many a malignant countenance as they saw the Son of God smitten with the scourge and spit upon? Did they see, or wildly think they saw, Him now put to shame, to lasting shame, in the face of the universe? Did holy angels, we say, see this joy of hell, this malice of damnation, this gladness of despair, at the sufferings and the shame of the Son of God? Suppose it, and then say, did they not see in it all the richness of iniquity, the very bottom of hell's hatefulness? Was ever the nature of sin so displayed? For these very spirits who thus assail the Lord of Glory, and rejoice when He is smitten, and are glad when He is scourged, were once pure servants, praising and serving Him, and bowing lowly before the throne. What awful transformation was this! It was the work of sin, and showed the nature of sin.

Yet the evil of sin was to be learned in the work of redemption on far higher and far different grounds. It was not enough that angels should see what sin is in men and devils; they must also see what it is in the eyes of a holy God. And had not God shown this in the expulsion of devils from heaven, and man from Eden? Had He not shown this when hell was kindled and the world drowned, and the cities of the plain overthrown under a tempest of fire and brimstone? Clear proofs of the Divine displeasure. Yet nothing so terrible as He gave that night, when He turned away His ear from hearing that prayer in the garden, and hid His face while the Redeemer was dying on the cross. As the substitute of sinners, the Saviour was dealt with as if the Judge had seen in Him all the sins of His people. It was with sin that the eternal Father was displeased, not with His Son. He was, in the midst of all His suffering, the beloved of the Father. It was sin that God was at war with—imputed sin.

To follow this train of thought clearly out, it behoves you to ponder deeply the estimation in which the Son of God was held by angels, and the adoration with which they served Him in heaven; and further to think well of the knowledge which these beings might have of the love of the Father to the Son. They must have known well that it was not possible that the glorious Emmanuel could be an object of hatred. If these things are borne in mind, you will in some measure perceive that, in the whole of these sufferings, the hatred of God against sin must have appeared in an awful light to the minds of angels. I know not at what moment the angels became acquainted with the grand principle on which redemption was to hinge; but, from that moment, the sufferings of the Son of God might move them, but would no longer perplex them. As soon as the grand truth opened before their minds, that His sufferings were vicarious, that this holy severity, this terrible vengeance, was falling upon Him because there lay on Him a load of imputed guilt, then would they see in every pang the evil of sin in the sight of a holy God. Not in the cry of a perishing, burning world, not in the groans of the damned, shall they ever have such proofs of the evil, as they had on that dark night, and that darker day, when His soul was exceeding sorrowful, even unto death. Those shall be but the sufferings of creatures; this was the anguish of the Son of God. After this, the universe never can forget, and never can need another lesson to teach, the light in which God regards sin. I have thus endeavoured to show how the work of redemption would tend to illumine the intellect of angels: I now proceed shortly in the third place,

III. To show how *angels would have their holiness increased by looking into this work.*

Those feelings or emotions which, when taken together, we designate holiness, depend in a great measure on the nature and extent of our knowledge. If our sentiments of God be just, the mind is so far fitted for holy affections. Not that we would say that knowledge is holiness. Nevertheless, a mind utterly ignorant can neither love nor fear God. Reverence and love, the main elements of holiness, result from the views and notions which we have of the Divine King. Now, if the work of redemption has tended greatly to enlarge these views and notions of God in the angelic mind, their reverence and love for that Being must have been greatly increased, and of course their holiness greatly improved. It is a knowledge such as a holy creature may have of the moral perfections seen in moral government, that produces reverence and love, that powerfully affects the mind. We may feel a momentary admiration and a slight emotion of regard for the

Divine Being, as we gaze on His works, that show His omnipotence, wisdom and goodness, in creation. It will, however, only be momentary, and will produce no beneficial effect. We only revere and love God aright, when we see aright His truth, justice, love and mercy. We love Him because He first loved us. Thus seeing God, our hearts expand with love and reverence to that good and glorious King. This applies with undiminished force, we presume, not merely to the moral nature of man, but also to that of angels. And we hold it to be plain, that if angels can have their notions of the moral perfections enlarged, then may their reverence and love for God be increased. But what is this but an increase of their holiness? Hence, they not only acquired new sentiments from looking into redemption, but also new feelings, or which is nearly the same thing, an invigoration of all upright notions.

But greater holiness is just greater happiness. It is of its very nature to produce complacency in the Divine Being. It leads to a nearer and dearer fellowship with Him. It is not so much the eye of the soul looking at God, as it is the very feelings of the soul, mingling with the feelings of divinity. I speak soberly: what says the Apostle? "Ye are made partakers of the divine nature;" and again, "Our fellowship is with the Father and with His Son," through the ever blessed spirit. This fellowship is the being made one with the Father and the Son. This is joy in the Holy Ghost. There may be a difference as to the mode in which men and angels share in this. There can be none as to the object; that to both is the same—God's love. The effect to both is the same—happiness; and that happiness just in proportion to the holiness of the creature. But an increase of holiness is an increase of dignity. Greater conformity to the divine character is just greater dignity of character. For what can more ennoble a creature than to become more like to his Master? Reverence and love for God leads to this near conformity. These direct, and possibly many indirect, advantages angels have derived from looking into the work of redemption. Did the seraph at the cross acquire his loftiest notions of the moral perfections? There also did his reverence, zeal and love acquire additional force and expansion. There new matter was found for praise, and that praise was uttered with a deeper pathos. Were not the harps of heaven struck anew to celebrate this matchless wonder of grace, and are not these harps struck with a profounder reverence, higher exultation and more ardent love, as these servants of the throne celebrate a Triune Jehovah in the work of redemption? My brethren, this is not fancy; these creatures, much as they had seen, never saw God so glorious in justice, so glorious in wisdom, so glorious in love, as when He appeared to save a world by the death of His Son.

And if these high creatures were for a while, as well they might be, perplexed and amazed, and knowing not what to think, as they gazed on the Son of God in an agony; if the sight astonished them beyond measure as they looked at Him, and upon one another, and at the Throne, and considered, and were silent, it was but to break forth into higher strains of praise than they had ever yet sung. It was but to have their feelings kindled with a more intense love and zeal, and reverence and joy. Oh! methinks that as they rolled back the stone from the sepulchre, and saw the mystery of God finished, there were new emotions felt in heaven, and the principalities and powers uttered their Hallelujah with an exultation which was never felt before. And as these glorious beings advance through the distant ages of eternity, in the high pathway of wisdom, their powers expanding, yet ever gratified with pleasures ever new and ever full, shall they not often revert to redemption as that work of God from which they gathered the noblest sentiments, and to which they are indebted for their highest emotions and richest pleasures?

CHAPTER IV.

THE TESTIMONY THAT DEVILS GAVE TO JESUS.

" They cried out, saying, What have we to do with thee, Jesus, thou Son of God ? "—Matthew viii. 29.

HIS testimony, although uttered by the possessed persons, who came out of the tombs, was really the sentiment of the devils that had possession of their minds. The terrible influence which fallen spirits exercised at this time over the souls of men was permitted by God for many wise ends. Among other things, it showed what these once holy and benevolent beings had become under the malignant influence of sin. It also showed how one kind of mind may influence other minds, and how sin and misery may be propagated from mind to mind—a fearful and awful lesson of moral contagion. And, in fine, it showed, in the deliverance which the Saviour afforded to the possessed, His power over the kingdom of darkness, and the nature of His own reign over the souls of men.

Before, however, proceeding to examine the remarkable testimony, which on this occasion devils gave to the Saviour, a few preliminary observations on the person and atonement of Christ may be useful.

The appearance of the Son of God in human nature to atone for the guilt of man was assuredly the most amazing event that has taken place in the universe. The whole is so extraordinary that it demands the most incontrovertible evidence, as to the facts, ere the mind can repose faith in the truth of the system. Great, indeed, is the mystery of godliness—" God manifest in the flesh." It is not wonderful that those who have heard the story of the Redemption from infancy, but have never thought earnestly on it, or believed in it, should feel neither astonishment nor perplexity. It has never occupied an hour of earnest thought. On the other hand, it is not to be wondered at that those who look with some attention at the facts of Redemption, but do not examine the evidence on which these facts rest, should either become confirmed sceptics, or fall into Socinianism, on the Divinity and Atonement of Christ. I shall not stop to strike the difference betwixt infidelity and Socinianism. Plainly those who deny the Divinity and Vicarious Atonement of Jesus cannot hope for the salvation in which Paul gloried. He gloried in the Cross of Christ. But what is the Cross of Christ to us, if Jesus was not divine, and His Atonement vicarious? As a creature, He could neither have offered Himself as our substitute, nor have borne the penalty of our sins. For the work He undertook to accomplish, He needed not only omnipotency but all the divine perfections.

It is, nevertheless, plain that the doctrines of the Divinity of Jesus and vicarious Atonement are the doctrines which cause many to stumble at Christianity. Remove these doctrines, say they, and we shall readily embrace Christianity. We love the purity of its ethereal lessons, and admire the moral character of its author. Even were the statement made in sincerity, and it were easy to show that it is not, yet what is asked can by no means be complied with. If God has taught these doctrines in His Word, man must not remove them, either to please his own fancy, or to gratify the caprice of others. Besides, to remove these doctrines were to expunge Christianity from the Bible, and to leave it a religion wholly unsuitable to the wants of man as a guilty, depraved and helpless creature. Guilty and depraved men need somewhat far more, and far other than a beautiful ethical system, plainly taught and fully illustrated by its teacher. If man needs a teacher, he also needs a Saviour. But, says the objector, I have no wish that any doctrine God has taught shall be discarded. All that I want is conclusive evidence that the Son of God did become man, and did, in His human nature, die to satisfy divine justice and save sinners. Than this demand nothing can be more reasonable. For to believe in these and kindred doctrines, without the most conclusive evidence, were monstrous credulity. We have said that the essential doctrines of the Christian religion are such as can only be received as matters of fact, and held as matters of faith, on the most irrefragable evidence. But, now, mark it, if such evidence has been furnished by the God of truth, wisdom and goodness, then there is nothing for man, if he would act rationally, but to search for that evidence, and when he has found it, give implicit assent to it. Surely it is not too much to ask man to believe what the great God has plainly taught.

But, then, it must be observed, that the whole force of this depends on assuming that the Bible is the revealed will of God. I cannot enter on the proof for this. A brief and, of course, an imperfect argument to those who have studied the question is not needed, and to those who have not studied it, would do more harm than good. Suffice it to say, that when we take fairly and logically into consideration the external as well as the internal evidence for the authenticity and inspiration of the Bible, no argument can be more complete. The Bible is proved beyond all reasonable doubt to be the revealed will of God. No evidence for the past or the distant, for the moral or the spiritual, can be more conclusive than the evidence we have for this.

The Bible, then, or, to express it in other words, God Himself, has given the most full, simple, and conclusive testimony to the doctrines of the Divinity of Jesus and His vicarious and meritorious sacrifice for the sins of men. He was the Child born, the Son given, yet the everlasting

God, Immanuel, God with us. He bore our sins in his own body. By His stripes we are healed. He finished transgression, brought in an everlasting righteousness. The word was, "the Lord our righteousness." It is thus that all the Prophets, from Moses to Malachi, speak of Messiah. I need not add that the New Testament writers not only speak the same truths, but give utterance to them with a fulness, simplicity and variety that give to their testimony a peculiar force and irresistible conviction. No candid man can search the Scriptures without finding three great truths most plainly taught: 1st. That there was to be a Saviour, the Messiah; 2nd. That the Messiah was in His person essentially Divine and truly human; 3rd. That the atonement which He made for sin was in the fullest sense meritorious of pardon to all that believe. On this view of the person and the work of Jesus has the faith of man in all ages rested.

But, not only did inspired men thus testify, angelic witnesses from heaven on divers occasions gave the same testimony. We take two instances. When the angel announced to Mary that she was to be the Mother of the Messiah, his declaration was: That He that was to be born of her, was "the Son of God," a phrase implying His proper divinity. And, again, when the angels came to proclaim His birth to the shepherds, they not only announced Him as the Saviour born, but as One who was to bring "glory to God in the highest, and on earth peace, good will toward men." These were the heralds of mighty truths which were understood but imperfectly at the time they were proclaimed. They answered great ends, the full meaning of which we may suppose they only found when looking at events when accomplished.

It is not wonderful that inspired men and angels give testimony to these high doctrines. But it is not a little remarkable, as we learn from our text and other passages, that devils also give testimony to the same effect. Thus it is that God cannot merely make the wrath of *man* to praise Him, but make *devils* utter a testimony to the praise of Messiah. But now,

I. Let me examine the testimony which devils gave to the person and character of the Messiah. And,

II. The personal feelings which they nevertheless entertained towards Him.

I. Let us examine their testimony.

In many cases the good character of a witness gives not a little weight to the testimony he furnishes. Yet every one knows that the most unprincipled witness may speak the truth, or may be made to speak the truth, and that the truth spoken by such is often of the highest importance. Devils are false—essentially false. It cannot be otherwise. They have entirely separated from the God of truth, and, as their nature is in direct opposition to His, they must be utterly false. Hence, Satan is said to be the father of lies. Yet these beings have often spoken a truth; sometimes compelled to do so, at other times that the truth they uttered might indirectly injure the grand system of God's truth. This trick has often been tried by the servants of the devil, and not seldom by himself. But, without going further into this, it is enough to say that the testimony or confession which devils on this occasion gave was a testimony to the very highest truths. Addressing Christ, they cry out: "Jesus, thou Son of God." This was, for substance, the confession of faith which every Christian then made, and does still make. For, says the Apostle, "Every spirit that confesseth that Jesus Christ is come in the flesh is of God." Is it not remarkable that devils should have given such a testimony as we have here?

Let us look a little closely at it. Observe, they call Him *Jesus*. This was a great name, and will be to all redeemed souls through eternity a precious name. It was the name given to Him by the angels at His advent, and the import of it, as to Him, was given at the same time. "Thou shalt call His name Jesus," said the angel, "for He shall save His people," not from their enemies, but "from their sins." The simple term, Jesus, signified Saviour. It had been applied to some who had been, as we say, the saviours of their country. But when the name Jesus was applied to Messiah, it bore a far other and an infinitely higher sense than it ever bore when applied to successful warriors and statesmen. Now, I cannot doubt that in the minds of the devils it bore the high and proper sense—the Saviour from sin. He was known to all the people as Jesus. This was His name, and it needed no spirit from the invisible world to proclaim that. But it was, nevertheless, true that although He came to His own they knew Him not. The Scribes and the Elders knew not this Jesus any more than the most ignorant of the rabble. They could not know Him, for their minds were blinded by prepossessions and prejudices; and they could not look at the evidence which the God they owned had given. To them He was merely Jesus of Nazareth, the son of the carpenter, the despised Galilean. A root out of dry ground, who had, to their eyes, no form or comeliness. Hence, they neither knew Him, nor loved Him, nor believed in Him. Not so with devils, for although they did not love Him they knew who He was.

These beings knew well that the person in whose presence they now stood was the Messiah that was promised in Eden, as the seed of the woman, who was to bruise the the head of the serpent. They knew that He was Jesus the Saviour, who had come to make peace betwixt God and man, to finish transgression and bring in an everlasting righteousness. In short they knew that this Jesus was to be the deliverer of fallen man from the power of the devil. This was a mighty truth which these demons knew, firmly believed, and uttered. This simple truth must have awakened in their minds the most strange and perplexing emotions. From the moment they held this belief of Jesus, they must have felt an intense desire to know what effect His mission into the world would have on the kingdom of Satan, and, knowing that in some way or other the effects would be disastrous, they must have felt the strongest desire to prevent, or, at least, to mar the great end of His mission into the world. Strange amazement, dread and hatred must have sprung from the views they held of Jesus, as the Saviour of men.

But all this admitted, yet we need not, and indeed *cannot*, suppose that they at all understood the mode by which Jesus was to accomplish the salvation of men. Their malign passions were so completely dominant in them, that their intellect would be incapable of drawing just inferences from the clearest premises. It is thus that pride, envy and malice give an utterly wrong turn to the most vigorous intellects. The malignant pride of devils would totally unfit them for apprehending the method by which the Saviour was to deliver man. What they knew was this, that He had come to do it in some way; but the way they could not with their pride and malice in the least comprehend. May we not suppose that devils held a set of opinions somewhat of this sort : That to the extent they could arouse popular indignation against Jesus, especially the wrath of the priesthood, so as to cover His name with obloquy and bring all kinds of suffering upon Him, they would so far mar His work and frustrate the ends of His mission. Nay, may we not go farther and suppose that, when they at length saw Him not only spit upon, buffeted, scourged, but actually crucified, they fancied that their malice against the Lord and His Anointed had triumphed and that the end of His mission had failed, under the violence and subtlety of hell. That these beings were most active, in bringing all kinds of suffering on Jesus, can not be doubted ; that they were most active agents in bringing about His death can as little be doubted. But, now, can we suppose that had they clearly seen the grand design and results of Christ's humiliation, sufferings and death, they would have been the active agents in all this? I cannot think it. They did not know that by His death He was to destroy the works of the devil, satisfy divine justice for the sins of man, and to all His followers take the sting out of death and take away the power of the grave. All this is now plain, so plain that he who runs may read; but ere events unfolded it, and Apostles explained it, did the highest minds comprehend it? I presume not. The disciples, before the event, did not understand the death of their Master: angels possibly did, for into this they desired to look so as to learn. And assuredly devils in no way comprehended what the death of the Saviour would accomplish, either as to God, to men, or themselves. These beings, so thoroughly disobedient, so thoroughly the victims of pride and malice, could never comprehend how a life of extreme poverty, of constant sorrow, but of perfect obedience to the Divine law, followed by an ignominious death of the most terrible kind, all submitted to by the Messiah, could ever be the sole means of saving men and of glorifying God. Their minds, blinded by pride and malice to the grand ends of the moral government of God, could never comprehend the lofty, wise, just and merciful bearings of this mysterious transaction. Their state of mind prevented them from either comprehending it in theory or seeing its results.

May it not be supposed that the theory which they had formed—if they had a theory as to the way in which Jesus would save men—would be one of mere power. He that was to come to bruise the head of Satan would come with might and accomplish the work by Heaven's lightnings and thunders. Hence, as it would seem, their utter perplexity as to the character of Jesus, and their subsequent attempts, if not to overwhelm him, at least to impair His glory and mar His enterprise. As their sin began in pride, so did the pride and the malice that springs from it utterly unfit them for comprehending this wisdom of God. To them it appeared foolishness that one born in a stable, and dying on a cross, should at once sustain the honours of the throne of God, overthrow the powers of darkness, and save men from perdition. We know that this has often appeared to the wise men of earth foolishness. It may have appeared the height of folly to the principalities of hell. If this view be near the truth, then their course of opposition to Jesus, on their theory, had a meaning in it. And yet we may say, as He Himself said in reference to others of His enemies, " They knew not what they did." Had they seen what God would bring out of all the suffering, shame and death of the Messiah, I cannot think they would have been the parties to it that they really were. What they did, they did as free agents, acting according to the motives suitable to their depraved nature. Hence, that God who makes the wrath of man to praise Him, in this matter, makes the wrath of devils to praise Him. Oh ! it is marvellous to see how God can make all the actions of the most wicked creatures, when acting voluntarily and from bad motives, instrumental in accomplishing His ends and glory, and yet in no sense be the author of sin ! It was thus that Judas, the chief priest, Pilate and the devils were all efficient instruments in bringing about the death of Jesus, which was to be the salvation of men. Yet they meant it not. To them, and with their motives, it was deep criminality.

But, although devils saw not what they were doing, while urging on the death of Jesus, yet the time came when assuredly they saw what they had done, and saw what God had done by them, and what He had done without them, and especially saw what He had done by Messiah to save the world. When Jesus arose triumphant from the grave and ascended on high, it then became, I presume, plain to the orders of creatures in heaven, earth, and also in hell, not only that there was a great salvation for lost man, but the *why* of it and the *how* of it became plain to all the spirits of darkness, as well as to the angels of light. The awful fact was now made plain, and that fact made plain spread a new joy through heaven, gave the hopes of earth a tenfold brightness, and, may I not add, gave to hell a tenfold darkness. For who can conceive the agony of that wounded pride, the misery of that disappointed malice, which these proud and malignant spirits must have felt, when they found that that Jesus of Nazareth whom they for a time despised, and then in furious wrath persecuted to the death, had by His death destroyed their power and marvellously advanced the Divine glory? Devils did not know, when they were striving to raise Jesus to the cross, that they were raising Him to His mediatorial crown, and that, by what they had done in their way of it, and by what He had done in His way of it, their misery was awfully augmented. Oh! the height and the depth of the wisdom as well as the goodness of God in this matter!

But, in fine, although the mode of salvation was hidden from devils when they uttered the words of the text, yet they knew the fact, to them a terrible fact, that the Saviour of man had really come into the world. They knew that Jesus of Nazareth is that Saviour—that they now stand in the presence of Messiah. Devils believe in God and tremble. They also believe in the one Saviour, and yet tremble. How strange their position! how perplexing their feeling! how strange their confession of faith! "We know thee, who Thou art"—Thou art Jesus the Saviour; but the confession went further, for, said they, "Thou art the Son of God."

CHAPTER V.

THE TESTIMONY THAT DEVILS GAVE TO JESUS.

(Second Sermon.)

"They cried out, saying, What have we to do with thee, Jesus, thou Son of God?" Matthew, viii. 29.

IT has, I trust, been satisfactorily shown that devils firmly believed that Jesus of Nazareth was the Messiah promised in Eden, who was to be, in the full sense, the Saviour of guilty man. But this testimony, wonderful as it is, is not all. Their testimony as to the person of Jesus is equally true, and in some respects even more remarkable; for, you will observe, they address Him not only as Jesus the Saviour, but as the Son of God. In this statement devils testify to the proper divinity of Jesus. Our business now will be to examine this part of the testimony.

The person of Christ was twofold: He was man, for there was in Him a perfect human nature as to all the essential qualities of soul and body. This was indispensable to the accomplishment of the mediatorial work; for He was perfectly to obey the Divine Law, and bear its penalty in His soul and body, in making atonement for the sins of man. His human nature was alone capable of this. But it was also necessary that He should be Divine, that He might bear the terrible penalty, and in every way magnify the Law. It was this union of the divine and human natures which constituted the person of the Saviour, and which everyway qualified Him for at once glorifying God and saving lost men. Devils had correct notions of the person of Messiah. No proof is needful to show that they knew that He was man; but, mark it, the text and many other passages furnish the proof that they knew that He was, in the proper sense, Divine.

As the expression, the Son of man, which so often occurs, teaches His proper humanity, so the phrase Son of God is employed to teach His proper divinity. No doubt the term Son of God sometimes implies the Mediatorship of Jesus, but then it ever implies His divinity. When devils, then, spoke of Him as the Son of God did they firmly believe in His divinity? This is the question with which we have now to do. It is plainly one not without its difficulties. To know if Jesus really was a divine person appears to have been a matter of the deepest interest to devils, especially from the time of His public advent on the bank of the Jordan, when announced from heaven as the well-beloved Son of God. It was immediately after this that the temptation in the wilderness took place. If you read that remarkable scripture with care you will not fail to perceive that whatever else Satan aimed at in that temptation one chief object was to ascertain the real character of this Jesus of Nazareth. There was much to awaken in the mind of Satan the apprehension that He was more than man, that He was different from and quite superior to all other prophets that had appeared. In short, the grand drift of the temptation was to ascertain if Jesus was in reality a divine person. You will observe that the hypothetical form in which the temptations are put was to ascertain this—if thou be the Son of God, do this—if thou be the Son of God, do that. The Socinians say, that the term Son of God simply means a good man. Now, it is not denied that sons of God and children of God often signify good men or men of God; but it is denied that the term the Son of God, when used emphatically, is synonymous with the term a good man. The mere term, of itself, might not prove the Divinity of Jesus, but the term in connection with other evidence is strongly designative of this. Besides, can it be supposed that Satan required to employ all these arts and peculiar temptations to find out if Jesus was a good man? Had he not had abundant evidence for this in the previous life of Jesus? Were there not good men here and there —good men such as Satan could see—and why this extreme desire to know if this person from Nazareth was a good man? This explanation is so utterly lame as to be absolutely absurd. Satan employed his temptations, not to find out what he already knew, if Jesus was a person of piety and had a moral nature of high worth, but to find out, what was to him far more momentous, if He had a Divine nature. Hence the demand he made : "If thou be the Son of God, command that these stones be made bread." If thou be God, says Satan, work a miracle, and that will prove it. Satan knew well that God alone could work miracles. And therefore he came, not as the foul fiend, but disguised possibly under some venerable aspect, professing to seek information and solution to doubts. It is surmised, said he, and what was uttered on the banks of the Jordan gave colour to it, that thou art more than man. Art thou Divine? If so, work miracles and prove it. If it be assumed, then, as correct, that the mind of the devil was haunted with the terrible apprehension that Jesus was Divine, the grand end of the temptation in the wilderness is seen to have had a peculiar significance in it. No truth could be more terrible to the minds of devils than this—that He who had come to bruise the serpent's head was a divine person.

Did the issue, then, of the temptation in the wilderness settle the question? Possibly not. From the way in which Jesus met the apprehension of His divinity, the truth may only have been deepened, but not yet wrought into a fixed conviction. We may well suppose that they would watch every movement of the Saviour in order to be satisfied fully on this momentous matter. And are there not grounds for thinking that the alarming apprehension that He was divine would deepen into conviction when they saw the many miracles which He wrought, not at their instance, but at His own volition ? They had, no doubt, seen many of God's prophets, such as Moses, Elijah and others, work miracles ; but they were too careful and profound observers not to perceive that the way in which these men wrought miracles and the way in which Jesus wrought them were wholly different. They performed them as mere instruments in the hand of God ; but Jesus wrought miracles as God. They were but secondary causes in this, the mere manifestors of a Divine power. Jesus wrought them as the first cause—wrought them as Divine, possessed of Divine power. The miracles of prophets, as done by them, proved—and that was much—that God was with them ; but the miracles as wrought by Jesus proved that He was God. Prophets and apostles cry to God to help them and ascribe the work to Him ; but Jesus speaks not as having delegated power but as having the power in Himself. To the dead He simply says: "Arise," and the dead arise; to the deaf ear: "Be opened," and the deaf hear ; and, when thousands are to be fed, He creates the food by His own power. Now, we assume that devils knew all this, and knowing that no miracle could be thus wrought but by God, they must from this, and no doubt from other grounds, have come to the conclusion that Jesus was, as they expressed it, the Son of God and a divine person.

But was this conviction held at all times with equal firmness ? All that has been said may be admitted and yet this be doubted. The prominent force of evidence depends not merely on the state of the intellect, but still more on the state of the passions. The intellect of these beings would take in the logical truth with great clearness, while their passions would sadly confuse that truth and sorely perplex them in drawing sound inferences from the plainest premises. One can easily see what work their pride, envy and malice would make among their intellectual deductions. Their intellect would assent to the evidence that He is divine. But think how their pride would confound them as to this. To their pride nothing would appear so irrational as the condescension which the incarnation of the Son of God implied. Of humility they knew nothing; of this amazing condescension they would understand nothing, while their malice would utterly unfit them for seeing aught of that love which lies in that expression, "God so loved the world that he gave His only begotten Son that whosoever believeth on Him should not perish but have everlasting life." A being, let his intellect be what it may, who is incapable of feeling love or understanding the workings of love, can form no just conception of the incarnation, the death or the life of Jesus. In short, devils would be sorely perplexed betwixt their intellectual convictions and the workings of their malign passions. Hence the conclusion to which I come is, that the doctrine of the divinity was sometimes held by them with great firmness; at other times held loosely, and possibly held oftenest with a mixture of doubt. Thus it is that a hated faith blended with misbelief or unbelief may be in fierce conflict in the bosom. This is the penalty which guilty creatures pay for abused truth.

Yet plainly there were seasons when devils were compelled to believe that He who was the Saviour of man was divine. When they addressed the words of the text to Jesus they did then so believe. But, mark it, when the divinity of Jesus was firmly held, the minds of these beings must have been filled with the strangest terror and amazement. May we not suppose them to exclaim: "What strange thing is this that has happened? what new thing is this? what meaneth this new manifestation of God? God has come down to dwell among men, how and for what?" Much in this must have been to them painfully incomprehensible. They could well understand how God should appear in majesty, as He did when He clothed His arm with vengeance to drive them out of heaven when they rebelled against Him; or that He should appear in majesty when He destroyed a guilty world with a flood, or when He overthrew Sodom and Gomorrah with fire and brimstone. All this from a simple knowledge of His justice and power they could easily understand; but how He should now appear clothed in human flesh and in human nature, go about poor, despised, not having where to lay His head, instructing the ignorant, comforting the afflicted and feeding the hungry, while those He was thus so graciously aiding were the poor, the guilty and the miserable, and, all the time He was scattering so many various benefits and blessings, should be hated and persecuted:—this, we say, these profound and malignant beings could not comprehend. God manifest in the flesh, under such circumstances, would not merely appear a mystery; it would seem an inexplicable absurdity. The matter looked at in this aspect, not only the Cross of Christ—the closing scene—but much that preceded it would appear to them as it has often done to men of the world, utter foolishness. And yet, it would have another aspect, or rather two other aspects to them. 1st. The proofs, as we have shown, for His divinity would be so conclusive, that they would be compelled to admit that, be it as it may, He that is come to save man is Divine. And next, from their knowledge of the wisdom of God, they could not fail to infer that, seeing that God has really become incarnate, it must be for some great ends worthy of His wisdom. They could not fail to infer that, some way or other, out of this shall come events which shall be for the overthrow of the kingdom of darkness and for the advancement of the glory of God in the universe. Whatever their passions might surmise, these would be the dictates of their intellect.

In fine, to sum up what has been said on this, we see that devils knew that He before whom they now stand is the Saviour of man, and that Saviour is the Son of God.

What a Saviour is He! not like other deliverers whom God had at different times sent for the help of His people, to save them from their enemies, such as Moses, Samuel and David, grand and great men, but still fallible men, over whom Satan gained many victories. But He, who has now come, is altogether a different personage. He is man—but more than man. This Saviour is Immanuel, God in our nature. They would see that He could neither be circumvented by subtlety nor overthrown by power, for He is the Son of God. "We know Thee, who Thou art," said they, "Thou art Jesus, the Son of God." This was a true testimony, given not by friends but by bitter enemies. Saul among the prophets—the devils witnesses to Christ; not willing yet true witnesses. Is it not strange that not out of the mouths of men and angels only, but out of the mouths of devils, God should thus perfect His praise? But,

II.—Let us proceed to notice the effect which the truth and confession had on their personal feelings. They exclaimed, We know Thee: "Thou art Jesus, the Son of God." Knowing Him to be such, how did they stand affected to Him? To answer this we have only to look with care at the other clauses of the text: 1st. Observe, they cry out, "What have we to do with Thee?" And 2nd. They exclaim, "Art Thou come to torment us before the time?" Let me briefly direct your attention to each of these topics.

1. The expression, "What have we to do with Thee?" plainly implies a complete disownment of all connection with Him, as the Saviour, and all reverence for Him as the Son of God. As a Saviour, they neither desire nor expect His help. Their language clearly implies this. There is no intimation given that there ever was any design of mercy for fallen angels. It is indeed expressly declared that the Son of God took not on Him the nature of angels, or, as it might be rendered, took not hold of their fallen nature to raise them from perdition, but He

took hold of the nature of man. Fallen angels, then, were not to be saved by the Son of God. I presume it may be safely admitted that this did not arise from the want of power in the Son of God to lift even them from perdition. If it had been so ordered by the sovereign will of God, I think we may venture to say that there was, or might have been, a sufficiency of merit in the atonement of the Son of God to have satisfied the claims of divine justice, even for fallen angels. But it was not so ordered. When we speak of God acting sovereignly, which is indeed the only way in which we can suppose Him to act, we must not infer that He ever acts without the highest reasons. Infinite wisdom pre-supposes this. Yet the reasons from which God acts, may be wholly beyond our apprehension. Now when the question is asked, Why did God manifest pardoning mercy to fallen man but not to fallen angels? we cannot, I presume, give any satisfactory answer. Yet, no doubt, infinite wisdom had the best of reasons for the difference, and for the election made. The following suppositions, which are not presented as certain solutions, but humble surmises, may possibly throw a few rays of light on this dark matter: There was no scheme of mercy for fallen angels, because,

1st. They sinned with far more light than man, were created with far higher powers, and had possibly experienced for many ages all the advantages of heaven. 2dly. Their sins may have had far more of malignity towards God, and may have been a far more direct attack on His moral government, than the sin of Adam. 3dly. Adam stood for his posterity, so that all his descendants were involved in his act, but each of these beings acted for himself. 4thly. Man was seduced from his allegiance by them ; but we have no reason to suppose that any other creatures seduced them. The revolt against God originated in their own minds. And, lastly, their sin may, although not in form, have had in it the elements of what is called the sin against the Holy Ghost—not so much a failure in some positive or moral statute as a daring blasphemy of God. But I do not go further into this. Suffice it to say, that whatever was the precise nature of their sin, or the guilt it involved, the Son of God was no Saviour to them. They knew that they had neither part nor lot in the work He had come to accomplish for man, so far below them in the original qualities of mind and the station they had occupied. They that were the younger and feebler were to be saved; they who were of the earthy, were to be taken up and repaired, while those who were once golden vessels in the upper sanctuary were to be cast aside as utterly worthless. Possibly, in their pride of heart, they once thought that heaven could not do without them, but now they find that heaven can do without them, and that their ancient places are to be filled by men of earth, redeemed by the Son of God; and that those whom they expected to drag down with them into a common ruin would be exalted to that glory and felicity which they had forfeited. How intense must their envy have been, as they beheld Jesus the Son of God, a Saviour to man, but no Saviour to them! Hence, they cry out in bitter resentment: "What have we to do with thee?" But,

2. Next, the expression, "What have we to do with thee?" taken in connexion with the declaration, "Art thou come to torment us before the time?"—the final judgment, as I presume—intimate very plainly their fear of, and intense hatred to, Jesus. It may take many words to unfold the sentiments of the brain, but a few simple words often express the emotions of the passions. This is seen here. It is the strongest aversion that is uttered in these words, "What have we to do with thee?" Away from us, or let us away from thee. Now, were not these beings wretched? Did they not need a Saviour, as much as lost man? Yes, but that is not enough. In order that the lost shall be saved, there must be the sovereign purpose of God, and ere any can embrace the Saviour, there must be confidence in Him, love to Him, and obe-

dience to the Divine will in the whole matter. But, as to devils, there was no divine purpose; so towards Jesus there was not only no love and no confidence, but the strongest aversion. They wished to have nothing to do with Him, either as Saviour or Lord. One would suppose that they might have uttered a cry for mercy. But they do not. Their pride and despair alike forbid it. Indeed we may readily suppose that their pride and malice were aroused to the highest pitch, when they saw the Son of God in human nature come to save man, and in that nature to be a judge of them. For they now seem to know that He who was the Son of Man, as well as the Son of God, would judge them at last, and was now on many occasions exercising a sovereign authority over them. Thus it was that they would extract nothing but poison from any view they took of Jesus.

The following inferences may be drawn: 1st. That the soundest creed may be held by minds deeply depraved.

2nd. That a sound creed held by such minds will increase the despair of the lost.

3rd. That the clearest and grandest views of truth, logically held, may be all perverted by the malign passions.

CHAPTER VI.

THE GOOD OLD WAY.*

"Thus saith the Lord, Stand ye in the ways, and see, and ask for the old paths, where is the good way, and walk therein, and ye shall find rest for your souls."—JEREMIAH vi. 16.

HE truth of God in revealed religion is often in Scripture compared to a path. The figure is simple, and pregnant with meaning. Progress to a definite end is one of the deepest laws of our being, and is indeed a law which seems to prevail in all the departments of the Divine Government. But motion is not progress, unless it be motion in the right direction. The traveller who would reach his destination, must first of all be sure that he is in the right road. The path of religion is that which leads the soul to God, to piety, virtue and life everlasting.

In illustrating the passage I have now read, I shall

I. Explain the general and broad principle in the text, viz. :—*that all reformation consists in a faithful return to God's truth*—here called the Old Paths.

At the time the text was uttered, things among the Jewish people were approaching a crisis. God forgotten ; idolatry prevalent ; impiety and immorality, as might be expected, had deeply and extensively affected the national mind. Sin in any degree is offensive to God. It is that

---

* Preached at the opening of the new Presbyterian Church, Scarborough, 3rd February, 1850. This discourse was published the same year, and was "dedicated to the Heads of Families connected with the congregation, as a token of the affectionate respect of their Pastor."

abominable thing which He hates. But when sin reaches a certain point, the Divine forbearance ends, and judgment begins. Yet, God does not smite without warning; nor smite before He has compassionately employed those various instrumentalities by which the thoughtless may be aroused and the erring reclaimed. Hence, the prophet Jeremiah was sent to this rebellious people with arguments and appeals well fitted to produce conviction and lead to repentance. The prophet was, indeed, admirably qualified for his work. And the *object of his mission*, whether he spoke the language of commination or of mercy, was to induce sinners to flee by repentance and reformation from the impending wrath of Jehovah. He tells the people of their sins—tells them in what their reformation must begin—in what it must consist—and the happy results that would flow from such a reformation as God required. In the name of God, he calls upon them to return from every way that is wrong—to turn from all those ways that lead to destruction—to the good old path that leads to God; and He promises them if they did so, they would " find rest for their souls." He calls upon them to take their stand in the old way, and to inquire, honestly and faithfully, if it be not the only path of safety. In a word, they are called upon by the prophet to turn from all that is new and false in their religion and practice to the old doctrines, worship and duties of the old, but Divine, religion. And not because it was old, but because it was of God and eternally true. It was thus that God, by His servant, addressed the Jewish people. He tells them that He had marked out a certain way for them —an old way—truth as old as eternity—duties, obligations and rewards as old as the first hour that God revealed himself to man, as his Creator, Law-giver and Redeemer. As all their sin and misery arose from their departure from this old system of Divine truth, so their only safety lay in returning to it. And is not this the essence of all true reformation—a thorough return to the faith and practice of what God has of old revealed, but which in reality is ever new, and to man ever of the highest moment?

On the same principle on which inspired prophets proceeded, did the great Protestant Reformers act ; and, just so far as they stuck to it, they were true reformers. The nations of Christendom had departed from the good old path, and were walking in ways not good—were worshipping the creature more than the Creator—were trusting to their own merits for justification, not to the merits of Christ—were punctilious in rites, but forgetful of spiritual and moral obligations. This state of things very much needed reformation, and certain men of God were raised up to accomplish it. They had got light themselves from the lamp of heavenly truth. They brought this forth, held it up, and called to their fellow mortals, bewildered with all sorts of delusions, "See the way—the true way that God has marked out for you; forsake all other ways, walk in this and it will lead you out of error, sin and misery to God, to piety, to life everlasting." Many heard and obeyed, and as many as did so had a blessed reformation.

Since that memorable time, Europe has had many reformers, and has needed them. But it is deeply to be lamented that not a few of those who have assumed that high and difficult vocation, should so often have forgotten a principle, quite indispensable to the success of their work. For I know of no principle that should be more fundamental with reformers than this:—That all reformation, to end well, *must begin in a return to God*. The work of destruction may be carried on very effectually to a certain extent, and this great truth forgotten. Nor is it denied, that in many cases there can be no reformation till much has been destroyed. Yet destruction is not it, and may never lead to it. The true reformer is not a mere demolitionist, but a wise master-builder. And he who would build wisely here, must never for a moment forget that a return to God, in the individual heart and conscience of men, is of the last consequence to the accomplishment of his work. Most candid persons will admit that more than a few of those terrible men, who arose during the French revolution, were possessed of vast intellectual attainments, matchless zeal, and, upon the whole, were enthusiastically bent on the reformation of society and the happiness of their country. They failed miserably. Alas ! poor men, how could it be otherwise. They knew not the old path of God's truth. They had only learned the new way of the infidel philosophy. That could afford them no safe guidance in their difficult task, but could only lead them, as it did, into helpless confusion and frightful ruin. Hence the terrible labours of these men, and the disastrous consequences—when compared with the labours of Luther and Knox, and the results that followed their efforts—furnish a *measure of singular accuracy*, by which we may arrive at the relative value of the two methods, by which it has been attempted to reform men, and improve civil and religious institutions. The one method assumes it as indispensable to all this that the Divine help be sought and vouchsafed ; and that man shall, first of all, return to that God from whom he has departed ; while the other method arrogantly affirms, that all the reformation that is necessary may be accomplished without any special aid from God, or any hearty acknowledgment of His government. It is true that bad men, acting from the worst of motives, might be made indirectly instrumental in preparing the way for great reforms, and so might a pestilence or shipwreck, by cutting off some powerful and tyrannical despot. It must, nevertheless, be borne in mind that all social or moral reformation, which is to yield permanent benefit to man, must spring from the great principles of Divine truth understood and believed by him. Not the ambitious and the selfish, but the wise and the pious, can either understand these principles or apply them. The world cannot too soon learn this, *and, let the lesson cost what it may*, it must be learned. To dethrone God from among us, and tacitly, if not avowedly, disown his truth ; and to give place to Satan, and to expect that *his servants*, mainly influenced by pride, avarice and selfish expediency, shall bring about reformation, is really to unite the madness of Bedlam to the impiety of Hell. My brethren, there can be no real reform in the family or the State—any more than in the Church— till there be reform in the bosom. But this has not so much as begun, till there is a return to the good old path of God's truth. For let it be concealed as it may by self-flattery, or the flattery of others, yet nothing is more certain than that the sole cause of all our maladies *is our departure from God*. This was ever a grand fact insisted upon by Old Testament Prophets, and they were the wisest, the most earnest and thorough-going of all reformers.

True, it is an old path to which men are called to turn. Now, with many, that a thing is old is sufficient reason for treating it with contempt, while the novelty of a thing is to them its main recommendation. Worth and worthlessness will not be settled by wise men on any such grounds. We are, perhaps, in our times peculiarly liable to err on this point. The present age is remarkable for new inventions, and some of them are, indeed, astonishing. Every new discovery should be hailed with delight, inasmuch as it not only enlarges the field of knowledge, but multiplies the sources of human enjoyment. But religious truth, on which the moral and spiritual well-being of man depends, is not a thing of human invention at all. To this human genius can make no salutary additions. Our religion is of Divine revelation—hence, the perfection of its truths and their complete adaptation to the condition of man in all ages. Had man invented religion, he might have improved it. He could not do the former : it is at his peril if he attempts the latter. But while religion leaves no room for invention, it, nevertheless, affords abundant scope for mental effort and progress in the investigation of its doctrines and duties, and in the faithful application of these. He who believes, and sedulously practises what God has revealed, is making progress in the highest and best sense. In a word, the principles of religion were not intended to be improved by man, but to improve him. Religion is a work of God, and is perfect. Science may analyze water from the purest fountain, or the rays of the sun, but cannot improve either. To attempt to improve what is perfect is folly; but to attempt to improve religion by human inventions is at once folly and impiety.

I have just glanced at a subject which, by two classes of thinkers, extremely remote from each other in many respects, has nevertheless been made the fruitful source, on the one side, of much superstition; on the other, of not a little infidelity. There is then no room for mental progress here, as men are bound down to principles that are old and unalterable ! Boundless room, my brethren; but motion is not progress, unless it be motion in the right path. A rigorous adherence to God's truth is the right path; for it leads the soul to Himself, to holiness, to happiness. The path of sin leads the soul away from God, and in the end conducts it to eternal death. Hence, when men are called on to return to the old path, this is not to retrograde but to advance. It is in the language of Scripture to begin to live—"to walk with God"—to go Heavenward.

Nor can this old path ever become unsafe for the traveller. For although it is of the nature of every human institution, after it has yielded the amount of influence it possessed, to decay, not so with this. Corrupt systems of religion are liable to decay. The particles of truth which they may have contained, once exhausted, the systems themselves must perish. But Christianity, as God has given it, can never by being old become inefficient. The reason of this is, that it is all truth, and that that truth is of universal application to man. When religion, therefore, has lost its divine energy in the church, or, which is the same thing, manifests little influence on the souls of professors, it is not because religious truth has lost its intrinsic force, but men have lost their hold on it. Their faith has decayed, not *the principles of faith.* Now, the remedy for this evil is not to set to work to invent new doctrines, or any new ecclesiastical polity, but simply, and with the whole soul, to return to the good old paths of God's truth. This, by the aid of the Spirit—and the Spirit will bless no means but His own—is the only way by which the Church can regain her lost strength and marred beauty. My brethren, it is even so. Would you have light that your darkness may be dispelled?—turn to the Sun of Righteousness. Would ye have warmth for the heart grown cold?—turn to that altar with its live coals. Would ye know what God would have you to be, and to do?—turn to that ark of the covenant and to the lively oracles. Would you have peace and hope?—turn to Calvary —look to a crucified Saviour. Would you be prepared for the conflict of life, and be fitted for the hour of death?— turn to that armoury in which you will find " the sword of the Spirit, the shield of faith, and the helmet of salvation." The remedy—the sole remedy—for darkness of mind, coldness of heart, deadness of conscience, is a return by a living faith to the good old path of God's precious truth.

Having thus explained the general sense of the text, I now proceed—

II. To illustrate certain doctrines, which naturally flow from the principle that has been established.

First.—*That for the salvation of sinners, the old doctrine of justification by the righteousness of Christ must be adhered to, and if it has been in any way abandoned there must be a return to it, else there can be no safety for the soul.*

Persons who are disbelievers in certain doctrines of religion must necessarily be indifferent on the whole matter. If man has no soul—if there be nothing of him that is to live eternally, there can be no sense of accountability to God, no right apprehension of guilt, no fear of hell, no desire of heaven. To such a man religion at best is but a useful element in government; at worst, a pestilent superstition, a cunningly devised fable. A cold indifference is the natural and, perhaps, the least offensive form that a sceptical mind assumes. But to all earnest men, who believe they have souls—who believe they are accountable for moral actions—dread guilt, fear hell, desire the friendship of God—religion is seen to be an affair of the last moment, and to them it presents itself under one of two aspects, *on either of which*, accordingly as their minds fasten, they attempt to obtain guidance and comfort. All men, earnest in this matter, hold in common that they are under government to God, admit that they have disobeyed Him, are exposed to His wrath; that it is, above all things, desirable to escape His wrath and to obtain the Divine friendship. They all see their need of, and to some extent all desire, salvation. But as to *the way of salvation*, their views differ widely on certain very essential points. Yes, say many, the Divine friendship has been lost, and the wrath of God incurred by sin; yet man, nevertheless, can do, in whole or in part, what will satisfy a merciful God and thus obtain salvation. It must be confessed that the views held by not a few, *of God's mercy* and *human merit*, amount to little more than a metaphysical speculation, by which they very effectually stifle conscience, and occasionally perplex an opponent. These men are but poorly in earnest. But not so with all, on the same side—the doctrines admitted take such a hold of their minds that *they work as well as speculate*, and if their works cannot, in the evangelical sense, be called good, they are at least numerous, and some of them very trying. Hence the painful rites of a spurious Christianity and the terrible sacrifices of an earnest Paganism. For it is a mistaken notion to suppose that to seek salvation by the works of the law is peculiar to guilty consciences, merely within the pale of revealed religion. Yet every system by which human merit is either in whole or in part made the ground of pardon and acceptance with God, is to seek salvation by the works of the law, and this is plainly condemned or rather declared to be impossible in the Revelation which Divine wisdom has made on the matter. The Bible teaches man to seek for his safety and happiness *far otherwise* than in what would disparage the holiness of God, or lower the claims of His justice. But every scheme by which fallen man is supposed to merit salvation really does this. To merit salvation is, indeed, a religion congenial to the pride of our nature, but altogether unsuitable to our present condition. By flattering self-sufficiency, it but deepens guilt, hardens the heart, and brings no healing to the soul, or real peace to the conscience. It knows not God, as at an infinite distance above his creatures; but vainly attempts to bring men to something like an equality with the Law-giver, and to make the Creator, *in a sense, a debtor to the creature.* The covenant of works, as God gave it, and as man would modify it, are two very different things. As God gave it, and as perfectly suited to the primitive condition of man, it has all the grandeur of justice and truth, and the simplicity of first principles. It is, do this—do all that God requires, and thou shalt live; but fail in one jot of the law, and thou shalt perish. This is plain, it is just; but to depraved and guilty man it is altogether terrible. It is a flaming Sinai, to which no fallen child of Adam can approach and live. But this scheme of salvation by merit, *as man modifies it*, is as various as his knowledge, his moral tastes, or his fancy. In the common view, I may say in every view taken on the matter by men, who would be justified by the deeds of the law, a holy and a just God is but imperfectly seen in their theory; while man's guilt and depravity are not taken into anything like full account. Hence the erroneous inference that by the works of the law man can be saved. Many, indeed, are the complexions which this system, with its ineradicable particles of truth and large portions of error, takes; but in all its forms, from the fanaticism of the Hindu, by which death is sought under the chariot wheels of his god, to the prim pharisaism, which says its prayers at the corners of the streets, it is but the religion of terror, pride and selfishness. How can it be otherwise? It is the vain attempt of man to meet God without a Mediator, and to obtain pardon without an all-satisfying atonement; *or, at the least*, to come with a righteousness which shall make a Divine Mediator little necessary, and His atonement scarcely more than supplementary. Hence the adherents of this system, when they look earnestly at God's justice, are filled with hopeless despondency; on the other hand, when they have what they call a clear view of His mercy, their gratulation has in it nothing of humility, and but little of that love and thankfulness which a profound sense *of unmerited mercy* can alone inspire. This is an old way; but not the good old way.

It is time, however, to enquire what is the Bible view of man, and religion adapted to man. As to man, the Bible lays down the truth, which it every where proves and illustrates, that he is not only under guilt, but of himself is impotent to remove it. He can make no satisfaction that shall meet the ends of justice, and yet very plainly justice requires perfect satisfaction. For God has added a penalty to His law. He had the unquestionable right to do so, and who will question His right to enforce this, if the law be violated? That penalty is death. Death, my brethren!—yes, but that implies much more than temporal sufferings, or the separation of soul and body. It implies separation from God, from holiness, from all happiness. Yet the soul is not to be annihilated, and to a creature of intellect, passions, moral wants and capacities, and destined to live for ever, that death must be unspeakably awful. He that shall endure all this, shall suffer the loss of all that is great, good and lovely; and, in addition, shall in various other ways, through every sense and faculty, have to suffer great torments. In a word, man's guilt is his liability to punishment, and that punishment to him shall be eternal. The reasons for this? My friends, many reasons might be given, but is not this one enough, and comprehensive of all others worth much? that the *Divine Lawgiver has said* that creatures violating His law shall be punished, and that this shall bring on them, "everlasting destruction from His presence, and the glory of His power"—has declared that when they shall go away from His judgment seat unpardoned, to meet the penalty, they shall go away "into everlasting fire, prepared for the devil and his angels." That is the curse, *and, till that curse in some way be exhausted*, there can be no acquittal. But man can in no way exhaust it. How can he? He is ever sinning, hence the terrible thought, that he must for ever lie under the curse.

But man is not only judicially but morally lost. Without holiness no man can see God—man wants holiness; he is not only a criminal at the bar, but morally unlike his judge—yea, hates a God of holiness; "for the carnal mind is enmity against God, is not subject to His law, neither indeed can be." If all this were not denied, or very feebly admitted, man would never dream of acquittal or acceptance with God in any way by his own merits. But to deny a truth is not to refute it, any more than to escape its consequences. To own what has been stated may humble, but it is the way to be saved. The penitent with his hand on his mouth, and his mouth in the dust, crying out "unclean! unclean!"—crying out "God be merciful to me a sinner"—is surely in the right way.

But revealed religion is not a mere announcement of man's guilt, depravity and helplessness. If there be a Sinai in it, dark and trembling with the presence of the Eternal Judge, there is also, blessed be God, a Calvary in it—trembling too, but trembling in the presence of the agonies of the Divine Saviour, dealing with man's case, that for him there may be mercy, *and yet justice be held sacred.* The announcement of a Saviour, suitable to the wants of a sinner, is what makes Christianity a Gospel to man. Oh! that was a day much to be remembered! Darkness was over much, as well as over the land; but then hope *was preparing* to step forth from behind that darkness and proclaim, in the midst of great light, that the law was magnified, justice satisfied, and man saved. This was the mystery of Godliness—Emmanuel identifying himself with us—taking up our lost condition—*exhausting the curse*, and so making justice and mercy meet together. He abolished death by taking that death upon Himself. He could do this; no one else could. And by what He did, and suffered, He put matters to rights. Hence He is "the Lord our righteousness"—hence all who believe in Him may find a justifying righteousness. The substitution was wondrous, the sacrifice was amazing! yet all in the highest degree suitable. For it was the voluntary substitution of Him innocent for us guilty—of Him in every sense all powerful for us in every sense all weakness and all helplessness. He drank the bitter cup to the dregs, then said "It is finished." Yea, my brethren, and was not that work most gloriously finished, for while mercy was crowned at the cross justice held the sceptre unshaken on the throne?

Nor did the Saviour merely work out a perfect righteousness for pardon; He also procured for His people all the Divine influences for holiness. He not only obtained for them a title to heaven, but also the means to fit them for it. He is not only "made unto them redemption," but "also sanctification." Not unto us, then, not unto us, *but to Him*, be all the glory of our pardon and acceptance with God, and all the glory of our holiness too. But for his atoning blood there had been no pardon; but for His mighty Spirit there had been no holiness for man.

Christ is then our hope—and He who was the hope of Israel must still be the hope of all who will be saved. The faith of the redeemed is simply this, that they are ransomed by His blood, sanctified by His Spirit, and shall at last be brought by Him to the heavenly inheritance. *This is the faith of the Saints*—this is good news to the sinner. And was it not for substance the Gospel of old? It was indeed the old path in which Abel walked, when he offered his sacrifice in faith. It was that in which Abraham walked, when he saw Messiah's day afar off and was glad. It was the path in which prophets and apostles walked, who all sought salvation in means by faith, not in merit by works. In this way they found joy and peace. The question is not how much did those ancient Saints, who "all died in the faith" of the promises, understand of the facts of the Saviour's work? There was much in this which the events could only explain; but did these Worthies firmly believe what they were taught of Him who was to come, as the substitute of His people? The value of a man's faith is not in the extent of the field of speculative knowledge his eye may wander over, but in the intensity of soul, *by which he fastens on essential points.* Those who walked in this old way found it the way of safety; by it they reached heaven, and are now "the spirits of just men made perfect." It is still the only way that leads to grace and glory. All other ways lead but from one delusion to another, and at last end in perdition. To the sinner trembling under a load of guilt, and asking what he shall do to be saved, tell him, oh! tell him of the way of salvation—point to this, and say to his troubled conscience, here is the way, walk in it, and thou shalt find grace and peace, and rest for thy soul.

Be assured of it—for all ecclesiastical history proves it—that during those seasons, when the Church has appeared "fair as the moon, clear as the sun, and terrible as an army with banners," she was then walking closely in the good old path of gospel truth. It was *this truth*, vividly seen and intensely felt, that enabled the first apostles of the cross so triumphantly to overthrow superstition and will-worship, and in a little while to change to a wonderful extent the whole moral aspect of society. Not in the gift of tongues, or in the gift of working miracles, lay the great strength of these men for their work, but in their firm faith in the way of salvation, and in their ardent love for the glory of their Master. It was this that made their tongues like flames of fire, that gave them a strength which no toils could exhaust, and a courage which no dangers could appal. We shall have successful missionary enterprises, not when the apostolic gift of miracles is restored, but when men shall go forth to the work with a *large measure* of apostolic faith and piety. And for a moment yet to advert to our former argument. Wherein lay the great strength of our reformers? Plainly in their ardent piety and extraordinary faith in the way of salvation. These men saw the world lying in wickedness, drowned in superstition, and they saw *but one hope* for it— the old way of salvation. Yes, my hearers, this is the pillar of fire in the wilderness. The God of glory and of mercy is there. The way of salvation, then, held, not as a popular hearsay, but in strong faith, as the best of all heaven's truths to man, and the Church will have life, energy, love and peace. And when it is asked, as it often is, in deep vexation of heart, what shall cure us of our spiritual feebleness and shameful coldness in religion?—what shall take away our criminal variance, emulations and strife? To my mind, there is but one answer. We must turn with a more ardent zeal and with a stronger faith to the good old way of salvation. We must get the whole soul filled, and warmed with right views of Christ—of His person, His work, His benefits to believers. As in this lies the hope of each individual for well-being and well-doing, so in it lies the sole hope of the Church. The Church that expects to find light and warmth elsewhere, than at the cross, is but deepening her blindness and increasing the torpor of her spiritual paralysis. But

Secondly.—To walk in the good old path *implies a thorough practical piety*.

The truth which we have briefly illustrated is the

heavenly seed. Whenever this is received into good and honest hearts, it will bring forth the fruits of piety—" in some an hundred fold, in some sixty, and in some thirty." Where there is not even the thirty fold, the seed has never taken root, or has withered away—the precious doctrines of the gospel have perished with the hearing, or gone off in wordy speculation. They have not been received in love, and are not held in faith, if there be no fruit. It is not my intention, however, at present, to insist on those acts of piety which are performed by all who walk in the good old way, but rather to notice a few points *in that temper of mind*, in which every duty should be performed.

1. Every religious duty *should be made a business of conscience*.

A good conscience is the soul listening with an obedient ear to the voice of the Lord—doing this, or eschewing that, because God wills it to be so. Such a conscience is the product of religion. It is also the instrument by which a man of piety will constantly work. A conscientious man may have a bad religion, and bear bad fruit, for he may have been ill taught; but a man without a conscience in religion will abuse the purest truths, and produce nothing from them but the most fatal results. And it is just all the worse, the more frequently he engages in religious duties. Such a man professes to be waiting on God; he is waiting on self. He professes to be desirous to hear what God will speak; but the desire of his heart is to hear his fellow-man speak him fair, and he says to himself, Peace, peace—" to-morrow shall be as this day," for all goes well. Very deplorable is the state of that man, who engages in religious duties merely to serve some low paltry end. He has more to fear than ordinary formality or hypocrisy. He may well fear, lest he be given up to utter judicial blindness. Can it be otherwise? He "holds the truth in unrighteousness," and is perhaps of all God's creatures the most criminally incongruous. *On the other hand*, to him who makes conscience of duty all is simple, consistent, definite. In the duties of the closet, the family, and sanctuary, he takes his part, not for form's sake, or the sake of reputation; but because God has required it of him. He prays, reads, hears and communicates, because God commands him to do so; and has promised an increase of grace, and the comforts of His Spirit to those who obey Him. This is enough to the man of conscience. He waits on God, and finds that he " is not sent empty away." And even if the duty be painful, and for a time appears fruitless, he feels that he dares not give it over. He is a servant, the Divine Master commands it. He is a child, his Heavenly Father requires it. He is a redeemed man, his Saviour enjoins it. Sloth may demur, a wordly expediency may plead, but to the soul listening to the voice of God, there can be but one course—simple obedience, and that obedience entirely on the Divine authority. O, blessed, O, gracious state of mind! For was it not this, wrought in them by the holy Spirit, that qualified martyrs and confessors for their trials, and enabled them to manifest that strong and serene moral courage, which adorned their profession and astonished and instructed the world? The soul listening with humility and love to the all-wise God, must become wise and good, diligent in duty, and in many respects *great in duty* as well as in trials; for he who has a heaven-enlightened conscience feels constantly surrounded with many sacred and powerful motives to duty. The command comes to him as a child of God, a follower of Jesus, a lover of his brethren. What force must every command laden *with such motives* have in sweetly constraining the Christian to seek the advancement of the Divine glory and the good of his fellow-men! Indeed, the language of his heart must be, I dare not leave these closet or family duties undone, be undone what may. I dare not forsake the assemblies of the Saints, or neglect any means by which I may get good or do good. My gracious Saviour's commands are on me, and He has added promises to His commands. Nor dare I do aught that would hurt the soul of one man, or mar the peace, or break the unity of the Church. My Saviour forbids all this. He has His eye on me. This, my brethren, is conscience in religion. This is the soul communing with itself—hearing, fearing, loving and obeying God.

Would that men in matters of religion were ever men of conscience! Pity it is that men carry the word conscience so much on their lips, but feel its power *so little* in their hearts! Let all its lessons be learned from the sacred page, and then let these lessons be deeply pondered. Let the dictates of an enlightened conscience influence you thoroughly in every feeling and duty in your religion. Would not this end much, and begin much in the Church? It would put an end to all the religion of mere pretence. For, is not hypocritical pretence but a Satan-devised substitute for conscience? It would end all that thing called fashionable religion and, in fine, it would end the religion of cold formalism. Till all this ends, nothing good can begin. That there is so much of cant, frivolity and formality in sacred duties, among professing Christians, is proof positive that many stand specially in need of severe lessons from an enlightened conscience. And surely it is not easy to conceive of anything more offensive to the eye of a holy God than a worship offered at his footstool, without conscience. God will have sincerity in His worshippers. But there is in this a total want of sincerity. Alas! is not this, of all wants, the most fatal! Such a worshipper is "sounding brass and a tinkling cymbal." It is not, what will men say of you, if you do this thing, or avoid that in religion? Man's approbation, or censure, is at best a small affair in this matter—it may be less than nothing; but the solemn inquiry is, What has God commanded? What will God say to you, if the thing is done, and what will he say, if you do the contrary? Will he approve, or will he condemn? My brethren, that is the point for you to settle. But that is just conscience in religion. To the right exercise of this you must come, if you would be found walking in the good old way. But if you feel that it hath not been thus with you, *but far otherwise* in your religious duties, then I beseech you, turn to that good way of making conscience of every religious duty. Make conscience of it in all the forms in which it can be looked at—in all the ways in which you go about it. If not so, then I must tell you that your religious duties, be they ever so punctiliously or decorously performed, do but dishonour God, injure your soul, and in various ways do mischief to others. Nor must it be the mere conscience of party or public opinion that you are to go by. This can never be a substitute *for individual conscience*. Indeed, party very often has no conscience, but only a loud voice; and woe to the man who takes that voice for guidance instead of the wisdom of God! If each for himself shall have to answer at the judgment day, then each for himself should have a conscience—should listen with a "*circumcised ear*" to what God the Lord doth speak, and constantly and faithfully do what he thinks God commands.

2.—*Those who walk in the good old way will worship God in love.*

Man, as he came from the hand of his God, and as he then stood related to Him, was in every sense a noble and a happy creature. He bore the Divine image, "in knowledge, righteousness and true holiness." To him God could speak, not as to the inferior creatures, *by the laws of physical instincts;* but in the language of *articulated wisdom and love.* And man could answer his God—and by an intelligent, voluntary and loving obedience own Him as his Creator and Lawgiver. Wonderful communion this betwixt the uncreated Mind and the mind of a creature. This was the first order of things betwixt God and man, and in it lay the chief glory of man, as out of it would have flown for him a full and lasting happiness. "But man being in honour abode not." His sin destroyed this order of things, and introduced the fatalest disorder. For, that man is now unfit, yea, averse to hold communion with God, is really the cause of all the other disorder and misery into which he has fallen. The Son of God came as a *Restorer*. Hence, the believer in Jesus is not only ransomed, but in many senses *restored to order*. For is not salvation the recovery of harmony betwixt God and man? Christ is our Daysman, and hath made *the peace*. And that Spirit, who at first brought order out of confusion, brings order into the bosom of those He regenerates, by making them fit to love God, and under the influence of that love to seek communion with Him. If this love be not felt, that communion cannot be sought. But is not communion with God the chief thing the Christian has in view in every religious duty? It is love that leads the soul to seek it, and prepares the soul for the enjoyment of it. No two men are more unlike than he who enters the sanctuary longing for communion with God, and he who comes there as the other, but neither desires nor hopes for this. These persons may differ in many respects, but the grand difference is this, that the former has love to God, the latter wants it. He who is without love to God may outwardly worship as the other, giving no sign of dissatisfaction; yet he cannot conceal from himself that in the duty he has no enjoyment, and reaps from it no spiritual advantages; while he who loves his God and Saviour finds every duty *a privilege*, as it affords him the means of the highest and most precious communion. In many things the want of love is the want of a power, which other and valuable qualities can but imperfectly supply; but in religious duties *the want of love* has the effect of *neutralizing all the other powers* and of turning the most sacred duty into a wearisome, if not a profane, ceremony.

It needs scarcely to be remarked that love to God in Christ, *in the bosom of a believer*, is an emotion far too complex to be comprehended in any simple definition. Indeed, human language is but a poor exponent of such emotions.

A delight in the excellencies of God—a desire to be like Him, and be loved by Him, assuredly implies not a little of what is meant by this love. And ought not this to be felt by all who would hold communion with God in sacred duties? That God should be loved seems one of the plainest of all aphorisms. Yes, and it has to the Christian an emphasis, which can be but imperfectly felt by those who merely see His wisdom and goodness in the beauties of nature, or only partake of the fruits of His goodness in the bounties of a common providence, rich and varied as these are. God in Christ is the God of the Christian; on Him the believer can look and not die. For this *manifestation* of God as He is, of what He has done, is doing, and has promised to do for poor sinners, not only superadds infinitely to the evidence which we have in nature for loving Him, but furnishes an entirely new and far more powerful kind of evidence, why we should love Him with the whole heart, soul, strength and mind. The earth is full of the goodness of the Lord, and men are plainly without excuse if they do not love Him. Yet the *riches of God's love* to man are in Christ, and what Christ is to us. It will not be expected that I should enter at length into this delightful theme. Suffice it to say that Christianity not only unfolds to our view, with amazing beauty and force, the perfect holiness of God as well fitted to awaken love in pure minds, but it also presents that holy Being in infinite wisdom, and with marvellous condescension, bestowing the choicest blesings on the undeserving. Christianity reveals God pardoning the guilty, arraying the degraded in everlasting honour, and communicating to the wretched "fulness of joy and pleasure for evermore at his own right hand;" and for the accomplishment of this, the WORD made flesh, Emmanuel dying on the cross. Oh! my hearer, dost thou really believe it? for it is this that will awaken thy love. Dost thou believe that, but for what a God of mercy hath done, thou hadst been a lost soul through eternity—but, because of what hath in mercy been done, thou shalt not be lost? Thou hast the friendship of God now, thou shalt forever be a holy and a happy creature in the heaven of heavens. Dost thou believe this and not love Him who first loved thee, and gave Himself for thee, that He might redeem thy soul from death, and ransom thee from destruction? Looking at the blessed Jesus, is not this the language of thy heart? "Lord, thou knowest that I love Thee"—feebly, alas! but yet, Lord, I do love Thee.

Well, then, you who can say so may engage in duty with the hope of honouring God in it, and of having enjoyment and profit from it. It was thus that ancient saints, who walked *in the good old way*, loved God and longed to meet with Him. "How amiable are thy tabernacles, O Lord of Hosts! My soul longeth, yea, even fainteth, for the courts of the Lord: my heart and my flesh crieth out for the living God!" And what else but this love caused *their hearts* "to burn within them, while He talked with them by the way, and opened to them the Scriptures?" Yea, and it was this love that made them exceeding glad, "as they believed not for joy, and wondered"—seeing the Lord. It was this, too, that brought a weeping Mary to the sepulchre, "early on the first day of the week," vainly seeking "the living among the dead," yet with ardent love seeking the Lord. And, my brethren, why should not *the same love* make you also long for the courts of His house, and make your heart burn within you, while He talks "with you by the way?" This love, *if felt as it ought*, will cause you to seek Him with sorrow when you cannot find Him, and will cause you to be exceedingly glad when you do find Him, *in the closet, at the Communion table*, or in any other ordinance. To His people Christ is, indeed, "the chief among ten thousand," and they will seek Him "whom their soul loveth."

Around the blind, every sort of beauty may be scattered in profusion, but it affects them not, for they do not see it; and to many, *even He who is altogether lovely* "has no beauty that they should desire Him." It is now, as it was of old, "the world knoweth not God." Fallen man is smitten with blindness of mind, and a far worse blindness of heart to the Divine excellencies. Wonder not that such feel no interest in the duties of religion. Indeed, the interest which they sometimes manifest is of so questionable a sort that it alarms one even more than their ordinary indifference. But what of the coldness of Christians? On this much might be said in the shape of argument, and in the tone of warning and reproof. And yet, methinks, a minister needs to be cautious in employing bitter censure against the dulness and coldness of his hearers. I dare not, for my part, say much in this strain, lest some pious soul, afflicted with the evil, might whisper "thou art the man!" My brethren, I know it: the Pulpit may, in divers ways, throw a freezing influence over the Pews. Yet let me remind you of what you should know, that there may also arise from the Pews a chilling influence which shall sorely affect the Pulpit. But be this evil in whichever quarter it may, I know of no cure for it, but an increase of love to God, our Saviour. Then shall there be more power in the preacher, and more comfort and edification in the hearers. But

3. *Those who walk in the good old way will worship God in reverence.*

Man must know God, or all his other knowledge is valueless for the great end of his being, and may prove in many ways pernicious. To what extent the knowledge of God is accurately held may with tolerable certainty be inferred from *the forms* of worship, but especially from *the temper of mind* in which a man engages in these. The childish follies, horrid cruelties and obscene rights of Paganism are simply the embodiments of the notions the heathen entertain of their gods. Whatever else contributed to the growth of superstitious observances in the Christian Church, there can be no doubt that *the decay of correct notions of God* was the main cause. The Reformation was the recovery of much, but of nothing more valuable to man than the correct view of God which was restored to the Church. For it is of the nature of this highest branch of knowledge that, when held in purity, it purifies all other kinds of knowledge and *turns them all into wisdom.* Indeed, without this knowledge all religion must be essentially and necessarily wrong. Hence, all false religions are characterized either by puerile levities or appalling terrors; but never by reverence or an enlightened adoration. Where God is known aright He will be worshipped, not with the mere fear which omnipotent wrath awakens, but with the love and reverence which a just view of all His perfections inspires.

Whatever may be the difference of form, the spirit of worship should be the same among God's children on earth as it is among the higher orders in heaven. Now, we know that angels and the spirits of the just made perfect worship God with the profoundest awe and reverence. *They veil their faces with their wings in His presence. They cast down their crowns before Him. They cry out, holy, holy is the Lord of Hosts.* This is the temper of mind in which these beings of excellent nature and vast knowledge worship Him. But the same holy, holy God is the Being that you worship. Is it with an awe and reverence at all similar to theirs who surround His throne? Do they revere Him much, because they know much of Him? Man's knowledge, it is true, is more limited, for he dwells not as they do amidst the unclouded splendours of heavenly truth, yet he is not enveloped in darkness. If God "keeps back the face of His throne" from man—shows him but "a small part of His ways"—still, much of "the invisible things of God" is clearly seen "by the things that are made" and *the things He has done in His providence and grace.* Hence, every Christian has abundant means for knowing that the God whom he worships "inhabiteth eternity," is omnipotent, omniscient, the Creator and Ruler of the universe, and is perfectly holy, just and good. All this, unquestionably, is more fully understood by angels in heaven than by man on the earth; still, every instructed Christian has the means of knowing enough of God's perfections and government to awaken great reverence in him when he draws near in acts of worship to that glorious Being.

And wherewithal shall we, who are but sinful dust and ashes, come before Him, or how shall we order our speech aright in His presence? To this momentous question there is but one answer: "We have an Advocate with the Father"—Jesus is "the way" to the Father. But, then, mark it, although in approaching God through a Mediator the fear that causeth torment is cast out, yet the reverence for Him is not on this account lessened, but rather vastly increased. If the soul never can see the Divine amiability in a light so inviting, as when by faith it sees God in Christ *reconciled and reconciling sinners to Himself*, so is it just when this view is taken, that His holiness, wisdom, truth, justice and goodness appear in surpassing grandeur. He who finds his reverence decaying as he becomes familiar with a sin-pardoning God has reason to fear *that somewhat* in the first principles of his faith is essentially wrong. For when all the principles of faith are sound, and *this grace itself* in lively exercise, the stronger it becomes the more profound will our reverence be. The believer sees enough to awaken the love of complacency, but not simply that—*adoring love* is properly *the mood* of his most sacred emotions.

It was thus that holy men of old felt as they worshipped. The Book of Psalms—the Prophets—the Epistles—are all full of evidence of a pure and fervent veneration. Nor is it unworthy of notice that the most favoured of these saints, such as Isaiah and John, were the most humbled and awed when they had special manifestations of the Divine Glory. He who has no faith can have no veneration. He whose faith is weak will adore feebly. But with the Christian, whose soul is in high spiritual health, it is not thus. He feels that worship *must be adoration*, or it is nothing, or worse than nothing. He knows that he is to worship " with reverence and godly fear," and this reverence influences his whole spiritual life, the *inner* even more than the outer. For while he loves, he adores; while he trusts, he reveres; and while with high joy he says, "Abba, Father," he lies in lowest humility at the footstool. And what but this high adoration, this reverence for Jehovah, so humbling yet so elevating, has given to *simple forms of family piety* and sanctuary services a dignity, a meaning and a purifying influence, which the scenic and gorgeous displays of a superstitious ritual can but poorly imitate: gorgeous displays of superstition, employed ostensibly to aid adoration, but much more truly *to hide the painful and conscious want of it?*

Yet, let me not be mistaken, the reverence in religious duties for which I plead does not by any means consist in the "disfiguring of the countenance," in a solemn and affected tone of voice, the upturned gaze, or the wild glance of the eye. A very little of this is a little too much. The Church cannot too soon get quit of it, if she would retain simplicity and sincerity. This is the reverence that we desiderate:—*The soul enlightened, and all alive to a present God in duty—seeing by faith the Almighty, the holy, just and merciful God as near to search the heart, to answer, to bless. To feel that thou art on the mount with God, and as if with God alone—seeing Him to be all glorious, yet condescending; and seeing thyself to be mean and vile, yet graciously admitted to a near and precious communion with Him.* This is the adoration of the soul—this is the reverence, or, if you will, *the cause* of the reverence, which should be felt by all who worship God.

My hearers, think ye that this is a very prevailing characteristic of professing Christians in our times? We may be favourably distinguished for some things in which our forefathers were deficient, but I fear that reverence for *the holy* is not among these. I may be wrong, yet I cannot but express my apprehension that in simple and ardent reverence the present age will not compare favourably with periods to which it were easy to refer. When religion in our day appears with somewhat of earnestness, it is so apt to go to *the house-tops* and stun all ears with feverish excitement and the glories of partizan triumph, that one feels sadly the want of that ancient reverence which, while it warmed and strengthened, awed and humbled! The Lord was not in the wind; the Lord was not in the earthquake; the Lord was not in the fire; but in the still small voice; and when the Prophet heard it, he "wrapt his face in his mantle." My brethren, when we are drawing near to God, and when *He is speaking* to us, should there not be a wrapping of the face, as it were, in the mantle? I mean that there should be awe, reverence and a loving adoration. To think that the word of God should be on our lips, or sounding in our ears, or the symbols of His love in our hands, yet no reverence for Him in our hearts, is sad. Brethren, it ought not so to be.

But I now come to the last topic in the discourse, and on this I must be extremely brief.

Those who walk in the good old way will strive to have a pure and consistent morality.

By this I just understand the keeping of the second table of the law. Love to God is the sum of the first table; love to our fellow-creatures is the sum of the second. It is pleasing to observe that all men whose opinion is worth much are settling down more and more in the conviction that morality can only be really effective when it has its roots deeply struck into religion, and is drawing all its nourishment thence. Even men of the world, *in their own way*, go far to admit this. Christians never had, and never could have, a doubt on it. For how is it possible that he who disowns the authority of God, and feels no love to Him, can either be just or merciful to his fellow-men? Atheism can furnish neither the *principles* nor the *motives* to this. Selfishness reigning in the heart, a man's principles are those of a narrow expediency, and his motives merely the impulse of the prevailing passion and the voice of public opinion. Morality, without religious truth as its basis, and no motives of piety as its support, has, under every variety of circumstances, been repeatedly tried, and has, in every instance, entirely failed. God has given to man a perfect system of morality, both as to principles and motives, and this has not failed and never can fail.

Those who *walk in the good old way* must walk strictly according to this. The Christian is no more at liberty to trifle with the claims of the second table than with those of the first. He dares not say " I love God," who hates his brother. But that man hates his brother who is false or unjust, as well as cruel. It is asked what, in that case, is to be said of certain high-flown religionists? Plainly this is to be said—that if they are false men, malicious, impure, or selfish, their religion is vain, and all the more vain for high pretensions. It is not a set of orthodox phrases, glibly or sanctimoniously uttered, that evidences a man's Christianity to be sound at heart, but *an humble piety* and a consistent and well-developed *Bible morality*. If Christ be anything to you, He is your Saviour-King as well as your Saviour-Priest. To talk of believing in Him and yet live in wilful violation of His authority, is a palpable contradiction, which you must get quit of, or stand charged with a miserable formalism or a ruinous hypocrisy.

Nor do we fear gravely to affirm that wherever the principles of the Gospel are held in faith, and where its true piety is fully carried out, there will be found among that people *a purity and strength* of moral sentiment and a broad and sincere application of *moral practice* in everyday life, which will be sought for in vain where religion is spurious, or where its heavenly doctrines are unknown. Not to see this is to be blind to the plainest of all facts. To see it and yet deny it shows a weak and bitter prejudice against the truth. For I hold it to be axiomatically plain, that when the Gospel of Christ has taken a firm hold of the understanding, the conscience and heart of a man, that man, although he may not be perfect, yet will in a high sense be rigorously moral. You who are professors of religion readily admit this. Well, how does it apply when each brings it home to himself? Dost thou adorn thy profession, my hearer, with truthfulness, temperance, purity, honesty and benevolence? Or is it far otherwise? Does conscience accuse thee of a lax morality? Then I beseech thee to consider thy inconsistent and dangerous position—inconsistent it is, with the profession thou hast made of submission to Christ's laws—dangerous it is, for if the context be looked at, it will be seen that the judgments threatened against the Jews were mainly for breaches of the second table of the law. Ponder this, ye who have departed from the path by any duty neglected, by any wilful sin committed, and instantly return to *the good old way.* Live in purity, love justice, do mercy. In a word, " love thy neighbour as thyself."

·I need scarcely remark to those who are accustomed to hear me, that partly from the nature of the text, as well as from a wish to make the discourse suitable to the present occasion, I have to-day departed very far from my usual method of handling a subject. Instead of confining myself to a somewhat close investigation of a particular topic, I have been led to take up many, and to dismiss each with but a brief illustration. And now, from a want of time, I cannot do more than offer a few slight observations on one of these great moral principles—truthfulness.

Satan is the father of lies—the author of falsehood. A false man is the child of the devil. Nor is there anything, if, perhaps, we except malice, which more clearly evidences this terrible and near relationship to the prince of darkness, than *an utter disregard to truth.* Than falsehood, no vice can be more directly opposed to the Divine nature, and the established harmony of the universe. Hence the false man is not only a child of the *Adversary,* but becomes himself a parent of confusion, and an adversary to everything that is good. The God of order, who is the God of truth, will not tolerate this. He has very plainly pronounced the doom of the liar. But God requires far more of His children than that they *do not utter* falsehood. They are to be true in the inward parts. First of all, true *in themselves*, and *to themselves*. They are to be true to their feelings, to the gentle as well as the severe emotions, so that the symbols of thought and emotion shall fairly tell what they ought, and what they are supposed to tell. This were a grand thing to see, and innumerable great and good things would flow from it.

Courage in any sense is a thing of some value ; but that moral courage which braces up a man under all circumstances to speak the truth promptly, the moment that duty calls—and that not only fully and fearlessly by his words, but by his very look and tone—is a thing of infinite value. He who has this courage will be afraid of nothing so much as a falsehood, *even by his very silence.* And upon the whole, is not he the most dangerous of all cowards, and the most meanly selfish of men, who never speaks the thing as it is, *because it is*, but speaks as he fancies it will please or soothe others, or save himself some uneasiness or bring him some paltry gain ? Depend upon it, whenever moral courage is low—when there is a want of that honest manliness, which cannot say yes or no, *as it should be*, let the yes or the no tell as it may—the fear and the love of God is low in that soul. And I entreat you to beware of being drawn into the path of falsity by these plausible but dangerous excuses—*a becoming caution—the interests of our party—amiable complaisance*—and the like. The Bible fact is, that the path of falsity leads to hell. There can be no good excuse for taking such a road. Be sternly truthful ; for is it not an established fact that the man who is sternly true is the man who, in the end, is found to have been wisely tender? Wickedness and folly may compel him to utter what is disagreeably severe ; but what help ? unless wickedness and folly are to be kindly smoothed down until ruin seizes its victim! This is often done. The world, indeed, is full of such kindness; just because overrun with falsehood. Clearly the man of truth is the man of wisdom and kindness. His *smitings* are those of a friend; often most painful to himself, but always salutary to the erring, if they have the sense and grace to listen, and not the infatuation to repel disagreeable truth, when prudently and honestly spoken. Whereas the false man, with his blandness, is doing mischief in many ways; and in the end will be found to have done nothing but mischief. God is true; Christ is the Truth; Heaven is a world of truth. Would you walk with God? Would you honour your Saviour? Would you be dwellers in Heaven? Then walk now in *the good old way* of truthfulness.

A word now in conclusion: The house which has been opened this day as a place of public worship, does credit to your taste and munificence as a congregation. You will, however, remember that it is the Gospel in its purity and fulness that can make any place of worship either an object of present interest or of future hope. *This is the true glory of the house.* I would fain believe that the force of this is in some measure felt by you. And, furthermore, that it is the ardent wish of your hearts that not only in your time, but for generations to come, the Gospel of the Lord Jesus may be proclaimed within these walls. God grant it may be so! And may He grant, that while from this pulpit the Gospel shall be preached *just as the Spirit of the Lord hath revealed it*, the men and women who shall in days to come sit in these seats, shall listen with believing and joyous acceptance to that Gospel of free pardon and perfect peace. But if the time should ever come, when in this house "another gospel" shall be enunciated, and shall be listened to with approbation, while the Gospel of Salvation through a crucified Saviour is forgotten or disrelished—then let the solemn inscription which is on the slab in the front of the church be erased and let "Ichabod" be engraven there.

CHAPTER VII.

THE RIGHTEOUSNESS OF THE SCRIBES AND PHARISEES.

"For I say unto you, that except your righteousness shall exceed the righteousness of the Scribes and Pharisees, ye shall in no case enter into the kingdom of heaven."—Matthew v. 20.

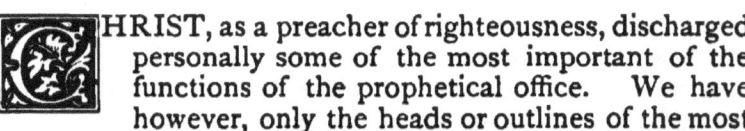HRIST, as a preacher of righteousness, discharged personally some of the most important of the functions of the prophetical office. We have however, only the heads or outlines of the most of His discourses. But the Sermon on the Mount appears to have been fully given by the Evangelist in all the richness of sentiment and illustration with which it was delivered. Hence, for depth of wisdom, simplicity of illustration and pointed application, it must ever commend itself to all persons of taste, judgment and piety as the most incomparable of all didactic and practical discourses, which have ever been uttered for the instruction of men. The character of the public instruction given to the Jewish people at this time was rather the perversion than the denial of the great truths of religion. For, if we except the Sadducees, who as a sect were not numerous, nor very active in propagating their opinions, there was no party among the people who disavowed any of the great doctrines of revealed religion. But the *perversion* of Divine truth, when this is accompanied with the introduction of human opinions, to which an authority is given equal to that of the word of God, may be as fatal to the piety and moral well-being of a people as an open scepticism. This was precisely the state of things when Christ delivered His Sermon on the Mount. Hence, we meet with so much

reproof, as well as direct instruction. But, indeed, Christ's reproofs were always intended to instruct and reform. The reproof contained in the text is directed against the Scribes and Pharisees, who at this time gave the tone to the religious feelings of the people. The Pharisees, as is well known, formed at this period the most popular and by far the most powerful sect among the Jews. They were punctual and zealous in their attendance on the outward rites of religion, proud of their Abrahamic descent, and bigotedly attached not only to the Mosaical ritual but equally so to a vast mass of human tradition, which they had gradually incorporated with the truth of God. This could not produce a healthy piety. Indeed, the religion of the Pharisees was perhaps as bad a display of religion as has ever been given by men possessing any measure of Divine truth. They were men of a thoroughly self-righteous spirit, possessing all the pride and bitterness of disposition which has ever characterized those who have fancied that their own works have secured for them the friendship of God. As the righteousness to which they trusted was that of ceremonial observances, their morality, as might be expected, was to the last degree spurious and defective. The Scribes, who are frequently spoken of as the lawyers, and never with commendation, were for the most part of the sect of the Pharisees. As their business was to expound the law, they came to be regarded as oracles of knowledge ; hence, in addition to the common faults and sins of Pharisaism, they were exceedingly vain of this speculative knowledge. We may, therefore, suppose that, as the righteousness to which the common Pharisee trusted was the righteousness of a pure church connexion, the Scribes' righteousness was that of speculative knowledge. This distinction must be kept in mind as we shall afterwards revert to it.

In theological language the term righteousness has two senses, which practically run into one. Man, as a sinner, needs to have his state put right with God. This is called justifying righteousness, or that righteousness in law which the sinner needs in order to escape punishment, and to stand acquitted and be accepted with God. This is what the inspired writers mean by the *righteousness of faith*, the *righteousness of God*, and the *righteousness of Christ*. It is called the righteousness of faith, because faith is the instrument by which man becomes possessed of it; it is called the righteousness of God, as it is such a righteousness as He can accept, and on which as a just Ruler He can act; and it is called the righteousness of Christ, inasmuch as Christ has, by His active and passive obedience, done what is needful to put all that was wrong betwixt God and the sinner to rights—betwixt a holy and just God and him who believes in Jesus. In short, righteousness employed in this sense is just the answer to the question: "How shall man be just with God?" How shall matters be put to rights betwixt a just God and the sinner? The answer on which faith fastens, and which will satisfy Divine justice, is Christ's doings, Christ's sufferings, in a word, His righteousness. This is the righteousness which has to do with man's state, as upon this the change from a condition of condemnation to justification can alone take place. It is the corner-stone of all religion; on right action on this everything depends. The whole moral duty of man, the moral commandments of God, the motives to the performance of the Divine will, must appear different to him who believes he is saved and put to rights in the sight of God, through the merits of Christ, from what these do to the man who thinks that he is saved by his own merits, and that his own doings have put all to rights. But the term righteousness is often applied to man's moral condition; and in that case it bears the sense of holiness of heart and life. In this sense a righteous man is a holy man, not merely free from condemnation, but brought to be like God, to love Him, and to serve Him. In this sense the term is used throughout the devotional portions of the word of God. Farther, as has been shown, both senses of the word righteousness run into one, and in every case practically do so ; so that in this compound state a man's righteousness is just a man's religion—his religion as it justifies him, his religion as it makes him holy, and as he lives by it, to God and for God. This is righteousness in the most comprehensive sense, and he who has this, and is this, is a righteous man. In further discoursing from these words I shall show :—

I. That the righteousness of the Scribes and Pharisees can neither justify nor sanctify the soul.

1. The Pharisees, as a body, trusted for pardon and acceptance with God to a punctilious observance of external rites. It is fashionable with some persons wholly to deny external religion. They allege as their reasons for their neglect or contempt of the outward ordinances of religion, first, the abuse which hypocrites make of them, and, next, that although gone about sincerely they can be of no avail in worshipping that God who is a spirit and must be worshipped in spirit. These apologies—for they are rather apologies than reasons for the neglect of outward religion—are often made, I fear, with little sincerity. The duties are disliked and neglected, and when the persons are charged with the neglect they find it needful to say something as an excuse. That hypocrites disgrace outward religion by their hollow professions is not to be denied. But if we were to consider everything useless that has been abused, we should find few things which we could value. Before a wise man treats everything as useless he will search for better reasons than that it has been abused by the thoughtless or the hypocritical. Besides, it is a great error to suppose that those whose general conduct belies their outward profession are in the proper sense hypocrites. Admit that there is a flagrant inconsistency betwixt what they would appear to be on the Sabbath and what they are during the week, is it too much to suppose that they are attempting to atone by a Sabbath sanctimoniousness

for the sins of the week? This, it must be confessed, is a pitiable form of self-righteousness, but it is far from being a well-defined form of hypocrisy; while to attempt to account for the neglect of the outward duties of religion from what these persons call the spirituality of religion, is to profess to be wiser than that King whom they profess to reverence. It must not be forgotten that God has not merely required His rational creatures to worship Him, but He has also prescribed the mode in which this is to be done. And surely God knows best by what means the sentiments of piety can be most suitably kept alive in our bosoms, and most suitably expressed for His glory. The man who neglects or despises the externals of religion is either grossly ignorant of its nature, or attempts to hide his aversion to all intercourse with God by plausible but groundless excuses. I thought it proper to state this much to prevent any misapplication of what is to follow; for true it is, man is so constituted that if he neglects all outward religion he cannot have the inward. If you neglect sanctuary duties, family duties, the means are neglected by which the knowledge of Divine things is acquired, and by which the sentiments of piety are cultivated, and the feelings of piety kept alive in the bosom. This fully admitted, there are several things that must be kept in mind, as, *first*, that, without the religion that is inward, there can be no outward religion that will be acceptable in the sight of God. If the outward be the means of aiding the inward, it is, nevertheless, the state of the heart that gives stamp and value to the religion of the life. Bodily service profiteth little, and mere bodily service, without the heart, can profit nothing.

The things needed are a righteousness of justification and a righteousness of sanctification. The thing assumed and acted on by the Pharisees was, that a punctilious attendance on outward duties would, in the sight of God, secure both. Now, suppose their attendance on outward duties to have been sincere, and we know that in many cases it was hypocritical—done merely to be seen of men —but suppose it done to be seen of God, how then does the matter stand? The man feels himself to be a sinner, deserving God's wrath both in this life and that which is to come. He goes to church, as the Pharisee of old went up to the temple to pray, reads the Bible, prays in secret and in his family, partakes of the sacraments of the church; now all these duties are of God's appointment, and if gone about from pure motives, and from proper ends, very great benefits might be expected. But the motives here are purely selfish, to the last degree mercenary. The man feels himself a sinner, he wishes to get pardon; he has the feeling—a feeling amply implanted in our nature—that God cannot grant pardon without a something being done which will furnish a reason for the pardon being granted; and the something which he does is to attend to certain external duties of religion, and he expects that this something done by him will furnish a reason for a just and holy God's granting him pardon and accepting him as righteous. In short, it is admitted that sin has put all wrong betwixt God and the sinner; but it is assumed that if the sinner attends to certain external commands, this will put all to rights—that the justice of God which has been offended will with these observances be satisfied. And by justice being satisfied, I understand something done which sustains the right of the Sovereign Ruler of the Universe, and makes it consistent with all His perfections, and His government over His creatures, to pardon the offender and accept him as righteous, and treat him as if all were right. God has prescribed religious ordinances; those are to be attended to. This is what the creatures owe as creatures to their Creator; *that* never can be an atonement for sins that are past—for the violations of the Divine Law—unless it shall be supposed that the performance of certain ceremonies of religion by a sinful man is a thing of such importance to the glory of God and the sustaining of His government, that this will be viewed as an equivalent for pardon and an atonement for guilt. This would be to make the Creator dependent upon the creature—the stability of God's government rest on the sinner's performing certain rites. But this was plainly the main ground assumed by the Pharisees in attempting to procure a righteousness for justification.

The righteousness which is of the law, the Apostle tells us, cannot justify. But this was a most imperfect form of even legal righteousness. The moral law implies far more than a mechanical and bodily performance of outward rites. It implies all the duties which, as moral creatures, we owe to God and to our fellow men. A man may be a most thorough-going ceremonialist, and make no attempt to keep the moral law. If legal righteousness be a shell without substance, the righteousness that is purely ceremonial, must be the very husk of the shell. But this is not all, it has been clearly shown that, unless the heart be right, the ceremonies cannot be rightly performed. The heart of the self-righteous ceremonialist is altogether wrong —he is ignorant of God's righteousness, ignorant in fact of his relation to God, and of God's relation to the universe. Hence, the wicked attempt by outward rites of getting pardon.

But, farther, such a man wants humility, or, rather, is full of pride. For he fancies that his service is of such importance to God's glory that his Maker specially needs it, and is ready to grant him the highest benefits for it. Such a state of mind, in the performance of any duty, so far from producing the righteousness of sanctification, must sink the person into the deepest depravity. To suppose that God can in any way be dependent on the creature is the height of ignorant presumption, and indicates a state of mind quite unfit for any worshipper of God. The first thing in a penitent worshipper, who is conscious that he is depraved and needs to be made a holy creature, is that humility which implies a complete abnegation of self. But the man who engages in the ceremonials of religion, with the view of obtaining a righteousness that shall justify him in the sight of God, can have no humility. Were it possible, therefore, for such a man to perform every religious rite with the most scrupulous punctuality, and even be, after a sort, sincere in going through these, that is, earnest in getting pardon and holiness by attending on these, still, if he wanted humility, it would avail nothing. I am far from thinking that all who engage in religious duties, even of those who become the children of God, do so at first from pure motives. Nor would I say to a man you must not go to church, you must not pray, nor read your Bible, till you are sure your motives are pure. These are means in which God is to be sought, and in which the most guilty and depraved are invited to seek Him. But there is a vast difference betwixt telling a man to seek God in these means, and telling him that he shall merit pardon, and heaven, and holiness by these means.

II. But, next, the righteousness of the Scribes is not more efficient as a justifying and sanctifying righteousness. That which the Scribe thought would put all to rights betwixt God and his soul, was his possessing such an extensive stock of sacred knowledge. These men sat in Moses' seat, and had their heads filled with Divine truth, and this they seem to have thought would be their safety. There can be no true religion without knowledge. We must know God before we can believe in Him or serve Him. Yet knowledge is but the instrument for the soul to work with. Very wicked men have had much sacred knowledge. Devils have it in no small degree. To those who have sacred knowledge and do not make a proper use of it, it will be a curse. It increases their accountability; it is a talent, and a talent abused increases guilt. Indeed, is not the greater part of the guilt of men but knowledge, to a greater or a lesser extent, abused ? The servant that knows his Lord's will and does it not shall be beaten with many stripes ; and the curse of Capernaum which Christ uttered was knowledge abused, the knowledge which the people there had heard from His lips, but by which they had not profited. But let us try to make this plain.

Knowledge is valueless while it merely remains in the memory. Memory is that faculty by which we retain sentiments, emotions and ideas, which may have been brought before the mind. Without this power man could draw no lessons from the past, could make hardly any use of the information or experience of others, could scarcely make any arrangements for the future. Indeed, without memory, man would be the mere creature of present emotions and of passing scenes. But this power, like others, but in a higher degree than most, is only useful when rightly employed. Were the memory filled with the highest truths, were these truths permitted to lie there, they could be of no use if not turned to some practical purpose. Faith must embrace them; the judgment must deal with them, digest and arrange them; the feelings must be moved by them; the conscience must apply them, and the life must be brought under their influence. When memory thus holds truth like this, wrought up and applied, it is of the last importance to have it well stored with truth. But the Scribes, there is reason to believe, did not keep truth lying as an inert mass in the memory. They were the expounders of truth, and there is reason to believe that some of them had an intimate acquaintance with it. We may well believe they read, wrote and talked much about truth—yes, *talked* much, and there the matter ended. With them, in short, it was mere speculation; and their speculations were so far from being pure or sacred emanations, that they mixed up the traditions of men with the word of God. But even had their speculations been perfectly sound—if truth was nothing more than a speculation—it must have been hurtful and not beneficial. Let the speculation be conducted on the purest principles, as to enquiry and as to teaching, that could not have produced a justifying righteousness. Because you know there is one God—know that he is in every sense perfect—know what you owe Him as a creature—know to what extent you have offended against Him—yea, know well by what way offenders are to return to God, what they have to do, and how they have to do it, as His children; now, say that all this knowledge is in the mind without one particle of error, that you think often upon it, often speak of it; and suppose all this is done not through hypocrisy, but done with earnestness, would that make any atonement for sin? Would the remembering of the Saviour's death, and the uttering of ever so much of God's truth, satisfy sin-offended justice, and repair the dishonour which your sin has done to His love and grace? To illustrate this—What would be thought of a criminal who had been condemned for some heinous offence, who would tell you that, true he is guilty, but he had no fears lest he should get pardon, as he had a great knowledge of the Prince and his government, and could speculate learnedly on the institutions of his country and its various laws! You might tell such a man, although you very much admired his extensive information, if he had the knowledge of the Prince and of the Law before he offended, that just made his offence the more heinous; and, as every one might have this knowledge, and was bound to have it, it never could atone for his guilt that he could speak learnedly as well as think clearly on these matters. The application of this is plain and apposite. Sacred knowledge is of the greatest consequence to the soul. No man can be saved without it. For how can a man believe in God as merciful, if he does not know God? And how can he trust in Jesus, if he does not know Him to be the Christ? But to know all this is not the man's righteousness for justification. If this knowledge becomes the ground of faith, and if by it he is enabled to make a personal appropriation of the Saviour's merit for the salvation of his soul, then it is well. But to think correctly over what God has revealed, or to speak it well can no more merit salvation than can the performance of mere ceremonies or rites. In the latter case it is mere bodily service, in the former case it is intellectual; but although this is really more valuable than the service of the body, yet in the sight of God, and intrinsically considered, it can no more merit justification than the other, nor is it a justifying righteousness.

All men who are not given up to practical atheism, who have not accepted the righteousness of Christ, will be found depending upon some sort of righteousness of their own; and among those who live at all within the pale of the Church, it will be found that almost all depend either on the righteousness of the Pharisees, which is a righteousness of a peculiar church-connexion, and a punctilious attendance on ceremonies—or the righteousness of the Scribes, a speculative knowledge of religious truth. But as it was of old so it is often now, both characters are found in the same individual. The man fancies because he attends to the duties of religion, and has a knowledge of Divine things, he is not only in a pardoned state, but for this will assuredly receive pardon. Alas! such a man is made the worse, not the better, for what he knows. He falls into a fatal security as to his condition. He thinks himself righteous, and despises others. Hence his religion makes him proud and bigoted, and in the end he becomes the victim of the worst of all passions—spiritual pride. His case is all but hopeless. Hence the declaration of our Lord in referring to the Pharisees, that publicans and harlots would enter the kingdom of heaven before them. Not but these persons were great sinners, and they, too, no doubt, when conscience troubled them, had their self-righteousness. But it was not of the kind that wrought such desperate delusion, and produced such a hardening of conscience as that which draws a force from the mad delusion that God is so blind as to make it a matter of justice that He shall pardon and accept the sinner.

CHAPTER VIII.

WHAT IS IMPLIED IN NAMING CHRIST.

"Let every one that nameth the name of Christ depart from iniquity."—2 Timothy, ii. 19.

IN the preceding verses of this chapter the Apostle puts Timothy on his guard against useless discussions, and points out the dangers of heretical opinions. He mentions two persons who by error had corrupted the faith of some professors of Christianity. Error when broached by those within the Church is peculiarly hurtful, for, apart from the mischief which it does to those who are the authors of it, and to those who may embrace it, it does no little mischief to many who are never ensnared by it. In stronger minds it awakens grief and shame that those who know the Christian religion should so grossly mistake or wilfully pervert its simple and precious doctrines; while in the feeble and ill-instructed it awakens painful doubts, which, if they do not endanger faith, in no small degree impair peace of mind. Such feeble and desponding Christians, when they look at the temporary triumphs of error, are apt to conclude that although for a while truth may keep the field, yet, in the long run, it shall be driven from the earth, and soon become the prey of mental darkness. All error is in some degree dangerous, some errors are damnable; yet the Apostle tells Christians that there was no fear of truth perishing from the world—that the foundation of God would stand sure, and that His chosen people never could be subverted by false doctrines. But, lest they should draw from this assurance the false inference that since the cause of truth could not fail, they need give themselves no concern about the truths of religion viewed as matters of faith, or things to be carried into practice. This has ever been the case with mere polemical wranglers. When these men cease to fight for what they call truth, its quiet and practical duties have no charms, and its great principles awaken no interest. To see a man zealous for the truth is a glorious spectacle; to see a man furious for his party and for party symbols, and calling this zeal for the Lord of Hosts, is a sight to sadden the heart of every reflecting Christian. Hence, while the verse contains a severe rebuke to those who fear that God's truth shall fail, our text contains an admonition which many a sturdy wrangler for doctrine would do well to study. But I proceed to discourse to you from the words of the text, and in doing so I shall, through Divine assistance, enquire—

I. What is implied in naming the name of Christ?
II. Show something of the product of this.

1. The term name, when applied to God and Divine matters, is much more than an arbitrary sign. Hence the word name frequently signifies Deity in all His perfections. Thus "the name of the Lord is a strong tower, the righteous run thereinto and are safe." That is they are safe under the protection of Jehovah. And again, "Not unto us, O Lord, not unto us, but unto thy name give glory." The name of God also often signifies His revealed truth. "I will declare thy name unto my brethren." "I have declared thy name, and will declare it." And, more strongly still, in the language of the prophet, "We will walk in the name of the Lord our God for ever and ever." These passages clearly fix the sense of the term name as it is applied to God; but does the same thing hold where the term name is applied to the Son of God our Saviour? The following shows clearly that it does: "To them gave He power to become the sons of God, even to them that believe on His name,"—that is, on Himself; and again, "that repentance and remission of sins should be

preached in His name," that is, repentance and remission of sins should be preached as bestowed by Him, and obtained through the doctrines which He taught. Such is the sense you are to attach to the name of Christ.

It comes next to be asked what is meant by naming this name?

It was the practice in ancient times, and is still to some extent customary, for the disciples or followers of any distinguished teacher to take the name of that teacher when they fully embraced his opinions. This was done by the followers of our Lord, for at an early period those who were attached to Him and embraced His doctrines were called Christians, and this application, as you are aware, has up to the present time been generally given to all that in any way profess the name of Jesus. Hence, in a loose and political sense, whole nations are called Christians. I need hardly remark that this is not the proper use of the term. For many of those who thus bear the name of Christ are His open enemies; while multitudes of others have no attachment to His person, and scarcely any knowledge of His doctrines, and manifest nothing of His spirit in their life. As the religion of Christ is a religion of facts and sentiments, there must be a knowledge of them, and a firm faith in them, in order to the production of suitable feelings and actions. Now, persons may assume a name, learn a creed, and perform certain external duties, and yet have neither the knowledge nor the faith of the religion which they profess. This applies not merely to those who live in popish countries, and where religion is comprised in the mechanical performance of rites, and the blind adherence to the beggarly elements of tradition, but to many who have been brought up under far more favourable circumstances. They have a name to live, but are dead.

In the Bible sense, to name the name of Christ is to feel and manifest the strongest attachment to His person, and to have faith in His doctrines. This you will observe is something quite beyond the mere nominal profession which many persons make. This implies, indeed, that the understanding is enlightened, as to Divine truth generally—that the conscience is awakened to a sense of sin and the need of pardon. Those who thus name the name of Christ are trusting in Him in all His mediatorial offices. They are relying on Him as the Priest who has offered an all-sufficient sacrifice for their sins, and whose intercession on the ground of that sacrifice cannot fail. They are looking to Him as their Divine Teacher, from whom they can alone learn the will of God perfectly; while to His authority as Mediator they are ever ready to give a sincere obedience. Such have put off the old man, and are renewed in knowledge, righteousness and holiness. They have put on Christ. They walk in Him, and are conformed to God as dear children. This is conversion, and nothing less than this can entitle any man to the high appellation of Christian. Such are the persons who can, and do in the scriptural sense, name the name of Christ. The Bible views man as guilty and deserving the punishment of God; at the same time it reveals the way of pardon through Christ, and as men are saved through Him, they who embrace the offer of God's mercy are called Christians. They are sincerely attached to the person, and have faith in the doctrines of Christ.

II.—We are to show somewhat of the product of thus naming the name of Christ, and that, in the language of the text, is to "depart from iniquity." Iniquity is a term implying whatever is offensive to God as our Lawgiver, Creator and Redeemer. God has in His word told us what we are to do, and what we are to avoid. In as far as we comply with His requirements, we depart from iniquity; and just in as far as we disobey God, whether it be by sins of commission or sins of omission, we cleave to iniquity. As accountable creatures we are required to love God with the whole heart, soul and strength. This implies all proper sentiments and feelings towards Him, and all those acts of piety which, as they must spring from faith, love, reverence and gratitude, at once manifest and cultivate these graces. We are also to love our neighbour, and this is to be shewn in justice, truth and benevolence towards him, in all the parts of our conduct. A conformity with this is holiness: the contrary of this is iniquity. But those who have named the name of Christ must *depart* from iniquity. The professing Christian is required to do all this.

And are others just to do as they choose in this matter? Many persons hold opinions which they would be ashamed and afraid to put into words. This I presume is one of them. You have not named the name of Christ, you have made no public attachment to His person, and have made no profession of faith in His doctrines, and therefore you may either cleave to iniquity or depart from it, just as you choose. What a monstrous notion! how unworthy of a rational creature! Has God made you and preserved you? Has He given you laws to keep? Has He declared that He will punish every violation of His law, no matter by whom it is committed, and are you at liberty nevertheless to disobey His authority, till you choose voluntarily to assume the Christian profession? This is nothing less than to abridge or set aside the Divine authority for the will of the creature. I tell everyone that this notion, in what form soever it is held, is a grievous error. The moment you can distinguish betwixt right and wrong, you are bound to obey, and every act of disobedience is sin, which exposes you to condemnation. If it be true that every Christian ought to obey, it is no less true that no rational creature is at liberty to disobey. What! because not professing Christians shall you neglect the most obvious and solemn duties, and plunge into the grossest sins, and all with impunity? The fact that you are not professing Christians, so far from being an excuse for other sins, is itself a very great sin. It is not more certain that there is a God, than that He requires all His rational creatures to obey Him. "Who is the Lord that I should obey Him?" is the language of atheistic impiety. The command to all is "depart from iniquity."

Still, we readily grant this comes with special force to those who have "named the name of Christ." For, in addition to the natural obligation under which they in common with all are laid, to "depart from iniquity," the profession they have made implies their hatred of sin, and their choice of God's service as good, and implies that they have felt and desire to retain His love. The position they occupy as redeemed men declares that they are not their own. The hopes they profess to cherish proclaim their hatred and loathing of sin, and their love of holiness and their delight to do the will of God. But all these principles are given up, if you do not depart from iniquity. But is it so that all that name the name of Christ do so in sincerity? I shall not say *perfectly* depart from iniquity. Alas! no. And yet ought it not to be the prayer of every Christian that he may not only be delivered from all presumptuous sins, but also be kept from all secret faults? Let me speak plainly on this matter to you, my brethren.

He that cleaves to any known sin does virtually renounce the theory and spirit of the religion he professes. The grand, I may say the distinguishing, characteristic of Christianity is *holiness*. By it men are brought back to God, and in some measure made like to Him in His moral perfections. But how grossly soever men may impose upon themselves in thinking that they are reconciled to God, while they are living in sin, no sort of folly can warrant the supposition that while they are living in sin they are conformed to God's image. In short, if they think at all, they must see they are not what the Author of Christianity requires of all who profess His holy religion. But, if what we have affirmed to be the genius of Christianity be correct, then we are required to present this truth in a stronger form. Those who live in sin virtually renounce the religion of Christ. They renounce it in its spirit; for the spirit of that religion is conformity with the Divine will. But sin is the opposite of God's will. They renounce it in its grand end, for the grand end of religion is holiness; they renounce it in its fruits, for the fruit of all holiness is happiness. And as those who live in sin are not holy, so neither can they be happy, as rational creatures ought to be. Thus you will observe that every wilful sin is just so far a practical renouncement of the religion of Christ.

Narrow views of what religion is and what it aims at are often not so much imperfect views as that they embody serious errors. Many when they think of religion, think of it merely as the means of removing guilt. Assuredly this is the grand end of the atonement. But although this is the central truth and that which gives efficiency to all others, it is not the sole truth in Christianity. Religion is not only a saving system, but a restorative system. The atonement of Christ saves the soul, but to suppose that this is the sole end of it, is a narrow and erroneous view. Among other things, it has given a very full and sublime development of the Divine perfections. By receiving the gift of the Spirit, it has made effectual provision for the regeneration of the human soul, and consequently has fitted man for glory, honour, and immortality. It has introduced a community of interest and feelings betwixt man and angels. It has taught many high and beneficial lessons to all intelligent minds; but these ends never can be fully accomplished but through the holiness of those redeemed. The guilty, redeemed and left depraved, could neither be honourable to God nor could they be happy. If you are cleaving to sin, then you are renouncing your Christianity, alike in its spirit and in all its practical bearings; yea, if all were to do so the Redeemer's work would, in a measure, and in a painful sense, be rendered vain. This cannot be. "He shall see of the travail of His soul, and be satisfied." The millions of the spirits of the just made perfect before the throne, and many who are now preparing for heaven, show that the end of redemption to them has been regeneration, and that their regeneration has been, or will be, finished in glory. Flee from every known sin then, and turn to God, for nothing less than this can furnish evidence to yourselves that you either understand or have embraced the religion, in its spirit and benefits, which you profess. But next—

We cannot have *peace* unless we depart from iniquity. Men may say "peace, peace," but the language of scripture is, "no peace, saith my God, to the wicked." Those who do not understand how a holy God must hate and punish sin, may have, if not peace, at least indifference on this matter. It cannot be so with the man who has read his Bible to any purpose. He knows that true peace of mind and holiness are things inseparable, just as guilt and misery must ever go together. Where there are any clear views of Divine things, the mind can only have peace when there is some evidence of peace with God. Now, Christ is emphatically to us the Prince of Peace. His atonement hath made peace. But what evidence have we that we are sharers in it? Just the evidence of having turned from sin to God. If you are cleaving to any known sin, you may say "Lord, Lord," but plainly He is neither your Lord nor Saviour. For, if He were, you would do the the things which he commands. But every wilful sin is just a violation of His commands, and darkens or destroys all evidence for a claim to the Divine friendship. How then can there be peace? But the want of peace is not some negative evil—a sort of want which something else may supply. If God be not our friend, He is our enemy. If we are not the objects of His love, we are the objects of His wrath. With God we cannot stand on neutral terms. Indifference to Him is rebellion against Him. Many cannot be brought to comprehend this. Hence, they have neither true peace nor are they filled with terror. They continue in a sort of dreamy state, which has neither the refreshing sweetness of repose nor the activity of senses fully awake. This shows a mind ill-enlightened, or a conscience partially seared. It is an unhealthy condition, and is far from being a state of happiness. In short, there is not true peace while the individual is liable every moment to be plunged into unspeakable terrors. A fit of sickness, or the approach of death, must awaken greatest anguish in such minds. Let a man have some good assurance of his pardon through the blood of Christ—let him know that God is reconciled to him—that justice, truth, omnipotency, and infinite wisdom are on his side, as well as goodness, and shall not that man have peace? If God be for him, who shall be against him? If the Almighty be his Father and his Friend, what can hurt him? This is what gives peace.

But, as we ought to guard against false peace, which, having no foundation in truth must, or may end in ruin, so do we need to guard against supposing that a want of peace and comfort is a proof that we want the grace of pardon and the love of God in the present life. It is enough that we shall be sustained now, and shall have feelings of joy and peace at God's right hand in heaven. The best saints have had wearisome days and nights appointed them on earth; and this has been done, not through a Divine enmity, but through a Fatherly tenderness. The best ends have assuredly been answered by those mental afflictions and that interruption of peace to which they have been exposed. Some severe outward calamity, the folly or sins of others, not unfrequently bodily indisposition, have been the causes of impairing the Christian's peace of mind. But when peace of mind is in this way broken up, God does not leave His children. Weeping may endure for a night, but joy cometh in the morning. So that the serenity which was for a time disturbed, is felt to be the more precious after it is restored. It is far otherwise when peace of mind is disturbed through a sense of unpardoned sin, and that sin indulged in. To such there can be no peace. "There is no peace, saith my God, to the wicked." And every man who has any measure of Bible knowledge, and has an accusing conscience, must realize the painful truth in this statement. But again—

If we do not depart from iniquity, we cannot serve God acceptably. The service that is acceptable to God must spring from the heart—be offered to Him by affections that are enlightened and pure. Bodily service in this matter profiteth little, and, if it be mere bodily service, it can profit nothing. The hypocrite and formalist may utter words and go through certain rites, but in all that they do there is no real service to God, nor can anything come from it that shall benefit themselves. Hence, Jehovah in addressing such by the prophets tells them that their service is a weariness to Him, that He cannot away with it. And the reason is plain; if we regard iniquity in our hearts, the Lord will not hear us. In this sense we cannot serve two masters. If we hold to sin, we will in our hearts hate God. Hence, all our service must be abominable in His sight, while we are living in any known sin. For to do so is really to disown His authority and openly to rebel against Him. But the mind can form no two notions more at variance than rebellion to lawful authority and service proffered. This is, indeed, to add insult to rebellion. And this, in the sight of Him who sees the heart, must be unspeakably loathsome.

But more: if we are living in sin, we are doing that which will wholly unfit the soul for the service of God. The understanding, conscience and affections must be all under the influence of truth, in order to perform any holy duty aright. But sin indulged in darkens the understanding, sears the conscience, and spoils the affections. I do not affirm that all sins do this to the same extent, with the same rapidity. Still such is the natural tendency of all sin; consequently he that is living in sin, is every moment more and more unfitting his soul for the service of God. All charitable and pious acts and habits are but the embodiment of the sentiments and feelings of the soul. But if the soul be debauched by licentious desires, hardened by avarice, or frenzied with malice, how can it engage in these acts which are pure, generous and benevolent? The strong man that keeps the house will utterly prevent any such movement within the breast. A mind that is cleaving to the dust, wallowing in the mire, must not attempt to arise on the wings of adoration, faith and love. Perhaps no spectacle is more offensive to God, and certainly few efforts are more painful, than for a bosom all disordered by sin, to make attempts by forced ecstasies to ape the fervour of genuine piety. Nor will this do long. The whole thing is so unnatural, and so utterly unproductive of good, that either the man who attempts it must become a shameless and unfeeling hypocrite, or the duty will be given up. If I am addressing any who have lived for a time in any known sin, and yet attempt to keep up the duty of secret prayer, or any other duty that specially demands the heart, they will understand very well the force of what I have stated.

And this brings me to remark that, if we are living in sin, we can do little good in *any* case, in many cases *no* good at all to others. Bad as the world is, it has some respect for virtue; and those who attempt to improve their fellow-men must themselves have some well grounded claim to the character which they profess they wish to see formed in others. It is true that some men can hide their defects or errors, and, while their hearts are like a cage of unclean birds, will speak or attempt to speak like angels. I do not say that such persons have done no good. For truth is still truth, let it be uttered by whomsoever it may, and God has often blessed His own truth even when it has flowed through very strange channels. But, admit that a wicked man may so order his words and conduct, that for a time he shall do some good to others, two things are worthy of notice: the extreme difficulty of playing this part in the presence of persons of observation; next, just the more successfully it is played, the more destructive it is to the soul of the wretched hypocrite, as no man can do greater violence to conscience than such a man. But suppose he could carry this out, alas! how short a way can he go in doing good. He has no principles which can lead to self-denial, and those sacrifices which love to souls so often demands. The hypocrite's efforts to do good are the efforts of words and of a moment. Such a man is feeble for everything that is really great and good. His heart loathes it, and his hand will not long perform it. And as soon as it is known—and that may be soon, and in ways that men little dream of—that the professor of religion is living in some known sin, his efforts to benefit others then become the bitterest satire on himself, and often an unjust satire on religion.

In fine, I do not mean to say that true Christians are or can be *perfectly holy* in the present life. But while sin cleaves to them, are they found cleaving to it? Assuredly no. They do not roll it as a sweet morsel under the tongue. They feel it a bitter thing. Their language is, "O, wretched man that I am! who shall deliver me from this body of sin and death?" Brethren, ye ought to be living epistles known and read of all men; giving to all a fair development of what Christianity is; and, if you have put on Christ, and are walking in Him, you will be able to give a just testimony to the truth, you will know Christ, you will edify souls, and you will have peace and joy in believing the gospel. Let those, then, who have "named the name of Christ, depart from iniquity."

CHAPTER IX.

THE PURIFYING INFLUENCE OF CHRISTIAN HOPE.

"And every man that hath this hope in him purifieth himself."—I. John, iii. 3.

OD has given to man the capacity to hope, and upon this his happiness, virtue, and intellectual attainments in a great measure depend. It is true that earthly hopes are often not realized, yet if they are such as can be entertained without debasing the imagination or hardening the heart, the effects will be found in every respect beneficial. But if our hopes are either extravagant or set upon what is vicious, painful disappointment and serious moral evils may be expected. It would not be proper, however, to affirm that all earthly hopes that fail are either extravagant or vicious. Partly from our own shortsightedness, but mainly from the uncertainty which characterizes all earthly objects and pursuits, many hopes must fail of accomplishment; yet, as far as these are innocent and rational, it is not wrong to cherish them. It is not wrong for a man to hope for competency in the world, and a measure of respect from his fellow men; or to hope for the virtue, health, and temporal prosperity of his children. Yet in all these things, from diverse causes, the most rational and best directed hopes may meet with the most painful disappointment. Still the cherishing of these hopes made the man all along a better neighbour and parent than he otherwise would have been. It is plain that, under the influence of these hopes, he partook of a large share of pure enjoyment, while his powers were vigorously exer-

cised; and this must have yielded, if not directly at least indirectly, a reasonable measure of substantial advantages. Hence, to hope rationally and to hope strongly is, for the time, the means of happiness and, in no small measure, the means of virtue and usefulness. This is so fully sustained by experience that it must commend itself to every man's judgment. But the principle thus briefly illustrated requires a mighty expansion when it is applied to those hopes which the children of God entertain. This is broadly stated in the text, "and every man that hath this hope in him purifieth himself."

It is plain from the context that the hope of which the Apostle speaks is the hope of what must be regarded as the purest bliss of heaven. Now are we the sons of God, saith he, and although our honour and happiness, from the relation in which we now stand, are both great, yet from all that we now have it hardly appears what we shall be, but this we know, that "when He shall appear we shall be like Him, for we shall see Him as He is." Without attempting fully to explain this rich and sublime language, it cannot admit of any doubt, that to see God as He is, and to be like Him, conveys the loftiest and purest happiness of heaven. To be like God is to be perfectly holy, and this is not only one moral qualification for heaven, but in this holiness the soul must find its chief honour and happiness. While to see God as He is, implies the nearest and most delightful fellowship which the eternal and sanctified soul shall have with God in heaven. As the friendship of God may be regarded as the foundation from which all the bliss of heaven flows, it may be regarded as that on which hope mainly fastens, when the soul is looking forward to heaven as its home. There is, therefore, a peculiar beauty and force in thus making the perfect holiness of heaven and the friendship of God as manifest there, the two great points to awaken hope. In a general sense, however, it is heaven in all its high service, and in all its pure and satisfying enjoyments, that is here presented as the object of hope. And this hope, says the text, will have a purifying effect, that is, will produce sanctification in the soul, or the growth of all holy principles. The Scriptures plainly teach that by an interest in Christ's atonement we acquire our title to heaven, and by sanctification are prepared for it. The Spirit is the grand agent in this. But He works by means, and hope is not the least powerful of these means in preparing the soul for heaven.

Whatever else makes up the religious sentiments or desires of men, the belief that Heaven is a place of happiness, and the desire to share in that, will be found to form part of the religion of every man who has the least pretension to the thing. But with many the hopes of Heaven are alike groundless and carnal; groundless, because they have never sought nor obtained the pardon which gives a title to Heaven; and carnal, because they never think of its joys as spiritual, and make no preparation for such joys. Such persons cannot be said to hope for the Heaven which God has prepared for His people. They wish for freedom from trials, repose from toil, and the carnal desires of the heart gratified; but a Heaven in which God is constantly seen in all the glory of His perfections, ardently loved, and faithfully served, is not the heaven they desire; nor can it, when thus contemplated, awaken hopes in their minds. It is only in the bosom of God's children that proper hopes of Heaven can be found to exist, or can exercise a beneficial influence. Nor can this be affirmed to any great extent of all Christians, for there are not a few whose knowledge is so obscure, and their faith so weak, that their hopes of Heaven are neither pure, nor strong nor effective. But where a somewhat full knowlege of divine things is possessed, and faith steadily exercised in these, the hope of Heaven cannot but have a most consoling and purifying effect on the mind. Hence it is that this hope of Heaven not only yields a large measure of present enjoyments, but is the direct means of preparing the soul for the future joy of the Lord. For "every man that hath this hope in him purifieth himself." I propose, through Divine assistance, to illustrate the text by the following considerations :—

1. The Christian, when engaged in the performance of religious duties, will consider these as preparing him for Heaven, and this consideration, in connexion with the duties, will have a purifying effect.

There must, in the common affairs of life, be a keeping betwixt our qualifications and the situation we would wish to fill, if we are ever to fill it with either credit or comfort. When this is overlooked from vanity, ignorance, or any other cause, and persons get into situations for which they have no suitable qualifications, they must fail in discharging the duties; and if they have any honour or conscience they cannot but feel very unhappy, even if they are permitted to retain their place. This is so well understood that all persons of sense and conscience make the greatest efforts to prepare themselves for important stations to which they may aspire. But every professing Christian looks forward to a place in Heaven, and there is no place there that is not one of high service, as well as of great enjoyment. Hence all that hope to fill stations in Heaven, if they act either rationally or piously, will carefully inquire what qualifications they have for these. I do not deny but there are many in Heaven who did not go through the training of means on earth. It is plain that all that die in infancy and go to Heaven go there without the training of the Church on earth, and it is equally plain that the Spirit of God might, in the hour of conversion, not only regenerate but sanctify the soul. But whatever may be affirmed of those who die in infancy, or die as the thief on the cross did, in the hour of conversion, it cannot be affirmed that those who reach years of reason, and have the means of grace furnished them, and despise these, can expect conversion; or, if this were possible, if after conversion they lived in the neglect of these means, could they ever be prepared for Heaven? Let it, then, be deeply impressed on your mind that without preparation, without qualification, your hope of Heaven is groundless; and if real, your hope in Heaven, without suitable qualification, must even there end in disappointment.

Knowledge, I think, must be viewed as an indispensable qualification for Heaven. Many of the works of God perform His will passively. They are regulated in all their movements by certain fixed laws and instincts. It is in this way that all the irrational creatures and inanimate matter may be said to perform the will of the Creator. But another law holds with man and all rational creatures. They, to answer the end of their being, must serve God with reason and with a willing mind. God is a Spirit, and those who would worship Him, must worship in spirit and in truth. But, if a rational and willing service be required of all the worshippers of God now, surely the same, but to a far greater extent, will be required in a future world. As the enjoyments of the future world wil' consist very much in the services to be performed, and as these services will be eminently services of reason and holiness, it is obvious that a large measure of sacred knowledge will be needful for engaging in these. For the performing of the duties of Heaven there must be a knowledge of the Divine perfections, of the will of God, of the character of those with whom you are to associate, and of the disposition and situation of those creatures, to whom duties may have to be performed. It will be observed that I am taking it for granted, that the happiness of Heaven is inseparably connected with duty—an eternity of inaction, or of something approaching to this, would be to such creatures as me, and I may say to any rational creature, an eternity of misery, if not of vice. But, as the service of heaven demands knowledge and wisdom, it must follow that the children of God, as they pass from earth to Heaven, will be the better prepared for its high service, and of course its pure enjoyments, as they have their minds the more fully stored with sacred knowledge : nay more, in proportion as they have had their powers enriched and purified by divine truth on earth, so shall they be qualified for the higher stations among their brethren in glory. And hence, I doubt not, that many who have filled but humble places in the world, will, through the treasures of wisdom and all other graces, be found prepared for occupying some of the highest trusts above. In our world presumption often pushes aside modest worth, and cunning circumvents high talent, and mere pretention gets the better of high attainments, so that places of great trust are often filled with the incompetent, while much genius and information are allowed to run to waste. It would be well if this were peculiar to the mere secular stations of life. In the Church, the same incongruity is witnessed. The highest piety and talent are frequently found, not in prominent, but in obscure stations. In Heaven, we may well believe, there will be found the most perfect keeping, the most exact agreement betwixt station and attainments, betwixt duty and qualification.

But although Divine knowledge is the basis of all moral worth, yet this is but one of the graces that qualify the soul for Heaven. There must, indeed, be all the graces, especially faith, hope, and love. Without faith, it is impossible to please God now, and whatever of its elements essential to a penitent believer on earth faith may drop when the soul enters Heaven, assuredly that part of it which implies unbounded confidence in God shall be greatly strengthened above. It is plain that the higher any creature is exalted in happiness, and the greater the prospects before him of that happiness, just in proportion must his confidence be in God, in order fully to partake of that enjoyment. The slightest doubt as to the wisdom, justice, or goodness of that Almighty Being in whom he depends for all that he has, and all that he expects, would destroy all the happiness of a saint in heaven. It is not only when he is going to heaven, but while there, that his confidence in God must be perfect.

The same may be affirmed of love. Not a single sentiment can be cherished in heaven without love, not a single note of praise uttered, not a single action performed without love. Without this grace, a man would no more be fit for heaven, than the most voracious brute would be fit for taking its place at the social circle, and discharging the most tender and delicate offices there. But on this, I do not further enlarge. Suffice it to say, that not only all the graces must be possessed, but these must have become habits of the mind—parts, as it were, of the moral man—so that the soul on reaching that world of glory shall find itself in its native element, having spiritual tastes for the joys and intellectual attainments, and moral habits for all the high and diverse duties to which it may be called ; so that whatever enjoyment God presents His creatures with, they may receive it with delight, and whatever duty He may appoint them to, they may be enabled to perform it to their own advantage and that of others, and to the advancement of God's declarative glory.

You all wish to go to heaven at death. But what are your expectations of that place? Are your views and wishes in reference to it low and carnal? The heaven which in a sense would suit you might be a mere place of repose, of delights for a depraved heart ; but that is not the place Christ died to purchase for His people, and which He has gone to prepare for them. The heaven which the Bible reveals is worthy of its glorious Creator, and suitable as an abode for rational and immortal minds. There God is known, confided in, revered, loved, and served. These holy creatures mingle with one another engaged in the diffusing of truth, benevolence and happiness, while they all engage in one form or another in celebrating the praises of their God, in studying His perfections, and in extending the knowledge of His name.

Without being more minute, let me ask is this really

the heaven that you hope for? Do you hope to exercise
your minds on the grand displays of God's perfections,
and in His service do you hope to be happy with intelligent and pure-minded creatures in their high and benevolent duties? These hopes embrace Bible views of heaven;
are they yours, and if so, what are the practical results
they are producing? If your hope of heaven be of this
sort, it will have a sanctifying effect. It will lead you to
attend upon every holy habit. The language of your
heart will be: I expect to dwell eternally in heaven; but
heaven is a place of such holy duty, as will demand much
sacred knowledge. I shall by all means endeavour to
obtain that knowledge now. I shall read and hear Divine
truth as I have opportunity, and meditate on what I hear
in Christ's school now. I shall endeavour to learn those
lessons which shall prepare me for the upper sanctuary.
And, as in heaven there will be a constant and perfect
dependence upon God, I shall endeavour now to cultivate that faith in God, which will fit me for implicit dependence on Him in a future life. In heaven there will
be a constant manifestation of love in its purest and most
extended forms. I shall now cultivate love on earth in
feeling, sentiment and in action that, through the love
and benevolence felt and exercised, I may be a fit companion for those who are perfect in love before the throne.
I do not deem it needful to pursue this train of thought
further. From what has been said, however, it must be
evident that the hope of heaven embraced on Bible principles has a purifying effect. If it leads to the getting of
sacred truth in great abundance, it must have this effect.
If it leads to confidence in God, as He has revealed
Himself to men, it must produce a sanctifying influence.
If it leads to the cultivating of holy habits, the benefit to
the soul must be great. For no man ever set seriously
about secret or family prayer until these became a gracious
habit, who did not derive from them a purifying effect;
and just so in the manifestation of love in the acts of

benevolence. Who ever set earnestly to work to instruct the ignorant, to reclaim the vicious, to help the poor, or to comfort the afflicted, that did not derive from one or other of these efforts a purifying effect? "Every man that hath this hope in him purifieth himself."

No; the Christian will never forget that it is solely to Christ's atonement that he is indebted for his title to heaven, and he will never forget that the Holy Spirit is the grand agent in preparing him for heaven; and no more will he forget that those whom Christ has redeemed are a peculiar people zealous of good works, and that every means is to be used for the preparation of the soul for heaven. Hence it is that the hope of our text is a powerful means to this. Under its proper influence the intellect is trained, the heart purified, and all the graces strengthened; so that every man that hath this hope in him purifies himself. But

II.—When under severe trials your hope of heaven will have a purifying effect. The declaration is still true that man is born to trouble as the sparks fly upward. And when we look at the sufferings of men, in the outward part of the dispensation, the inference which we will draw is that, in this, there is one event to the righteous and to the wicked. But when we look at the inward or moral effects of suffering, no two things can be more widely different than the influence that suffering has on the wicked, and the influence it has on the righteous. In general, for there are exceptions, the effect of suffering on a wicked man is either to make him fret against God or sink him into a state of apathy and despondency. If the former, all his malignant passions are roused into force, and sometimes open rebellion against the God that smites. If the latter, hope perishes in the bosom, and all the powers of the mind give way, and he is heard crying out: "My punishment is greater than I can bear." Without stopping to enquire which of these conditions of mind involves the greater amount of guilt, it is plain that neither of them can produce any benefit, as there is in neither any just views of the ends of suffering, nor aught of that repentance which suffering should awaken. Hence, as far as suffering produces a hardening or a stupifying effect, it is punishment, not chastisement; and it is a painful conviction that those who thus lie under it are, from the sins committed, only treasuring up wrath against the day of wrath. But, as has been stated, the child of God may have to endure as great suffering in the outward part of the dispensation as has ever been inflicted on the most wicked of men in the present life. Sickness is not less painful to him than to others, while from the superior delicacy of his mind, and purity and benevolence of his motives, certain losses and disappointments may be even more exquisitely painful. Yet, under all this, how different is his temper of mind from that of the wicked when under suffering! He is awake, but not fretful; he is resigned, but not apathetic. His language is: It is less than I deserve. "The Lord gave and the Lord hath taken away; blessed be the name of the Lord." He sees that the suffering is just; he hears the rod, and Him that appoints it; searches himself; casts out the old leaven; he is humbled under the stroke, and goes to God for help to bear it. In a word, he regards all his sufferings as needful discipline to purify his heart and life from sin, and as the means to prepare him for future blessedness. But at the same time, it is plain that all these views, sound as they are, could be of no avail but for the hope spoken of in the text. Patience can only have its perfect work from faith. Take away hope, and patience would soon end in despair. The Christian, amidst all his toils and sufferings, turns with delight to that happy world where there shall be no more suffering, nor sighing, nor sin, nor death. And while he lies under the suffering, he hopes that his Heavenly Father will give him strength as his day shall be. This leads him to God in prayer, and he gets grace. He hopes that all he endures now will just the better prepare him for glorifying God on earth, and for serving and enjoying God eternally. In a word, his eye turns upwards to that world where all is peace, love, health and joy.

"I shall not," says the child of God, when under severe bodily pain, "fret or despond; my God can raise me up, or, if He take me away in the midst of my days, and this earthly tabernacle shall be dissolved, I know that I have an house not made with hands in the heavens. I hope that this body, now so feeble and full of pain, shall at last be made a glorious body, free from all weakness and pain, and with a perfectly sanctified soul in that body. I hope to be forever happy with my Lord." "I have lost my earthly property," says another, "but I have not lost all. I hope I have mansions above—a kingdom with Christ—a crown of glory that cannot be lost, and these I shall inherit forever. I miss my earthly wealth, but if the want of it makes me more anxious to lay up treasure in heaven, I hope it shall be all the better for me at last." "I have lost, unjustly lost, my reputation," says a third, "and this is painful. But if I have lost my good name among men, I hope I have my name in the Book of Life, and out of that it cannot be lost; and although I should be covered with reproaches now, the Judge at the great day I hope will own me, and on that day say: 'Come, ye blessed of my Father.'" While another is heard saying: "True, I have lost my earthly friends—some by death, and others in ways more painful than by death; the loss is painful, yet over them all I do not sorrow as those who have no hope. Some of them sleep in Jesus, and with these I hope to meet, where there shall be no more tears shed, and no more partings. Besides, I hope to meet with innumerable friends in heaven that I never can lose. My Saviour is there to be seen in His glory, to be conversed with and eternally loved; and angels are there who were ministering spirits on earth, and in heaven shall be companions throughout eternity; and the spirits of the just are there who were companions on earth, and shall be so through lasting ages in heaven."

Yes, my brethren, true, most true, ye may have heavy trials, and heart and flesh may faint and fail under these trials; yet, though cast down ye cannot feel that ye are forsaken; though in distress, ye cannot sink into despair; for he that has the well-grounded hope that he is in covenant with God, and the hope of heaven burning in his bosom, will be sustained in the midst of the severest trials; and he that hath this hope under these trials will purify himself. He cannot prove rebellious, who thinks that he needs all the affliction that his Heavenly Father sends, in order to prepare him for an eternal weight of glory. He cannot become stupid under affliction, or sink into despondency, who thinks that it is but for a moment, and who hopes when that moment of suffering is over, he shall enter into an eternity of unspeakable happiness. He cannot mourn sinfully over losses, who believes himself an heir of God, and who hopes to be a joint heir with Christ in heaven. With such a hope in the furnace of affliction, faith, meekness, joy and peace must all be improved; but, as these graces are improved, the soul is sanctified, and hence it is that every man that hath this hope in him, when under affliction, purifies himself. But

III.—When under temptation to sin, the hope of heaven will be found to have a purifying effect.

Whether we are tempted by the world, the devil or the flesh, the two grand means employed by the tempter are pleasure and profit. Something to gratify, and something from which gratification may be obtained. Man will have pleasure of one kind or other, and if he has not a relish for pleasures that are rational and spiritual, he is apt to be led astray by those objects which profess to gratify his depraved passions and appetites. That temptation, under certain circumstances, may overcome even good men is as little to be doubted as it is deeply to be deplored; and this should make all pray and watch against temptation.

But of all the means which have been furnished by God to enable us to resist temptation, next to faith, there is no one more powerful than the hope spoken of in the text. He that has godliness, in its spirit and substance, is even now in possession of much real pleasure. He enjoys truth in its enlightening and purifying influences; he has fellowship with the Father and the Son, through the ever blessed Spirit; peace of conscience and fellowship with Christian men, with all the precious benefits that flow from a sense of pardon and sanctification, in all its principles and fruits; so that he might well say: I have a pleasure in religion, which the world can neither give nor take away. Now, he that hath this pleasure, when tempted by the pleasure of sin, is so far fortified against temptations. It is, however, mainly in hope that his strength is found to resist temptation. Does the Christian hope to be like God—that is, to have a nature in Heaven as holy as any creature is capable of, to be like God in knowledge, righteousness, and purity? and shall he listen to those temptations which would spoil his soul and make him like to the devil, or the brutes that perish? Shall not the hope of approaching near to a likeness to the God of all perfection cause us to repel with a holy indignation whatever would prevent this?

Whatever else the expression "to see God as He is" implies, it certainly conveys this notion, that saints in a future life shall have the nearest and most delightful fellowship with Him who is the source of all wisdom and excellence. This, indeed, must be the highest bliss of heaven. But of this, sin deprives creatures, for it is sin that separates betwixt them and their God. Let it be deeply impressed on your mind that there is such a contrariety betwixt the holiness of God and sin that minds tainted with it never can enjoy the Divine friendship. But if you are hoping, on Bible grounds, for heaven, the enjoyment of the Divine friendship constitutes the main part of that hope. Now, when tempted to sin, you are just tempted to forego this, and when you embrace the offers of sin, you just say, as plain as actions can speak, I would rather have this pleasure and profit from sin than the friendship of God, and I will take what sin offers, and give up all hopes of fellowship with God for ever. But shall it be thus with the Christian? Shall he give up the friendship of his Father in heaven for all that the devil can offer? No, my brethren; if he has this hope in him he will resist the temptation. He will say: "No; I cannot give up the hope of seeing my Heavenly Father, and of sharing in His love through eternity, for all that the world or the devil or the flesh can offer;" and in a holy indignation he will exclaim: "Get behind me, Satan; what are thine offers but shameful insults to reason and to piety? I hope for the friendship of my God in heaven, and I know that an hour of that will be far better than ages of sinful pleasure. And are eternal ages of that to be lost, or to be put in peril, for an hour of sinful pleasure?" Every man that hath this hope in him purifies himself. But sin has its profits, or at least its pretended profits, which it offers. Well, are these to be embraced at the risk of losing the treasures of heaven? Time forbids me to enlarge on these treasures. The terms under which they are spoken of, such as an inheritance, a crown, a kingdom, show at once their fulness and their richness. Assuredly the treasure of heaven will be abundant as the capacities, and diverse as the holy tastes, and lasting as the existence of the immortal beings that dwell there. But all the treasure of heaven is sure to the Christian, and then it has all been secured for him by the merits of his Redeemer. Believers, what say you to it, when sin holds out its profits? Are you willing to give up all right and title to these treasures, or at least to put all these in peril, for the profits of sin? An heir-apparent to a great throne, giving up his right to that throne, or putting his right in peril for a few pence or a mess of potage, were wisdom and noble mindedness to this. But will the Christian, in whose bosom burns the hope of that heavenly treasure, and who looks at it under the light of Divine truth, and in strong faith, pander to sin with the treasures of heaven? We say, with clear views and strong faith, for there is much in this. Ah! my brethren, when sin overcomes you, is it not when faith is weak and hope obscure? Who with heaven open before him, as it was to Paul and John—who that beheld, as they did, its material glories, and its far higher moral glories, its society and the order and converse, and the songs of that society—who, after having seen and heard these unutterable things of bliss, would turn round and exchange it all for the profits and pleasures of sin? That could not be; the cry would be, away with the thought, as madness and folly. But, my brethren, why should not hope and faith produce at least something like the same results? Are you a child of God? Then that treasure is yours. It is laid up for you. A few days or a few years, and you shall enter upon it, and shall find it to be far more than eye hath seen or ear heard, or than hath entered into the heart of man to conceive of. "Every man that hath this hope in him purifieth himself."

CHAPTER X.

THE OCCUPATION OF THE SAINTS IN HEAVEN.

"Him that overcometh will I make a pillar in the temple of my God, and he shall go no more out; and I will write upon him the name of my God, and the name of the city of my God, which is New Jerusalem, which cometh down out of heaven from my God; and I will write upon him my new name."—Revelations iii. 12.

WITHOUT faith and hope the mind must sink under severe trials. These graces support it. But the faith and hope of the ancient Christian, when under trials, were upheld by the promises of God, and thus they were enabled to resist temptations, and firmly to endure the greatest persecution. But the promises which support the Christian graces draw their main strength from the prospects which they unfold for the soul in a future world. To those who are struggling under trials, and are faithful to their Saviour, our text contains a promise distinguished for its sublimity of thought and the consolation it is fitted to confer. Our Lord promises that those who overcome in the spiritual warfare shall be made pillars in the temple of God. It is necessary in a passage so highly figurative to explain the language, before we proceed to illustrate the doctrines which it contains.

The Jewish temple was a sacred building, consecrated to the service of God, in which He was worshipped, and where He gave many visible proofs of His power. But the temple spoken of in the text was no earthly sanctuary, but the heaven of heavens. It is promised that the faithful followers of Christ shall be pillars in this temple. Pillars are erected in public buildings either for support or monumental ornaments. The latter is the sense of the figure employed. God alone can support the heavenly temple. But while no creature can share in supporting heaven, holy creatures may be made its ornaments. The redeemed are monuments of His glory in heaven. But when the figure of a pillar is employed to designate an individual, it is descriptive of very high worth and of high standing. Thus Paul on one occasion speaks of Peter and James as pillars of the Church. Pillars which are set up to commemorate events, or in honour of an individual, have generally inscriptions upon them. And the moral and spiritual pillars mentioned in the text are spoken of as bearing these inscriptions : the name of God, the name of the city of God, and Christ's new name. The meaning of these sublime and significant inscriptions may be thus briefly explained. That the redeemed in heaven shall be publicly known as the sons of God, and shall visibly represent the Divine image. Next, they shall be the citizens of heaven, and fully entitled to all its privileges. And, lastly, their relationship to Emmanuel—for that is Christ's new name—shall be plainly and eternally recognized. This, I think, is a just, though brief, explanation of these remarkable expressions. The words thus explained, we find that the passage unfolds several great and consoling doctrines. At present I can only attempt to illustrate one of these.

The redeemed who have been faithful to their Lord, under trials while on earth, shall be advanced to a very high standing and great honour in heaven.

Perhaps no creature in the universe presented a more strange and instructive subject for contemplation than man when looked at in his moral condition. At first created in the image of God, his soul was endowed with the purest knowledge, righteousness and holiness. A creature thus endued, and secured of immortal existence, possesses capabilities of great usefulness to others, and is fitted for tasting varied and lasting happiness. Such was man as he came from the hand of God. But being in honour he abode not; his fall into sin destroyed at once his happiness and moral beauty, and rendered him incapable of serving God acceptably. A mind hardened by sin, enslaved by the vicious passions, and hating what is wise, just and pure, cannot but be miserable and depraved, and very offensive in the sight of a holy God. The powers of thought and passion which remain in such a mind—as in the case of devils—but tend to render the degradation the more visible, and the misery the more complete. In man, these powers of thought and passion survive the loss of the image of God. And the history of our race furnishes ample and frightful illustration, what a creature of intellect and desires becomes, when he disowns the law of God, and is entirely destitute of the Divine love. Although sin in the proper sense did not destroy the reasoning faculties of man, yet it made him far less capable of happiness suitable to his nature, than the lowest creatures which retain the place assigned to them in the scheme of Providence. Hence, the powers which man retains after he has lost the image of God tend but in one way or other to dishonour the creature and increase the sum of human wretchedness. That God makes the wrath of man to praise Him, and often brings good out of evil, merely shows the Divine power and wisdom, not that the depraved heart possesses any tendency to glorify God or do good. Had man been left in this deplorable condition, it is easy to see that his wretchedness must have been as lasting as his rebellion.

But God had mercy on man. Redemption is a scheme of restoration. Man, by a free pardon through the merits of Christ, is restored to the favour of God, while regeneration by the Holy Spirit restores the image of God to his soul. When we look at the guilt and depravity of man we may well exclaim: How shall the Ethiopian change his skin and the leopard his spots? How shall he that is accustomed to do evil learn to do good? The answer is, the Spirit of God is the agent in restoring man to holiness. He is omnipotent and can do it. And when this is done, the soul is again put in possession of knowledge, righteousness and holiness, and all its powers fitted for endless happiness and improvement. Men might be pardoned, but without holiness they never could taste happiness, or properly exercise their powers for the glory of God.

When we affirm that all that enter heaven are perfectly holy, we mean that their faculties are delivered from the power of sin. They know the will of God and sincerely love to obey it. Still we do not affirm that all who have been redeemed from sin and death have equal intellectual endowments, or have made the same attainments in holiness. They have all the graces, but not all in an equal degree. We know that as one star differeth from another, so will there be a difference in gracious attainments among the redeemed in heaven. Those who possess eminent piety now will shine with peculiar glory hereafter. Yet all in heaven shall be happy. As their relation to Christ is the same, and their holiness the same in kind, their happiness shall be the same in kind, though not in degree. The little child that just lisped a Saviour's name and breathed out its soul in the arms of its mother, and the Apostles that converted nations and died as martyrs at the stake are both in heaven, and both happy to the extent of their capacities, though not to the same degree. Restoration to holiness was restoration to the dignity and happiness which saints possess in heaven. Without holiness no one shall see the Lord. Without it His friendship cannot be enjoyed, nor can any of His rational creatures without this serve Him aright.

Knowledge of the highest sort is an essential element of this holiness. It implies a knowledge of the divine perfections—of the ways and dealings of God with His creatures—of what he requires of them, and what He promises to bestow upon them. Whatever else we may know, if ignorant of these grand truths, our souls can neither possess dignity nor moral beauty. But he that possesses this divine wisdom is possessed of great enlargement, elevation and purity of mind. This, to some extent, is seen in every true Christian in the present life, even while this sacred knowledge is mixed with error, and its operations greatly marred by affections imperfectly sanctified. It is far otherwise in heaven. We do not affirm that even there the highest of creatures know all things. The great book which had opened for their view will be but imperfectly read after millions of ages have passed away. But what we affirm is, that all this knowledge is pure, and that all this knowledge in them is wisdom. They possess with perfect accuracy all the essential elementary truths, and are continually adding to their stock of knowledge. They have the most just notions of the perfections of God, and as far as opportunity affords scope for observation—and this must be vast—their notions of the providence and works of God are perfectly accurate. Such knowledge must give to the human mind a wonderful dignity. Those who possess it are monumental pillars in the temple of God—pillars of wisdom that adorn the heavenly society.

But mere knowledge, even of the highest sort, will not confer dignity or moral beauty on its possessor, or ensure him of happiness. Devils have capacious minds, furnished with a vast mass of great truths, and yet remain wicked and miserable. And we have all known men of extensive information, who have been very wretched and mischievous in the world. Man is not a mere creature of thought and sentiment, but is endowed with feelings and passions and, if these are malignant or impure, he will be degraded and miserable, let him know ever so much. Hence, *he must be made holy in his affections*, as well as in his understanding. He must possess meekness and humility, and above all he must possess love in all its modifications. It is only when the affections are reduced to perfect order and purity, that the powers of intellect can be properly exercised—that the soul appears in the charms of beauty, and is fitted to partake of durable and rational enjoyment. The graces of the affections are the graces of the Spirit. These are given in the hour of regeneration, and are perfected in glory. If the knowledge of the redeemed be vast, so are all their affections pure and amiable. These taken together make up what the inspired writers mean by the image of God restored to the soul, and constitute what in common language we call holiness of character. The reason of man fully enlightened—his judgment accurate on all matters—his memory stored with the most lofty and valuable truths, and his affections in perfect harmony with the Divine will, must present a character in the highest sense beautiful and noble. Such is the character of the redeemed in heaven —hence they are monumental pillars—spiritual ornaments in the temple above. Without holiness they could not be there. Their high holiness gives them distinction among the society of heaven. But next—

The duties which the redeemed perform in the heavenly economy give them a high standing among their associates.

It has been already shown that the souls of the redeemed are richly endowed. But the gifts of God are not intended for display, but for use. On earth the servant that hid his Lord's talent was condemned. No servant in heaven can do this. The gifts they have are employed. They serve God day and night in His temple, without ceasing. From what is revealed of the heavenly state, it is plain that active service is its prominent characteristic. Not but finite natures may require repose, that their limited powers may not be exhausted, as well as to afford variety to their emotions and time for meditation. Repose, however, seems the exception, and action the general rule of their existence. Hence, angels are represented with wings, and as flames of fire—figures which show their motion and activity. But this truth rests upon fact. We find that the angels have been frequently employed in our world, in working out some of the most important parts of the scheme of providence. Sometimes they have come as ministers of mercy, at other times as ministers of vengeance. But Christ tells us that after the resurrection the redeemed shall be made like unto the angels. This likeness I take it will consist in holiness, happiness, and in the service they shall be called upon to perform. But this statement, although strong enough to warrant our inference, is by no means all that we have to rest our argument upon. Have angels been commissioned to come into this world? so have glorified saints. Moses and Elias came from heaven to converse with our Lord before His suffering on the cross. And who shall say that this was the only mission in which they and others of their brethren have been sent to earth?

They shall, says Christ, be on a par with the angels. And we know it was so in those visions which John had of the heavenly service. The active services and the adoration uttered seem to be shared alike by angels and saints. They stand together before the throne—join in the songs of praise—walk in white, and together hold intercourse with God. But is their service wholly confined to those times when they approach the visible Shechinah, and adore Him that sits on the throne? Do they never leave the heaven of heavens, and serve their God by doing His will throughout the universe? We know that angels have often done this, and do it still, but the redeemed are on a footing with the angels, and, as we think, share with them in the service of God in various parts of the universe. To be minute here, were to attempt to be wise above what is written, yet we over-step not the bounds of revelation and right reason, when we affirm that some of the higher duties which are performed by the instrumentality of creatures are performed by the redeemed from among men. The promulgation of the truth of God is one of the highest and most benevolent services in which creatures can be engaged. May we not suppose then that Paul and Peter and James, with others who promulgated truth on earth, are now communicating to distant portions of God's universe certain truths of the knowledge of which other rational orders may be benefited? Not that these worlds have sinned—not that doctrines of faith and repentance need be preached there, for the reason they are preached among men. Yet many who do not need the direct benefits of redemption may, nevertheless, be benefited by a knowledge of the principles and doctrines which this mighty work unfolds. Angels, we know, who do not need a Saviour, desire earnestly to look into the glorious mysteries of a Saviour's work. But why angels alone? Would not all other rational creatures who love God desire to do the same? Would they not all learn much by having a full development made to them of what the Son of God did when He appeared as Mediator betwixt offended Heaven and a guilty race? It has been shown angels were appointed to unfold to man the Saviour's work before He came, and, as the work is now finished, may not saints in heaven be commissioned—for they are now equal with the angels—to carry the wondrous tale from world to world, and to proclaim from system to system the glories of this mighty work of Jehovah? No order of holy creatures can learn the amazing doctrines of the cross and not acquire a more ardent love and a more profound veneration for God.

When the Apostles stood around their Master on Mount Olivet, His mandate to them was: "Go ye into all the world and preach the Gospel to every creature." They did this and fulfilled their course on the earth. But when the same men ascended on high, and were clothed in white, and crowns placed upon their heads in heaven, did they not hear another mandate from the throne not altogether dissimilar to the first—might it not run thus: "Go into all the universe and proclaim the glories of my cross? Tell it from world to world, how mercy and justice have met; how righteousness and peace have embraced each other; how God can be just, yet the justifier of the ungodly!" Indulge me on this theme for a moment longer, my brethren. If truth is thus promulgated, are Apostles the only messengers? No, may it not be at this very hour; there are some of those whom you knew on earth—*the world knew them not*—who are employed in carrying forth from the Throne of God great truths to be diffused through distant worlds. On earth they were men of God, of ardent piety, yet no man regarded them. They are now pillars in the heavenly society, and they are honoured in promulgating the truth of God among other orders of intelligences. Nor can I quit this part of the subject without remarking, that if redeemed men are thus employed, the service will yield to themselves great happiness and afford the means of vast improvement. In promulgating the truth we do great good to others, and in the most direct way glorify God. This cannot but yield the highest gratification to a holy mind. But with such powers as the redeemed possess this exercise will afford great scope for improvement. The new regions they visit, the new orders they hold intercourse with, the modes of thought and of action that prevail there, all by the appointment and under the government of God, cannot fail but open to such minds boundless sources of knowledge, and the purest gratification. But, further, suppose the knowledge communicated to be the view given of the Divine perfections as manifested in the work of redemption, are not the redeemed from earth, on many accounts, admirably fitted to communicate this knowledge to them? They understood it well, possibly better than the highest angels. The deep personal interest which they feel in it will animate them with the greatest zeal to make others acquainted with the whole system of Gospel truth. When on earth there was no theme on which they loved so well to speak, and shall this feeling not be the same, yea, far more intense in heaven, or in any other part of the universe? It is no fancy to suppose that wherever they can find rational creatures to listen, they will tell them of a Saviour's love and condescension. And they will do this that others may love and revere God more, and that Jehovah may be more glorified by all His creatures. Hence will be fulfilled the sublime declaration of the Apostle—Eph. iii. 10.

I need hardly remark that this reasoning proceeds on the supposition that there are many other worlds besides ours, and many other orders of creatures besides men and angels. Who can doubt the former that looks at the thousands of bright luminaries seen by the naked eye in the aerial heavens, or thinks of the millions more which are seen by the help of glasses? I cannot doubt but all these worlds are the abodes of life, of intelligence, of law and love to God. These worlds are the abodes of rational beings that know and serve their God. Not all the dead matter or merely sentient beings together can show forth the glory of God like one rational intelligence. It is the rational soul that is the true mirror of the Divinity. Hath God, then, who does all things well, created suns and systems innumerable, and placed no one there that can know or love Him? I, at least, cannot think so. All His works praise Him; and all His saints love Him. The praise that arises from the worlds He hath made must be the praise of rational service springing from grateful hearts. Now, shall we suppose, that that work of God which of all others is most fitted to unfold the Divine perfections so as to awaken the reverence and gratitude of creatures is kept secret from the greatest part of the universe? Earth, it is true, was the platform on which the work of redemption was accomplished; man the object to whom its benefits directly apply. No other creature shares in the pardon of Christ's atonement. But all other holy creatures may share in the beneficial effects of those truths which spring from the knowledge of that atonement. Hence the indirect benefits of redemption may extend to every race, and its mighty truths be known in every world. Well might an Apostle exclaim : " Great is the mystery of godliness, God manifest in the flesh, justified in the spirit, seen of angels."

There is abundant reason for thinking that on the great, the final day of reckoning, when the Son of God shall appear to iudge men and devils, the whole universe shall be assembled to witness that mighty event. And possibly lessons shall on that day be taught, which shall be throughout all eternity of unspeakable importance to all finite minds. But it is easy to see that the transactions of that day can be but imperfectly understood without an intimate knowledge of the work of redemption. This knowledge, if needful, will be communicated in order that the vast assembly of principalities and powers and various orders may be prepared for witnessing the final judgment. Now there are two ways by which we can conceive God to make other worlds acquainted with this knowledge—either by direct inspiration or through the instrumentality of such agents as He may employ. Both these means have been employed in our world. The first, however, has in all cases been made subservient to the second. When men or angels have been inspired it was not for their own special benefit, as far as we know, but that they might be qualified to communicate the will of God to others. We have every reason to believe that this order of procedure shall continue. Angels and men have both been employed on earth to promulgate the will of God, and shall not redeemed men, when on an equality with the angels in a future world be employed as well as they to transmit Divine truth into other portions of the universe? And thus shall the rational offspring of Jehovah be made acquainted with the ways of God, especially with the work of redemption. What a wide field shall thus be opened up for the exercise of the expanded and sanctified powers of redeemed men in heaven ! But if the service be great so is the honour attending it. Now their sphere of labour is confined to a family or a small community; hereafter that field of labour may be vast and varied, beyond the loftiest conception. God shall fit them for their work—shall mark it out for them—and shall bless them in it; while it shall be seen to all the heavenly society that they are moral pillars in the temple of God. But, lastly,

Saints in heaven have a high standing from their intimate relation to the Son of God.

There is a vulgar remark pregnant with much wisdom, that "fools should never judge of half-done work." The sense of the adage is that those who understand a thing but imperfectly ought to give no opinion upon it. But nothing is more common than for these very persons to offer opinions, and often in a way that shows as little modesty as wisdom. They condemn what they do not understand, and ridicule what they never have studied. Alas, that this should be applicable to the highest of all subjects—the redemption of Christ. Many who ought to understand it better are extremely imperfectly acquainted with it. Hence, they treat the whole with indifference, frequently with gross contempt. This is seen when some of its most sublime and consoling doctrines are discussed. These are regarded as the dreams of enthusiasts. No doctrine has been more exposed to treatment of this kind than the union of Christ and believers. I shall at present only offer a few remarks on this union, and that with the view of showing the high standing of believers in heaven.

This union is of the most intimate kind. Christ in the covenant of grace is the head or representative of His people. But this Divine person in assuming this relation to men assumed their nature. This was done for the highest reason—that He might have something to offer. The thing which he offered was His soul and body on the cross, or, in other words, the human nature which he assumed. But the nature which was thus humbled in making an atonement for sin was afterwards highly exalted. That glorious Person whom John saw—whose face was like the sun, and whose eyes were like a flame of fire—was Emmanuel in His glorified human nature. In that nature He appears in heaven, and through it the whole of the heavenly inhabitants have a constant and vivid manifestation of the Divinity. But every saint will possess the same nature which his Divine Master wears. This must make the connexion betwixt the Son of God and His redeemed people more intimate, and altogether of a higher and dearer kind than betwixt Him and any other creatures. Our Lord intimated this very plainly to His followers after His resurrection. He spoke of them as *His brethren*. It is, therefore, not a mere covenant relation, but a fraternal connexion. If not in degree, yet in kind, their bodies will be like His glorious body. And this likeness shall be eternal. He has a fellow-feeling with them, for the sympathies of His soul are human sympathies. Hence, human nature in Emmanuel is exalted to a far higher pitch than the angelic nature ever can be raised to. And the brotherhood which Christ recognized on earth shall be eternally recognised in heaven. He that is in the midst of the throne leads His brethren— leads them to fountains of endless bliss. And shall not those who are regarded by Emmanuel as His brethren be looked upon by all the inhabitants of heaven as monumental pillars in the temple above? Will not all who see this connexion—all who adore the Son of God—look with peculiar love and respect on those whom He has redeemed and whose nature He wears? The grand fact that the Son of God died to redeem those whose nature He assumed and wears must stamp saints with peculiar excellence in the eyes of the heavenly society.

CHAPTER XI.

BACKSLIDERS CALLED TO REPENTANCE.

"Repent, or else I will come unto thee quickly, and will fight against thee with the sword of my mouth."—Rev. ii. 16.

THE Church of Pergamos possessed much that was pleasing in the eyes of her Divine Master. For although Christians in that city were surrounded by many forms of wickedness, and exposed to severe persecution, yet they continued to hold fast the doctrines of the gospel in their purity. This was much. A church that retains the essential doctrines of religion, has still within herself the grand elements of spiritual life and reformation. And we find, indeed, that the Church of Pergamos stood in need of reformation. There are certain sins mentioned as practised by some of the members of this church, and as it would appear connived at by many others. A holy God loves His children too well to permit them to indulge in any sin. While our Lord, therefore, commends the doctrinal purity of this Church, He utters at the same time admonition and threatening against those sinful courses into which some had fallen. Were admonitions listened to, threatenings would not be needed. Were threatenings laid to heart, neither chastisement nor punishment would be required.

I shall first direct your attention to the admonition, and next to the threatening.

I. The admonition and call to repentance.

Repentance towards God is comprehensive of so much that it may be regarded as one of the chief branches of revealed religion. It is called in our Catechism a saving grace. Indeed, without it a sinful creature could have no religion that would be acceptable to God, or beneficial to himself. There is a repentance which even needs to be repented of; for, as it springs from mere selfish motives, and has no reference either to the holiness or justice of God, it can only, by the sorrow it awakens, work death to the soul. But *true* repentance is a high spiritual condition of mind. It is indeed the soul, by an act of faith, uniting the past with the future, so as to see abused obligations in consequences, and yet at the same time discover a hope of mercy which leads to God and to newness of life. This cannot fail to produce just thoughts, and all kinds of healthy mental action. Hence the repentance to which men are called in the Gospel, implies not only sorrow for sin and separation from it in heart and life, but also a return to God in faith and practice. Sinners have departed from God, and are in rebellion against Him. The call to repentance is a call to return to God and submit to Him as His obedient servants.

But, important as this doctrine is, I can only devote to it a very brief space. The guilt of man makes repentance necessary, while the mercy of God through Christ makes it not only possible, but in the highest sense beneficial. Angels need no repentance; for they have never sinned. Devils need repentance. But as there is no scheme of mercy for them, they only tremble while they believe but do not repent. But although man is a sinner yet he is within the scope of mercy, as for him there is a Mediator. Hence, any sinner may say: "I will arise and go to my Father;" for the declaration of his Father is, "Turn ye, turn ye, why will ye die in your sin?" Were there no Gospel there could be no repentance unto life. The sinner mourns aright when he looks at Him who was pierced for sin.

Take away the cross and sorrow for sin becomes despair, out of which can only spring intense hatred and aversion to God. But while all sin must be offensive to a holy God, sin in His own children must be peculiarly dishonourable to Him, and if it brings not down upon them His wrath, as a Judge, it cannot fail to awaken against them His fatherly displeasure. Yet painful as it is to admit that the people of God often fall into sin, it were a criminal folly to deny it. But as God hates sin in them, He calls them to repentance. His dealings with the Jewish people, while in covenant with Him, strikingly illustrate alike the tendency of professors of religion to go astray and the Divine procedure towards such. His people are counselled, warned and threatened, and, if they repent not, are severely chastised. There are degrees of guilt in moral acts, but there is no sin so little as not to need repentance. Are you living in any known sin, or in the neglect of any known duty? The call to you is, repent. Turn with hatred and loathing from everything which God forbids—turn with a loving and obedient disposition to all that God requires. This is repentance in its principles, and out of it will spring all the fruits meet for it.

A faith in God's truth is essential to evangelical repentance. The more a man knows of the truths of the Gospel, he is all the better prepared to listen to the call to repentance. Assuredly a man's principles and practice may for a time be sadly in opposition. This, however, cannot last very long, unless he so plays the sophist with himself as to make truth subservient to a wicked practice. For he whose mind holds fast the great doctrines of religion has that in him well fitted to arouse conscience, and to warm and enlighten the heart to a true repentance. The Church of Pergamos was in this respect in a favourable condition to listen to the admonition in the text. To call a man to repentance who is ignorant of the grand doctrines of the Gospel is not a hopeful task. There must be principles on which faith can fasten ere the appeal can be felt. True, many that know their Lord's will may, for a time, under the influence of strong temptation, fail shamefully to do it. Still it is plain that the conscience of such men, if not seared, is in the best state for being aroused to a sense of danger, neglect of obligations, and the claims which God their Saviour has on them. These undutiful children know of the holy, just and merciful Father they are offending, know much of the Saviour they are dishonouring, and know something of that Spirit they are grieving, and may know not a little of the joys and hopes of that religion they are abusing. It is sad that under any influence a soul with all this knowledge should even for a brief period depart from God; yet that knowledge will render the time of departure a time of wretchedness, and will prove mightily instrumental to the return of the soul unto God.

It were not wise to suppose that such departures are extremely rare. Alas! if the best faithfully try their heart and life by the Divine requirements, they will find ground enough to confess that they often depart from God, and by sins of commission as well as of omission grievously offend Him. Woe be to us! if we find in this apology for committing sin or repose in lying under it. It ought to produce grief, humiliation, watchfulness, in a word, repentance. Christians at Pergamos were sound in the faith, and men of courage and zeal, yet there was also among them much that was offensive to Christ. Hence the call for repentance. Examine your heart and life by God's requirements, my brethren, and do it as in His sight, and you will also find cause for repentance. Are there no duties left undone? Or, what may be worse, done formally and hypocritically? Are there no sins indulged in? No temptation trifled with? No mercies overlooked? No opportunities for doing good neglected? An honest answer to this cannot but awaken regret, shame and remorse. But remorse is only a means to an end. The end here is repentance. Your regret, shame and remorse are vain, unless you have done with everything which you would be afraid to carry with you to a death-bed, and unless you begin to do everything which you would wish you had done when you shall stand at Christ's judgment seat. He that does not cast out the old leaven of every sinful passion and appetite, and who does not say, and say it with the whole heart: "Lord, what wilt Thou have me to do," is not listening to the admonition in the text—repent. And against those who will not listen to it, Christ threatens to fight with the sword of His mouth. He has many ways of chastising. This is one of them. It sounds very strangely. And this brings me—

II. To speak of *the nature of the threatening*. "Except ye repent," said the Saviour, "I will fight against you with the sword of my mouth."

God often employs the sword of war as well as the sword of pestilence to punish the guilty. But the sword which He threatens to employ against His erring children is Divine truth. The term *sword* is used figuratively. It is the Divine word. This at first sight may seem a strange instrument of punishment. The word of God is spoken of under the figure of a sword in several passages. In Ephesians, vi. 17, the Christian is commanded, among other portions of the spiritual armour, to take "the sword of the Spirit, which is the word of God." And in Hebrews iv. 12., the word of God is said to be "quick and powerful, sharper than any two-edged sword," and in Rev. i. 16, where Christ is represented as holding the seven stars in His right hand, out of His mouth proceeded a two-edged sword—plainly His word. Now, when Christ threatens that if His people repent not He will fight against them with the sword of His mouth, it is plainly His word that is to be the grand weapon to punish. God's word is compared to light, as it gives direction—to bread, as it nourishes the soul—to water, as it purifies—to honey, as it delights the spiritual taste. These figures are full of meaning, and highly appropriate; but, it may be asked where is the appropriateness of comparing the word of God to an instrument that wounds and kills. The figure is indeed highly significant. For the word of God is not only a sword to pierce the heart with conviction, to divide the soul from its lusts, but also to pierce the heart of the impenitent with killing agonies, or to inflict painful wounds on the conscience of the backslider. And thus Christ fights with His word against His offending people. This seems a strange instrument in the hands of the Saviour for such a purpose. If rightly thought of, the threatening is very awful, the punishment inflicted very terrible, and although often, yet not always, salutary.

We must try and make this plain. Man in his present state may be punished either in body or in mind, or in both. But as man is properly mind, so is mind the proper seat not only of his exquisite joys but of his bitterest woes. A stroke on the body may be severely felt, but it is not, either in degree or kind of suffering, at all equal to that which is felt when the heart is pierced. And, then, the arrow that pierces the heart may come on one or two winged words. A few words may tell you that your highest hopes are to be realized. No mere physical gratification can equal the joy which these few words awaken. Or, again, a few words may blast in a moment all hopes and all joys, and produce suffering far greater than any bodily illness you ever felt. The figure that it goes to the heart like a dagger, is scarcely too strong. What a creature is man! how mysterious his mind! The heart may be made to live or die by a few words. A word may make all light around you and open up a golden vista far into the future, or a word may plunge you into darkness or sink you into despair. Words are but wind, but they may be a whirlwind that rends and scatters every hope and joy, or it may be a gentle breeze that bears on its wings fragrance, music and health.

But, to illustrate what I have further to say, I shall notice that the threatenings of God must produce exceeding anguish of soul.

If a word of threatening, uttering the true and the terrible, by a fellow-creature, produces great pain while it merely points to temporal ills, shall not the word of the great God produce incomparably greater anguish when it points not only to temporal but eternal ills? For this there must be faith in the utterances of God. He who does not believe His word, but merely says he does that he may not put himself to the trouble of denying it, will not be moved any more by the most terrible threatenings of God than by the pratings of a child. This non-faith, or negative belief, is the real condition of many. These men have false repose, not peace. But where there is a faith positive, men will hear and fear when God threatens. And if their faith be strong they will be filled, as well they may, with intense anguish, when they hear the omnipotent and just God declaring Himself their enemy. They will feel, in some measure, as the guilty monarch felt when he saw the writing on the wall. It was the hand of God; well might his knees smite together. They will feel as the Jews did on the day of Pentecost, when the word of God pierced their heart, and they cried out: "Men and brethren, what must we do?" or as David, when the prophet, in the name of God, said to him: "Thou art the man." An angry word from God would appal the mightiest angel, yet men are stout of heart when God threatens. The angel would believe, men do not. But when man does believe he is appalled and trembles; his knees smite together, and his heart is filled with unutterable anguish when the word of an angry God enters his soul. The threatening is like a sword, or, to use another figure of an ancient patriarch, "the arrows of the Almighty" then stick within him, and the poison thereof drinketh up his spirit—the terrors of God set themselves in array against him.

Many have realized this when under convictions of sin. Some have confessed that when they first saw the law in its just claims, the penalty in its terrible meaning, their sins in the sight of a holy and just God, and His omnipotent arm ready to punish, they felt as if environed with the pains of hell. Yet no stroke had touched their bodies, no blight had fallen on their temporal interests; they were in health, prosperous in the world, respected and beloved. All was well but the bosom. That was smitten by the sword of the Spirit. God's truth, in the form of a few simple words, had reached the understanding, and awakened conscience to the sad past and the awful future. God had said "the soul that sinneth it shall die." This they believed. He had said, "Cursed is every one that continueth not in all things written in the Book of the Law," and they believed Him. He had said, "the wages of sin is death," and they had come to believe Him. He had declared that the wicked shall go away "into everlasting fire prepared for the devil and his angels," and they had come to believe it would be so. But there was another solemn fact, in addition to all this, which they had also come to believe—that they were the persons, the very persons, to whom all this is applicable. Assuredly, my brethren, without faith in these, and the like, as God's statements, and faith that He means as He says, and faith in making a personal application of these statements to themselves, they cannot awaken in you fear, shame, and remorse. But where there is faith in the threatening, as God's utterance, one sentence from Him of this sort will, like a sword, pierce the guilty bosom.

But, it may be said, this only applies to the impenitent in despair or to the penitent in conversion. Without faith in God's word there could be no despair. Many die easily, as they die in utter stupidity, or in a sad misbelief, if not disbelief. It is some faith that makes despair, as it is the want of enough of it which confirms despair. Yet let it not be supposed that God's word only produces anguish in the despairing, or when the soul first awakens to a sight of the lightnings of Sinai. The backslider who, by his sins, has darkened his hopes, brought his adoption into question, and thrown his evidences into confusion, will feel, when aroused to a sense of his danger, that every threatening of God has to him of all men the most direct and terrible meaning. It is to him not only the sword of God but that sword bathed in heaven. When the Apostle denied his Master, the Lord turned and looked upon him. The Saviour looked Divine Truth into Peter's bosom, or, what is nearly the same, that look as a flash of light kindled up much truth that was lying in his bosom. And he went out and wept bitterly. No torture of his most malicious enemies could have equalled what he suffered. " The spirit of a man will sustain his infirmities, but a wounded spirit who can bear?" But what sword can wound the spirit like the word of God?"

For, mark it, the backslider, till he finds peace by a new application of the blood of Christ, must really see every threatening in a more terrible aspect than he saw it in the hour of conversion or when living carelessly in sin. He knows far more now of a just and holy God, far more now than then of His law and its claims. And he has now not only to look at the despised justice of God, but at His abused goodness. If he has not crucified the Saviour afresh, and put Him to an open shame, he feels he has come fearfully near it. If he has not done despite to the spirit of grace, he feels that he has at least sadly grieved that Holy Spirit. And he knows that to be a true saying, that the servant that knew his Lord's will and did it not shall be beaten with many stripes. In short, every threatening must have a far more terrible meaning to the backslider than to him who has never named the name of Christ. No wonder that such a man feels that every threatening is as a flaming sword, turning every way to keep him from the tree of life, and has in it, to his eye, an image of eternal death. Hence, if his conscience be not utterly seared, and if he be not given up to judicial blindness, every threatening pierces his bosom like a sword. It is fearful to think that to backsliders every page of the Bible in which threatenings are found sends forth flashes of lightning to scorch their souls. Every historical incident in which a wicked man is doomed by God to ruin, reads them a frightful lesson of what is to be their doom. The word of God is to them what the prophet was to the wicked King of Israel, a denouncer of evil and not a messenger of good, and just for this reason, that they have forsaken the good and chosen the evil. But,

III. I shall endeavour to show you how the promising part becomes also a sword to pierce the heart of the sinning Christian. All men live by hope. Take it away— take all hope away, and men will go distracted, or sink into idiotic despondency. But the life and movements of the Christian depend especially on hope. By this chiefly he has the earnest of his heavenly inheritance. Hence his hope is nearly the measure of his joy. But, again, hope depends on that faith which lays hold on the promises of a covenant-keeping God in Christ. A full pardon, a finished sanctification, Divine protection, the consolations of the Spirit, and heaven at last, with all its varied and satisfying joys for eternity, are the rich and suitable promises which God has given to His people. They are, indeed, the manna, the water from the rock, the cloud by day, the pillar of fire by night to the Christian in this wilderness of toil and affliction. He that can appropriate the promises of God will have a joy and hope which the world cannot give nor take away. The Christian who is walking closely with God by a living faith can do this.

But far different is it with him who is living in sin, either of omission or commission. Such a man may not be a cast-away. No ; God, in mercy, may snatch him from the jaws of destruction; he may be plucked as a brand from the fire, from the very edge of the pit. Such triumphs of grace are wonderful, and they have not been few. It is not my intention to notice symptoms of reprobation—a sad and difficult task—yet assuredly there could be few symptoms more alarming than this—that while rolling sin, as a sweet morsel under your tongue, you could profess at the same time that with a keen relish you are tasting the sweetest of God's promises. This were, indeed, the last infatuation—holding in a most frightful form the truth in unrighteousness, and by a most destructive sophistry turning the grace of God into licentiousness. When men have reached this point, they are given up to believe a lie. Conscience is dead, or utterly debauched. Even the sword of the Spirit no longer pierces these hearts.

This is not the condition of all; we hope, indeed, of few. Those who have been instructed in God's truth have to fight a hard battle with conscience in their departures from him. They know far too well what is required of God's children to suppose that while they are serving the world, the devil, or the flesh, they can appropriate the promises of the covenant of grace. The backslider may be a justified man, but while living in known sin he dare not appropriate to himself the promises of pardon and acceptance. He may be one of the adoption, but while living in known sin he cannot lay hold on promises of the inheritance of faithful children. The best robe and the ring may be ready for him, but till he arises and goes to his Father, he cannot say they are his.

It will not do to affirm that, seeing he is now living in sin, he cares nothing about the promises. This may be if he is past feeling, and working all manner of wickedness with greediness. But many who fall sadly, do not fall so low as this. They do care about the promises; for they have not yet completed their covenant with death and agreement with hell. They have a painful impression of the good they have lost, or may lose eternally. Their knowledge is adverse to their false peace. They know too much of a holy God to think that He can own them as children while living in sin. They know that justification implies adoption, but that both must be evidenced by sanctification, and this must be seen in the fruits of holiness. But they see their blossoms gone up into dust; hence the just fear that the root of the matter is not in them. No; my brethren, with lusts nourished, duties neglected, sins committed, lying on the conscience unrepented of, you cannot put forth your hands and partake of the promises. You read: "Blessed are the poor in spirit, for theirs is the kingdom of God." But you cannot appropriate that promise if you are living in pride. You read, "Blessed are the pure in heart, for they shall see God." But you are not pure in heart; you dare not appropriate the promise. You read: "I will never leave nor forsake you," but conscience tells you, you have forsaken Him, and the promise is not yours. You read: "As a father pitieth his children, so the Lord pitieth them that fear Him." But you are undutiful children, and do not fear Him. The promise is not yours. You know that God is infinitely good; but how can you claim that goodness if you are not serving Him? You know that God is able to protect; but how can you claim that protection if you are acting in opposition to His Divine authority? In fine, you know that heaven is a place of perfect happiness; but by sinning you have lost sight of your title to that heaven. And just so with every promise in the covenant of grace. Each is full of comfort to the obedient child; but to the disobedient, every promise, like the cloud to the Egyptians, turns its dark side. Oh! is it not a fearful thing when a man has sinned himself into that state that he becomes afraid to look into God's word? Every threatening is a sword to pierce his soul, and every promise is that sword with a keener edge. The most terrible sounds that the guilty hear are not the sounds of the earthquake, the whirlwind, and the thunder of God's alarming providences, but the still small voice that comes from the Bible, in a just threatening, or an abused promise. God's book is on God's side, and, depend upon it, will fight against you, while you are fighting against

Him. Ye, then, who feel alarmed at the thought of having such a being fighting against you with such a weapon, listen to His admonition—*repent*. Be ye separate from sin. Touch not the unclean thing. Turn to the Lord with your whole heart, and seek His mercy through Christ, and do works meet for repentance; and then shall ye hear Him saying to you: "I will be a Father unto you, and ye shall be my sons and daughters, saith the Lord Almighty."

CHAPTER XII.

WITHDRAWING ABUSED MERCIES, THE RULE OF GOD'S GOVERNMENT.

"Whosoever hath not, from him shall be taken away even that he hath."—Matthew, xiii. 12.

FROM the time the children of Israel were constituted into the visible church, they possessed the choicest moral and spiritual privileges. That these were, by great numbers of that people, during long seasons of their national history earnestly improved, and were productive of great spiritual advantages, is a cheering fact which may be learned from many passages of the Old Testament. It is, nevertheless, abundantly plain that these peculiar privileges were often neglected, and otherwise very grossly abused. They forgot God—turned to idols, and in various ways destroyed their own mercies. But great as their advantages were, while they enjoyed the regular services of their priesthood, and the teaching of their prophets during the long tract of ages that the Mosaic economy was in force, it will not be questioned that their privileges were vastly increased when they heard Divine truth from the very lips of its Divine Author. It was in many senses true, that no man, priest or prophet, had ever spoken as He did. Yet we learn from the context and many other passages, that they understood but imperfectly the doctrines He taught. So that neither the sublimity of His matter, the ineffable simplicity with which He unfolded it, nor the heavenly charms which His life threw around what He uttered;

no, nor the force of the miracles which He wrought, could commend to the understanding and conscience of the bulk of the people the lessons of wisdom which He taught. The cause of this is plain. They had not improved their former privileges and ordinary spiritual advantages; hence they did not profit, even under the teaching of the Son of God. Great privileges are solemn trusts involving deep responsibilities; and, if not improved, must be followed by fearful results. The talents that God gives cannot be hid, or otherwise perverted, with impunity. In this God is jealous of His honour, so that those who abuse His gifts shall at the day of reckoning not only be called to account, but even in the present life God often withdraws the misused talent.

Nothing is more certain than this, that privileges not improved shall not be utterly futile : God will either withdraw them, or they will prove curses to him that perverts them. Than this, no dispensation of God can be more just. His gifts are all precious, bestowed for high ends; it is at man's peril to neglect them, but when neglected, it is but just in God to withdraw them. A moment's reflection will show you, if consequences be thought of, that this is a matter to be deeply pondered and conscientiously applied, by all who have trusts, and by all who are misusing these trusts. The withdrawment of misused talents is the doctrine taught in the text. There is, as you will observe, a peculiarity in the words, "To those who have shall be given." Have what?—plainly, have improved their means or talents, and their graces; more means, talents and graces shall be given. But next, "From those who have not"—have not what? —have not improved their talents or privileges, even these privileges or talents shall be taken away, which they had. He who buried his talent in the earth, had it not only taken from him, but was condemned as an unprofitable servant. We repeat it, that God justly calls in neglected talents, and thus even in the present life, punishes the abuse of His gifts.

How does God do this? What is the mode by which He withdraws misused trusts? The question admits of no specific answer, at least of no answer that will apply to all cases. This need not be wondered at. Our knowledge only extends to facts, and a few of their relations to each other; but the inquiry, By what mode does God call in neglected talents? is not a question as to facts, but as to the mode of the Divine operations. Of these, properly speaking, either in Nature or Providence, we do not know anything. You cast certain seed into the ground; you know it will produce a certain crop, but how the seed expands into the plant, and the plant into the stalk, and how upon the top of that you find the precious wheat, the wisest man cannot tell. Indeed, as to modes of operation, it is a vast hidden machinery, moved by the invisible hand of God. The eye of man cannot see it—his wisdom cannot comprehend it. Our education, as well as our useful benefits, must now be sought, in fairly dealing with facts. When we attempt to go beyond this field, we do not grow wise and happy, but speculative. With our eye on the doctrine before us, the question is: Is it a fact that misimproved talents are called in?—does the Bible teach this?—and does experience more than hint this? Then, let no man weaken the force of this awful fact by vain and perplexing questions, as to the mode by which God withdraws misused privileges.

But what is a talent or privilege, in this sense? Anything by which God may be served and honoured, and the soul bettered. These gifts of God—for they are all His gifts by which we can work in this way—are of divers sorts. Some are in their nature more refined and spiritual, others more common and, as it were, earthy. To illustrate the doctrine of the text we shall select,

I.—A few of what are called the natural gifts of Providence, which ought to be made subservient to the glory of God and the good of the soul; but, when not employed in this way, may by the great Giver be justly called in.

1. *Health very properly takes the first place among these gifts of Providence.* Nothing of an earthly sort is more precious than this, or rather, as all men know, nothing on earth, without health, can be precious. It is this which gives a value to every possession, and a talismanic charm to every enjoyment. The poor man that has health is often *not* poor. The rich man that *wants* it is poor indeed. The infirm and sick understand the meaning of this. But, pity it is that those who possess the blessing most largely seem often to comprehend its value the least. Yet health is not grace, nor does its possession necessarily imply either the getting of grace, or the increase of it. There is, indeed, no essential connection betwixt health of body and health of soul. There have been many healthy bodies, connected with souls sick unto death, and many bodies full of sore and loathsome diseases in which the soul was vigorous with the grace of God, and very beautiful with His holy image. Nevertheless, is it not true that, although health is not even among the primary means, it is yet an admirable means for getting good to the soul and for glorifying God? In our present state, the mental and corporeal are so intimately connected that the mind cannot well perform some of its most important functions without the aid of bodily health. If in a great measure destitute of this, you cannot attend at all on some of the duties of religion. If sorely oppressed with infirmities, the public ordinances of religion must be wholly given up; while the private duties, such as the reading of the Word, prayers and godly converse, are attended to under great disadvantages, unless the soul is in a very high state of spiritual health indeed. Persons, by no means strangers to piety, have owned that in severe sickness they felt extremely unfit to attend to any religious duties. Pain so distracts the mind, and scatters the thoughts, that it is difficult to read, hear, or pray to edifi-

cation. Oh! it is sad to think how much is left, by most persons, to be done on a sick-bed, and how unfit a place it is for such momentous work! The thoughtless do not realize this when in health, while men in sore sickness have their anxieties so enlisted, as to their bodily sufferings, that they do not comprehend how little they are doing, or, humanly speaking, *can* do for the interests of the soul.

If you have spent your years of health in serving God, then has this precious talent been well employed, and when sickness comes you will not have the greatest of all works to begin, but may be enabled, under the heaviest affliction, to exercise strong faith, bear patiently and hope to the end. But even in this case is not the talent called in? In the sense of the text, it is not. The talent of health is withdrawn not till it has answered its ends, and not till God puts other talents in its place. Health was given as a talent by which God was to be served in action: sickness is the talent now given, by which God is to be served by the good man in patient bearing. But, now, let me ask how would it be with you if laid on a sick bed—your bones filled with sore pain, every nerve and muscle racked with suffering? How would it be when you looked back? Should you, in conscience, feel that you had employed the precious talent of health in the service of God, and for the good of your soul? Ah! no: with many, the frightful conviction would be that they had spent the talent in the service of the world, the devil and the flesh. For many a long year, God had continued this talent with you, and often in various ways had He admonished you to occupy the talent for high and holy ends. But you never did this. Nay, did you not often take occasion from the very fulness of your health to dishonour God all the more, and do all the deeper a damage to your own souls? But the talent is now gone. No more can that sick man go to the house of God. He may lie for months—it may be years—in his sick bed; but never more shall he hear another sermon. Nay, he cannot even attend well upon the more private duties. His prayers are but wild exclamations, his meditations misty, scattered thoughts. He cannot read—he cannot listen to edification. Weary and woe-begone, how shall he begin the great work? He may be saved; but oh! what a want is the want of health in commencing and carrying on the business of the soul's salvation! My hearer, didst thou never see a man in this state?—sick in body but sicker in soul? My hearer, art *thou* one of those who misuse the talent of health? Fear, oh! fear, lest God may call it in. What wilt thou think when on thy sick couch, when in sore conflict with bodily infirmities, yea, with the king of terrors, and the soul has never been attended to, and eternity so near, and health so needful, to set about the work! But health is gone; an offended God has called in his talent, and is now about to call in thy soul to His judgment bar to answer for the abuse of the talent. " From him that hath not shall be taken away even that he hath."

2. *God may withdraw the use of the senses because they have not been employed aright in His service.*

It has been already stated that all talents or privileges are misused when not employed in the service of God and for the good of the soul. The senses are those wonderful bodily instruments by which mind holds fellowship with mind, and intercourse with the external world, and by which the soul gains its primary ideas and, to a great extent, its materials for thought and feeling. The least reflection as to what you gain for the mind by the use of sight or hearing must satisfy you as to the importance of these instruments, not only for corporeal gratifications, but also for supplying the mind with its most refined material. But it is needless to enlarge on this—every man of reflection admits the great value of the senses. Let me ask, what are they valuable for? and to what uses do ye turn these talents? Valuable for many purposes assuredly; but do ye consider their highest value and their greatest use to consist merely in administering to bodily gratification? Do ye rejoice merely in the senses of sight and of hearing in order to obtain wealth, or to secure any sort of low gratification? Alas! how often are these senses employed in fatally corrupting the heart, the fancy and the conscience. Surely, surely, if man has a soul that is rational and immortal, these noble gifts of heaven ought to be employed for far higher purposes than to cater for mere bodily gratifications, and never, never ought to be employed in debauching either the heart or the conscience. As they are precious gifts of heaven, they ought to be used for the service of God and the good of the soul.

My brethren, have you so used them? Have you employed the sense of sight in reading what God has written of Himself in the great volume of creation? As you have gazed upon His face and mighty works, and saw how His hand had scattered beauty and beneficence around you and above you—from the glorious sun in the heavens down to the little flower in your path and the golden harvest in your fields—were your hearts filled with adoration at His greatness and wisdom, and with gratitude for His goodness? And, still more earnestly, have you employed the sense of sight in reading the wonders of God —wonders of wisdom, justice and mercy—as recorded in the volume of inspiration? Has your sight often grown dim in reading that blessed book which has brought life and immortality to light, and in reading other books which wise men have written to explain how God can be just and yet the Justifier of the ungodly? If so, my brethren, the talent has been well used. And, furthermore, as to the sense of hearing, has your ear been often employed in earnestly listening to what wise and good men had to say of the dealings of God with His creatures? What He has done for them, requires of them, promises to the obedient and threatenings against the disobedient? In a word, are the things of God and the things of your soul's eternal welfare, the matters on which you have employed your eyesight and your ears, hearing that the soul might be filled with instruction for guidance, warning and comfort? If so, then have these talents been rightly used. Much do I fear that if some of my hearers were to speak out their declaration would be : We have not done so, and we cannot comprehend all this. What were our senses of sight or hearing given for, if not to aid us to get wealth, honour and sensual pleasure? Hast thou a soul, my hearer, or art thou a brute that has merely animal life? Thou dost start at the question, thou art ready to cry out "I *have* a soul, rational and immortal." Even so, yea, even so, my brother. Thou hast a soul that can know God, that can be saved, that can be damned. And if thy senses are admirable instruments for the good of the soul, why are they not employed for its good, in its service? I tell thee that these senses of sight and hearing—for I fix mainly on them for illustration—are the choice gifts of God, and if thou hast, for long, long years, employed them not in His service, but for His dishonour—not for the good of the soul—hast thou not cause to fear lest God take them from thee? God may call in His abused talents. He may smite thee with blindness or deafness, so that thou canst no more see His works, read His word, nor hear His precious truth, and thus thy dark soul shall be left forever in darkness.

I think this reasoning sound, and the appeal sober. Yet, as the appeal may not be felt, so the reasoning may be perverted. You may be ready to say ; "Yes, it is true, that neighbour of ours who has lost his sight, or hearing, has been unfaithful, and the talent is called in." This opinion may be right, but what right have you to make it? The affliction may not be a wrathful judgment but a fatherly chastisement. The talent may not have been withdrawn until it has answered the high ends for which it was given, and the very withdrawment of it may be, so to speak, to make room for greater talents with which the soul is henceforth to work for the glory of God and its spiritual welfare. On such matters judge not, or do it very charitably, but rather judge yourselves than others, and even in judging yourselves see that there is righteous judgment. For truly it is with ourselves that we have mainly to do in such matters. The home question with every man should be, not how others are employing their talents; that may be a question, but the main one is, how he is employing *his*. And oh! let it be a question with you whether these fine instruments which God has given are employed in His service, or are only employed to work for pride, for the flesh, for the world, for the devil. If so, need ye wonder that God should call in His misused gifts? But do not these senses decay in all? In most they do, and in some they become extinct long before life ends. Does not this, then, weaken or neutralize the force of our argument? Nay, for we again ask, was the soul enriched through them with Divine wisdom ere they failed? If so, that soul is not in darkness. The gift has not been withdrawn in anger, it has answered the ends for which it was given, and, as we said before, it is removed to make room for other talents; faith, patience, and hope, by the blind or the deaf, are now to be more fully exercised. But with you it may be all otherwise. The gifts are not used but abused, the soul got no good but much harm, and they are now gone or going, and oh! what darkness and 'confusion is the soul still in! and like to be locked up in that frightful darkness and confusion for eternity! Sad spectacle this, my brethren! Let it never be forgotten that the body is for the Lord and that all its senses should be for the Lord. And if one or other of these is not employed in His service, is it not just that He should call in the talent, and condemn the unprofitable servant?

II.—*The public ordinances of religion, which are precious talents, may be withdrawn, if not improved.*

There is obviously a strong tendency in our times to slight the public means of grace. A man may wholly neglect these, yet his standing in society not be the least affected. He is spoken of as an honest, kind-hearted, neighbourly man, although he utterly disavows all regard for God. What is worthy of commendation—and there may be certain traits of character even in godless men entitled to a certain approbation—ought assuredly to have its measure of approbation, but only its measure; and while I cheerfully admit that there are, among those who practically disown God, persons who possess some worthy qualities, yet I dare not speak in unqualified commendation of such men. To do so shows a looseness of principle which is at once pitiable and dangerous. Those living without God cannot live well; they are not safe companions; they are not trustworthy friends. But the evil to which we advert assumes a more dangerous form when men fancy that they can themselves be in a tolerably fair spiritual condition although living in the neglect of public ordinances. Indeed, the matter in either form is a frightful delusion; it is, in fact, a mode of atheistical indifference to God, which, although not so horrible to the ear, yet may not be less fatal to the soul or dishonourable to God than theoretic atheism. To admit that there is a God, that He has appointed ordinances, required attendance on them, and threatened His vengeance against those who wilfully neglect them, yet wilfully to neglect them is grossly to dishonour God, and practically to deny Him. This is not the language of bigotry, but of common sense, as well as of the Bible, It is a wretched apology which some make for this neglect, that public ordinances have been turned to an ill use by the superstitious and the hypocritical. That they have made an ill use of them will not be denied, but is not the wilful neglect of them a gross abuse? God's talents neglected are misused.

Most true, ordinances will not save you—the pulpit cannot—sacraments cannot save you. The Lord Himself and the Spirit of the Lord can alone do that. But God's means, as means, are no more to be set aside than God's *Son*. He who slights the means that lead to the Saviour and by which He is honoured, slights Himself. The public ordinances of religion, the preaching of the Word, sacraments and prayer, are to returning sinners and growing saints literally invaluable. Yet multitudes slight these means. For high ends they are given: if not improved, it is just in God to withdraw them. The candlestick may be removed, or the shepherd of the people may be called to another sphere of action, or his labours may be closed in death, so that the whole of the public spiritual machinery among a people may, as it were, stop. The pulpit no longer utters its instructions, warnings, comforts. Men go not up, or have not the opportunity as formerly to go up, to the house of God; the seasons of solemn assemblies have ceased, or come but seldom and bring but partial benefit. The candlestick is removed and there is a darkness that may be felt. On this ministers need to speak with caution, delicacy, and even with trembling; yet wise men do not need to be told that no community can sustain a more serious loss socially, morally and spiritually than in the loss of the regular public means of grace. Yet when this happens to a people who have made a right use of them when they had them, we cannot think that God will long leave them comfortless; He will come to them again. But, mark it, if the Word has been long and faithfully preached, and hath not profited, and the sacraments often administered and have not profited, and if men have grown careless, formal, vain and disputatious, under all these means, may not God in justice withdraw them, so that there shall be a famine, not of bread, nor of water, but a famine of hearing the word of life?

Besides the loss of the public ordinances in the way adverted to, there are other modes by which God may withdraw this talent. Men who never had a hearty regard for religion have nevertheless for a time attended its public services. But not having the root of the matter in them, their attachment which was but whim, fancy, partizan feeling or outward appearance, at length withers away. These are truly the stony-ground hearers. Where the Gospel is faithfully preached such men will hear much to offend and little to gratify their tastes. It is, therefore, not wonderful that they turn their back on the House of God. Admit that they got little good, yet where are they to get the good now? To say it is better that they should be off and have done with all shamming in this matter expresses the truth so far well. Yet, upon the whole, it is not a pleasing nor a wholesome statement. From the public means of grace they derived little or no good, and having flung up all these and gone to the world, how are they to get good there? The state of such men is to the last degree melancholy. Nor is it rendered less so when they try to cover their retreat from public ordinances, either by high pretensions or by poor, most poor apologies. This is adding falsehood to unbelief. If the Gospel has not gone from these men, they have gone from it, who have cut all connection with its public ordinances.

There is another mode, my brethren, by which this precious talent may be withdrawn or lost, and that is where persons remove entirely beyond the pale of the sanctuary and get out of sight of visible sabbaths. I do not say that this in all cases is wrong. In such a country as this, when the wilderness has to be filled up, the thing I refer to in many cases must be done. And when good men go into new settlements carrying with them not only civilization but a healthy Christianity, they may be instrumental—nay *have been*—in making the wilderness to blossom and rejoice as the rose ; but it is quite another thing when men gospel-hardened, men grown careless of means, loathing Sabbaths, sermons and communion seasons, quit a region of gospel light and take up their abode where neither churches nor ministers are ever seen. These men, alas, feel well enough pleased with their silent and secularized Sabbaths, and the whole atheistic state of things around them. Like him of old they have gone out from the presence of the Lord, and whatever they build they are not likely to build for eternity. "From him that hath not shall be taken away even that he hath."

In fine, if you have not made a right use of the public means of grace, we fear that these in some way or other may be withdrawn. The talent may be called in, or, which is the same thing as to you, the talent may be lost. Little may you understand what you have lost. Nay, you may madly rejoice, or at least feel complacent in the loss, nevertheless, no words can utter the amount of your loss. For Oh! may it not lead to the final loss of the soul. "From him that hath not shall be taken away even that he hath."

CHAPTER XIII.

DARK DISPENSATIONS OF PROVIDENCE.

"But it shall be one day which shall be known to the Lord, not day, nor night: but it shall come to pass, that at evening time it shall be light."—Zechariah, xiv. 7..

OOKING to God for His blessing, I intend from these words to illustrate this topic:
That the providence of God as seen in the lot of man, in the present life, has much of obscurity about it.

Light and darkness are figures often employed by the inspired writers. Light represents knowledge and happiness, and very often is the figure used for holiness, which is comprehensive of both. Hence heaven is a world of unclouded light. There is no night there. God is light, and in Him is no darkness at all. Christ is the Light of the world—the Author of all knowledge, holiness and happiness, to His people. Darkness, on the other hand, is a figure for ignorance, sin and misery. Hence wicked men are said to be blind, to walk in darkness, while Satan who is the author of sin and misery is the prince of darkness, and hell is the place of utter darkness. But mental vision, or the want of it—knowledge, or the want of it—is what the figure in the text specially teaches. You will observe, however, that in the language of the text, it is neither all day, nor all night; neither fulness of light, nor thick darkness, but an obscure dawn. Such is the figure. The truth we adduce from it for illustration is, that the providence of God, although to Him so well known that

He sees the end from the beginning, yet to man is neither all clear, nor yet all dark, but often in many parts very obscure. Somewhat is dimly seen, yet much not seen at all. There is perhaps no moral question, which more readily commends itself to the reflecting mind than this. It has puzzled reason in all ages. It is clearly seen when we turn to Job and his pious but bewildered friends, and see them labouring to find solutions to dark dispensations in Divine Providence. The wisest of men have felt that, if all be not dark in the Providence of God, much is often very obscure.

It will be observed that we assume that man's lot is appointed by his Maker. None but an atheist will deny this. And it is a sublime and cheering reflection that the Providence of God extends to the most minute as well as the greatest of things. The hairs of our head are all numbered, and not a sparrow falls to the ground without the Divine permission. It was thus that the Saviour taught the nature of Divine Providence, when He would lead men to draw consolation from it, and in faith cleave to it, as a grand fact. But then there lies close by it another fact, which meets us every day in the practical movements of that Providence, which is, that to us it is not all light, nor all darkness, but often seems a scene in which light is mysteriously struggling with darkness. Were the light perfect, we should see all the movements of Providence so clearly as never to be perplexed. Were the darkness complete, we should stumble at every step, or sink down in utter despondency. But as man's lot in the Providence of God is neither all dark nor all light, but often very obscure, man is often sorely perplexed and at his wits' end to know what to make of some parts of it. The truth is, that the Providence of God is often so dark as not to produce despair in His children, yet frequently so obscure as to demand a constant exercise of their faith in His infinite wisdom and Fatherly guidance.

When men speak of a dark Providence, it is some

dispensation which is painful to them. Man in his present state is a compound creature. What painfully tries his physical nature cannot but be felt even when the soul is cleaving to God, and finding its supreme enjoyment in Him. Hence, if a man suddenly loses the property which he has gathered by patient toil and frugality to meet the claims of parental affection, and is at once reduced to beggary, the dispensation is called *a dark providence*. And so it is, when a sudden stroke of disease paralyzes the bodily powers, or some mental disease crushes the mind into imbecility, or drives it to frenzy; or some youth, the hope and support of those near and dear to him, is smitten by death in the morning of life, and the widowed mother and helpless sisters are left sorely bereaved; or children taken away one after another, until fond parents are written childless; or a man's reputation is blasted, so that with the mark of opprobrium on him, he totters into the grave, blighted, forsaken and forlorn. Any one of these trials is painful—and when several of them come together, as you have sometimes seen—and all the earthly happiness of a family is swept away, men are ready to exclaim: "How dark, how trying the dispensation!"

Assuredly there is truth in the statement that the dispensation is trying. But is it not also true that, just because it is exceedingly painful to flesh and blood, you think it mysterious? If it were agreeable, you would see no mystery in the dispensation. It is because it is painful that it perplexes. But why, my brethren, should you reason so poorly? The dispensation is sent by a God of infinite wisdom, He cannot err; by a God of infinite justice, He cannot do wrong; and by a Father of infinite mercy, who can make all things work together for good to His children. He is all this when His providences are painful, and He is all this when His providences are pleasant. But, then, as they are pleasing, we do not fret under them, or think them dark. We get perplexed because we are pained.

Still there are many of the dispensations of God in our lot so truly painful and dark, that without strong faith we could not bear them, and even in the exercise of faith the perplexed and suffering child may be ready to cry out : "All these things are against me." Yet this is wrong. For, although it is not all day with him, neither is it all night. He is only in obscurity, not in darkness. But in order to guard against misconception in this, as well as to show how the providence of God is often obscure to His people, I remark

I.—The mind of man sees but little of the inner movements, and still less of the remote ends of the moral providence of God.

The human mind is capable of understanding many things partially, but nothing perfectly. In material nature it sees facts, and the relation of these to one another, yet how much in the operation of these facts is hidden from it! Indeed, man only sees the surface of things, and can only deal with practical results.

The carpenter can employ the wood of a tree in fifty different ways that may be useful ; but he cannot explain, nor can the philosopher, how the seed unfolds itself into a tree. And if man understands but imperfectly the providence of God in material nature, is it wonderful he should comprehend but imperfectly all the wheels and springs of His moral providence, and should fail to see all the ends God intends to accomplish by its complex movements !

When at any time—and that is not seldom—we find in our lot what is dark, would it not be well, ere we despond under the trial, or foolishly arraign the providence of God, that we quietly and modestly conclude that the feebleness of our vision sufficiently accounts for the obscurity around us ; and that there is perfect order where all to us is confusion ; perfect justice where much appears wrong, and perfect goodness where we see nothing but severity? Let the afflicted say : "It is the weakness of my mental vision, or the weakness of faith, and not an unjust providence that is the cause of perplexity." But this, my brethren, implies that humility, without which nothing is seen aright. A proud self-sufficiency, while it attempts to scan all things, and account for all in the providence of God, is proof of the most fatal blindness. The humble wise man will conclude that in all things his Heavenly Father does right, and that it is only his own imperfect knowledge of the movements and ends of God's dealings, or his feeble faith in God, that perplexes him. Abraham was tried with the darkest providence that has perhaps ever been in the lot of any man, when God commanded him to offer up his son Isaac. All that he knew —and this was enough—was that God had given the command. He, therefore, went on to the top of Moriah simply determined to do what God bade him, and leave the issue with Him, who never errs in justice, wisdom and goodness. This was the faith which staggers not in the midst of the greatest darkness. How can it, for it holds fast by the hand of God! In a thousand dispensations that are painful, the eye of reason is bleared and dim. Blessed is he who is conscious of this, and who holds fast his confidence, that although he cannot see what God means, yet God ever means what is right. But

II.—In addition to a conviction of our own weakness to comprehend fully the providence of God, it should be borne in mind that the present life is but the beginning, not the end of man.

What a difference betwixt a thing in its beginnings and the same thing in its finished condition. The house building and the house finished, how different! The former is all apparent confusion; the latter all order and design. Nothing can be made of man without assuming that the present is but the commencement of his existence. If his journey ends at the grave he is the most unhappy and the most inexplicable of creatures. With powers incomparably higher than the other creatures, he has often a far less share of mere sensuous enjoyment, and tastes miseries of which they are wholly incapable. To suppose that the human mind that can wander through space and gather thought and emotion from distant worlds—can draw upon the remote past and the distant future for thoughts, motives, enjoyment, misery—with passions as deep as hell or as high as heaven, or as dark and foul as the pit, or as pure and gentle as the light of heaven, is to end its course at death, is not only mysterious but utterly anomalous and inexplicable; and it becomes all the more inexplicable when you admit that a God of infinite justice and wisdom rules over all.

No—the grave is not the end—man is not a little organized matter. Death does not close his destiny. If it did, we might well exclaim as we look up and recognize a God of infinite wisdom and goodness: "What mean these dark and trying providences in the lot of a creature who has played out his part when he drops into the grave?" No, verily, death is not the end, but only the beginning of his great existence. Now, my brethren, what appear to be obscure or dark providences are only so because we can only see the beginning, not the end. In short, we do not see what is to come out of them; what influence they are to have not only on future life, but on the condition of the soul through eternity. But it is only the order and beauty and glory of the finished condition that can explain the apparent confusion in the beginning. It was at the very time when the ancient Patriarch was about to enter with his family on the greatest happiness and honour, that he exclaimed, as he looked at the dark providences of God: "All these things are against me." Thousands have uttered the same exclamation, while God was, by what to them were dark providences, preparing them not for an earthly Goshen but for a heaven of glory.

We repeat it, we are but in the beginning of our existence, on the lowest form in the school, learning the elements of our moral and spiritual education. But, then, this elementary knowledge may be indispensable to the highest acquisitions. Let me illustrate this. The boy at school feels the learning of the alphabet and the learning of the names and the simpler powers of figures a drudgery. But the wise parent or teacher knows that unless he passes through this drudgery, he never will make any higher attainments. Indeed, is it not true, that the beginning of all things has in it much apparent confusion, much that is unmeaning, and much that is painful? There is nothing for it, however, but patient toil if we would reach the completion, which shall have in it beauty, order and happiness.

The application of this is simple. We are now little children in God's school on earth. But we are there learning what will fit us for the service, the joys, the glories of the heavenly sanctuary. To be fitted for doing God's will on *earth* is a great end, but not the greatest end of an immortal soul. The child of God is to enter the household above, is to take his place near the throne —is to follow the Lamb whithersoever He goeth—is to be the companion of angels and the sharer of their joys and services through eternity. This is the high condition of man's being. This is the completion of his spiritual nature. But, at present, we only see the beginning of things—only see the day of preparation, with its tasks, its toils and its apparent confusions. And why should we wonder that this training of man is a painful one? He is not merely a creature of feeble powers that need to be strengthened, but of deeply depraved faculties that need to be spiritually changed ere he can be fitted for the grand ends of his being. The grace of God can alone do this. But remember that, although grace is communicated directly through the Spirit, it is matured in the soul, and the soul cultivated by it, through many a dark providence. Jacob, Job and David were men of God before they were tried by some of His darkest providences. Indeed, but for their piety, they could have learned little from these, still it was in passing through these dark providences that their grace acquired its greatest beauty and strength. Possibly those who occupy, in every sense, the highest positions in heaven are those who had to pass through the darkest providences on earth. God does nothing in vain; does not afflict his children for nought, and He knows best what is necessary to prepare them for their eternal condition.

It may be plausibly objected to this, that God might prepare His children for glorifying and enjoying Him without leading them through the furnace. But let it be remembered, apart from all hypothesis, as to what God might do, that *men* cannot be trained like *angels*. Man not only needs to be instructed, alas! he needs to be corrected, that he may be instructed; he needs not only to be pardoned to be accepted, but to be sanctified that the acceptance may avail him. And he needs not only to be polished in his sanctification—he needs to be refined. In a word, the dross must be taken away ere he can be a vessel fit for the Master's use, or a gem fit for the Saviour's crown. Ponder it, then, when under dark providences, that you are but in the beginning of your existence, and that to be prepared for your *grand* existence in your Heavenly Father's house you need to be tried in the furnace. Corruption, which is so engrained in us, would utterly spoil us for heaven. God employs His dark and trying providences to clear the soul from its pollutions. Those that are before the Throne have come out of great tribulation. They are now clothed in white. They did not wash their robes and make them white in their tribulations, but in the blood of the Lamb. But in their tribulations they learned how to keep these white robes unpolluted and how to wear them. In fine, fasten on this, that the present is but the infancy of our being, that if looked at apart from our grand existence it is all perplexity, obscurity and darkness, when environed by the painful dispensations of God; but when looked at in connection with our grand existence in heaven, it is not all dark. It may not be day, but neither is it night. To the best there may be much in their lot that is very obscure, yet when they think of the great end of their being—of their grand existence in eternity—of the wisdom and goodness of their Heavenly Father, of the terrible corruption that needs to be taken away ere they can either glorify or enjoy Him; they see a meaning, a precious meaning, even in the most painful dispensations of His providence. While heart and flesh are like to faint and fail under some sore and complex trial, the afflicted sufferer may not be able to say: "I see it all, I see it all clearly;" yet he will be able to say: "it is not all night, my Father is here—my God is doing it—even so, Father, it is right." It will be right for eternity.

III. But a third reason why the providence of God is often obscure is, that one man's condition and future destiny are often mysteriously linked in with the condition and destiny of others.

No man can live for himself. Selfishness that attempts this is as unwise as it is wicked. No doubt the selfish man who dissociates himself from the feelings and interests of others will avoid many sorrows and escape from much that is painful in the course of providence. But this selfish isolation will end not in happiness, but in wretchedness. He that will only mind his own things will soon find that he has little worth minding. Man leans on man, heart is closely knit to heart, so that in the little social circles of life, when one member suffers all the members suffer with it. This is God's arrangement. It is at man's peril if he deranges it.

Let me illustrate this:

1. As to the physical relationships among human beings. The father of a family of helpless children is suddenly cut off. The dispensation so common is dark and trying—for the children are left without guidance or

protection. Or take another trying dispensation. A son or daughter, the main support and comfort of aged and feeble parents, is snatched away by death. In these houses a blight has fallen. Joy has vanished, hope has gone out. Assuredly these are painful providences, but whence springs the pain? Plainly from that beautiful arrangement which God has made, by which one depends on another, and by which human bosoms can pity, love and succour one another. If we could not pity and love, we should be freer from many cares and sorrows. But then we should no longer be men but brutes or demons. He that sheds no tears, and has none for whom he can weep, is not the best and happiest of men, but is very depraved, and probably extremely wretched. It is because we lean on one another, need help and can give it—can love, pity and rejoice with the hearts of others—that our own hearts are so often pained by dark providences. Had the Patriarch not felt the most ardent parental affection, he had not cried out, in an agony of grief: "Joseph is not! and Simeon is not!"

2. The moral relationships that subsist among men are often the causes of intense suffering from certain dark providences.

Christian parents of enlightened affections not only desire that their children may have bread to eat and raiment to put on, but that they may be wise and pious, and, in the best sense, honourable and useful in the world. That this wish may bear its fruits, they educate their children, watch over them, counsel them, pray for them. Now, there is a command and a promise on this. The command is "train up a child in the way he should go," and the promise, "when he is old he will not depart from it." The principle in the promise is general, but not without, at least, its apparent exceptions. Good men may give counsel, but cannot give grace; may set a godly example, but may fail to lead their children heavenward. Hence, those in whom they feel the deepest interest may disappoint their hopes and fill their bosoms with deepest grief. The child that was expected to be the honour of the house may prove its shame; who was looked to with the tenderest joy of the heart, may break the heart; and who was the chief hope of the bosom, may fill the bosom with darkest disappointment. Was not this David's case when he cried out: "Oh, Absalom! Absalom! would to God I had died for thee, O my son! Absalom!" These are among the most trying dispensations in the lot of a good man; for all the tenderest feelings are lacerated, the fairest hopes blasted, and many of the holiest joys of the heart perished.

Now, it is true, if the parent utterly failed in his duty, this dispensation is more painful than dark. Alas! it is plain enough. But suppose he was upon the whole faithful in duty, whence springs the pain from the moral relationship? It is just, my brethren, because you feel a deep interest in the spiritual and eternal well-being of those nearly related to you. It is this deep interest that makes you labour so much, hope so ardently, and feel so bitterly when hope is disappointed. This disappointment, mark it, will be in proportion to the depth and strength of holy affection, and to the reasonableness and ardour of your hopes. But now, it is asked, why should such a dark providence befall the wise and the good? Ah, my friends, they were not perfectly wise and good. Even they may have in many ways failed so sadly in their duty that the dispensation is not to themselves all dark And, yet, it is not all light, for they did much work that was good, and now they do not reap as they expected. For, as to their earthly expectations, they may be said hardly to reap anything but disappointment. Is there no light then in the dispensation? Yes, surely there is, for if this dispensation, or any other alike painful, lays pride in the dust, and teaches a higher humility, and draws off the heart from sinful attachments to the creature, and fixes it in simple and stronger faith in God, then for themselves through all eternity the dispensation will be found to have wrought well. Their labour, then, was not lost. No real labour of faith and love was ever lost. Yet we are so wondrously connected together socially, morally and spiritually, that one string snapping, all the music of the heart is spoiled, and there is nothing but disharmony ever after in the bosom, which will not end till the soul enters amidst the perfect harmonies of heaven. In a word, then, our lot in the providence of God is not all day nor all night, but often very obscure. My brethren, let us walk by faith and hope, that when the day-spring from on high visits us it will be all day. When the immortal soul enters the heavenly world, clouds and darkness shall flee away, for there will neither be night nor obscurity.

CHAPTER XIV.

THE DUTIES OF SUBJECTS TO THEIR RULERS.*

"Let every soul be subject unto the higher powers."—Rom. xiii. 1.

IN these words the Apostle requires subjects to be obedient to their rulers. The grounds on which this obedience is enjoined, and the various ways by which it is to be exemplified, as well as the benefits that result from good government, are concisely, yet very distinctly, stated in the context. It is also worthy of notice, that the obedience required is not to be rendered merely to those who fill thrones, but to all who are in authority—to all who are entrusted with the cares and discharge of any of the functions of Government. Hence says another Apostle: "Submit yourselves to every ordinance of man for the Lord's sake, whether it be to the King, as supreme; or unto Governors, as unto them that are sent by him." 1 Pet. ii. 13, 14. Obedience to the sovereign *power* implies, of course, obedience to all subordinate officers; still, there is much wisdom in making the claim of obedience explicitly commensurate with the various *powers* of Government. For no error in theory could be greater, and few more mischievous in practice, than the supposition that allegiance might be rendered to the Sovereign with perfect fidelity; while Governors and Judges acting under, and by appointment of the *supreme*

---

* Preached at Scarboro', on a Thanksgiving Day, immediately after the Canadian Rebellion in 1837-8, and published the same year.

power, might be violently resisted, or treated with contempt. Let successful resistance be made to those who hold delegated authority—made to men of ability and integrity, even in the lower departments, and the profession of submission to the Sovereign will be found to be a mere phantom of the imagination, or more frequently a screen artfully employed to conceal the movements of sedition, until sedition is ready to break forth into rebellion. These remarks, I trust, not only illustrate an important idea in the text, but also tend, if I mistake not, to unfold a principle to which, in all fairness, may be traced much of that seditious spirit, whether open or disguised, that lately threatened the destruction of this Province. If the authority of the Government is not felt and respected, in *all its servants*, its efficiency for good hath come to an end.

As it is my intention in this discourse, rather to give a plain exhibition of *certain* important duties which subjects owe to their rulers, than to discuss abstract principles, I do not feel called upon to inquire minutely into those questions that refer to the origin of the magistrate's power; the grounds on which obedience is rendered ; the extent to which it ought to be cheerfully yielded ; the point at which, under certain circumstances, it may cease ; and resistance, on the high principles of justice and mercy, become a sacred duty. You will easily perceive, that were these propositions to be thoroughly discussed, the discussion would yield matter rather for a volume than for a portion of a sermon. When such topics are fully investigated on purely philosophical principles, by a man of ripe faculties, the inquiry must afford to the intellectual labourer rich enjoyment, and be productive of substantial advantages to others. Yet, in truth, all men of good sense, and of virtuous dispositions, feel no difficulty, under ordinary circumstances, in coming to just and satisfactory conclusions on these and similar inquiries. At the same time it is well known that these very questions have furnished inexhaustible themes for the Demagogue and the political Empiric. Out of these they have often brought *darkness*—not light, *confusion*—not order. For what is more easy than for an ingenious sophist, or even a determined wrangler, to lay hold upon some recondite principle in politics, or religion, and out of that start difficulties and objections which, in the eyes of the ignorant, may have an air of learning and originality, yet do not possess in fact one particle of solid wisdom, and serve no other purpose save to weaken the understanding and corrupt the conscience of men. It were really amusing, if it were not so exceedingly mischievous, to hear men of the most moderate powers of mind prate about laying the foundations of Government, as if this were yet to be done; and they, forsooth, the only persons capable of doing it. It would be prudent in certain men to avoid, as much as possible, all discussions on Government that turn on abstract principles.

On the questions to which reference has been made, I shall only make a few simple remarks. And (1) I observe, that how much-soever the *form* of Government may be liable to alterations, from the changes incident to all communities of men; and much as human wisdom in all cases must have to do in making suitable modifications; still it is abundantly plain, both from scripture and the light of nature, that civil government is of divine appointment. God is the author of this, as well as of every other good thing which His creatures enjoy. Justice, Truth, Wisdom, Power and Benevolence, the essential elements of all good government, have been, and ever will be, the same. But these elements wherever found to exist are from the Author of nature; and, if I may so speak, are parts or reflections of the grand principles of His own moral government. The powers that be—or the principles that remain—are ordained of God. Now, whether we think of these principles, or of the constitution of nature —the latter rendering government so necessary, and the former making what is so necessary so unspeakably beneficial to the human race—we cannot but conclude that civil government is an ordinance of Heaven. In what part of the universe soever innocency needs protection, or the virtues admit of cultivation, there this ordinance will have place. But (2) all this being admitted, it must follow that obedience, in the broad and natural sense of the thing, should be freely rendered to the Government under which we live. The word of God and right reason alike demand this. And (3) rebellion never can be justifiable, or right in the sight of God, until the government has nullified its own claims to obedience, by having in some way or other wilfully destroyed the essential principles—and in all cases there are such, whether expressed or implied—in the relation or compact that exists between rulers and subjects.

With the last, by far the most trying of these general topics, you, my brethren, are, I believe, as little liable to be perplexed as you are disinclined at present to hear it discussed. Indeed, its frequent discussion proves clearly that either the Government is extremely bad, or the public mind is in a most unhealthy state. It is folly, nay, wickedness, for men to rack their imaginations in fancying cases in which resistance to Government may become their duty. Every man who knows when he should obey, and does obey authority from right motives, will know when and how to resist oppression. It will be time enough for us, my hearers, to give our mind to this inquiry, when the Government under which we live has ceased to be a Government of law and of justice. To this pass things have not come. To say they have is to utter the language of falsehood or sheer folly; and out of hollow professions to make a cloak to hide the odiousness of the late rebellion. Most mad and wicked attempt! And let us, my brethren, this day, with hearts full of *sanctified* gratitude, adore Almighty God for the late deliverance. He hath saved us from ruin. He hath broken the arm of the wicked. He hath brought to light the *hidden things of darkness.* He hath restored peace, and preserved order among us. The Lord reigneth, to His name be the praise.

But ere I proceed further, I beg to guard you against supposing that I wish to inculcate a blind passive obedience to any Government armed with power to enforce its villanies. This were not to support, but to subvert the fundamental principles of our admirable Constitution. Of its genius they are grossly ignorant who think that it makes provision for arbitrary power; and they are its enemies who would seek thus to uphold it. Arbitrary power cannot be established without tearing up the British Constitution from its very foundation. I revere that Constitution because I do, from my soul, regard it as the *nurse* and *protector* of genuine liberty. I urge obedience to the Government under which we live, because I believe it to be substantially a Government of law and of justice. I stand up zealously in its defence because it is my solemn conviction that whatever has been wrong in its administration may be corrected by constitutional means, while I would regard its overthrow as the sorest calamity, of a temporal sort, that could befall this Province. And say, does not the word of God demand obedience to such a Government? Does not a just sense of your own best interests—a regard for the welfare of millions that may yet inhabit this vast and fertile country—make it imperative on you as men, as Christians and fathers, to stand up for a Constitution and Government under which you have enjoyed such perfect security, and have had, and do still possess, such a large share of temporal blessings? But I remark,

I.—*That it is the duty of all good subjects to pray for their rulers.*

"I exhort, therefore," says the Apostle, "that, first of all, supplications, prayers, intercessions, and giving of thanks be made for all men: for kings and for all that are in authority," 1 Tim. ii. 1, 2. This injunction, so explicitly laid down by the inspired writer, was faithfully attended to by the primitive Christians. These pious men prayed fervently for all rulers. On the importance of remembering our rulers at a throne of grace, little needs to be said to those who believe in the efficacy of prayer. They will readily admit that believing prayer is one of the divinely instituted means by which blessings are obtained for others as well as for ourselves. No one more earnestly desired the prayers of his fellow Christians than did the Apostle. "Brethren, pray for us," was the affectionate request made by him to those on whose piety and sympathy he could rely. Nor will it be doubted that he whose mind was illuminated by the Spirit of God must have had clear and just conceptions of the connection between the performance of believing prayer and the bestowment of blessings. But he who desired the prayers of others when labours and trials pressed heavily upon him, earnestly exhorts all Christians to pray for their rulers. The Apostle's exhortation is to us a divine command. The reasons for this command will become strikingly apparent if you reflect—

1. That the duties of rulers *are extremely weighty*, and their station *highly responsible*.

There are rulers, it is true, who do not feel the burden of office, nor, to any good purpose realize the responsible nature of their trust; men without principle or habits of application to business, to whom office is a place for repose, not a field for labour. Such men, it must be confessed, will suffer little from the toils, and less from the anxieties peculiar to their high station. But, alas, their ease is without innocency, and their repose without honour! Yea, such persons, how great soever their talents may be, are the scandals of Government, and the curses of their country. No statesman can be negligent without being highly criminal. His sins of omission are often sins of the deepest dye. This admitted and you will not fail to pray that your rulers may be kept from falling into a criminal and dishonourable forgetfulness of their responsibilities and duties.

It were, however, in my opinion, far from true to suppose, that, as the Constitution is *now* constructed, and the various departments of Government balanced, and check-bound by one another, indifferency to their duties is, or can be, common in British rulers. To them office, especially in the higher departments, is not a bed of roses; its duty is something widely different from an elegant recreation. Indeed, the ruler who feels his responsibilities as he ought, and labours faithfully for the good of his country, will have all his powers tasked to the severest toils, and his mind fretted with cares and anxieties of which the greater part of men can form no conception. Such, in fact, is the constant and severe friction that this sort of labour produces on the intellect of faithful statesmen, that minds of the most solid structure have often given way under it. And if it be—as it certainly is—far more honourable to rule nations now than when men were uncivilized, and in a state of slavery; so is it far more difficult, and demands an incomparably greater degree of labour. The toil of the ruler now is mental toil; and is every day becoming more severe. The matters which in the present age require his attention—and in no country more than in Britain and her dependencies—are so various and complex, and the changes so great and sudden, not to speak of the conflicting interests and the fierce and perplexing movements of the different political parties, that plain it is that the statesman who would watch, anticipate and arrange as he ought, must possess various powers of a high order, and these powers must be constantly on the stretch. Nor ought it to be forgotten, that the highly artificial form which society has assumed in modern times —the rapid changes to which vast masses of property are liable—the human mind rather stimulated than nourished by political knowledge—the contempt manifested by so many for all that has hitherto stood by prescription—the strong desire felt by various classes to break away from the positions which they have long occupied, and suddenly advance to new ground—the numberless channels which have of late been opened up for the gratification of the passions of avarice and ambition :—all contribute to render the situation of rulers eminently difficult and laborious. The question is not, do these striking characteristics in modern society augur good or ill for human happiness? but, do they not greatly increase the ruler's duties, and make these at once more delicate and more toilsome? Of this I think there cannot be a doubt. In order to fill their places well, rulers would require the patience of saints, and the wisdom of philosophers. To please all is impossible. To do justice to all is often difficult, and a single false step, O how fatal! Generations may feel and deplore the evil, yet may find it impossible to correct *in an age* a measure that was passed *in a day*. On the other hand, how many precious blessings have, under God, been secured to a people by the wisdom, integrity and firmness of a Prince, or a single statesman. A slight acquaintance with history will sufficiently illustrate both these positions.

My Christian brethren, think not that I make these remarks merely to display the duties and difficulties of those in authority. No. They are made simply from a wish to impress your minds with correct notions of the necessity of praying earnestly for men whose duties are so arduous and their station so responsible.

2. *The temptations to which rulers are exposed* is another powerful reason why subjects should pray for them.

An elevated station—great and, to some extent, imperfectly defined trusts—a keen sense of shame—ardent ambition, and vast means for its gratification—will naturally expose even solid virtue to serious danger. From these, and similar causes, rulers are liable to peculiar temptations, and to each temptation under peculiar disadvantages. Those who move in the humbler walks of life, exposed to temptation, yet retaining their integrity, and keeping a good conscience, are possibly not always aware to what extent they are indebted for all this to the narrowness of their sphere, and their very limited means. Let no one sneer at this as a sly bow to greatness or a heartless compliment to poverty. I am sure a little reflection will convince you that those who occupy the higher places, and hold the greater trusts in Government, have their virtue often severely tried. They are, indeed, tempted on all hands, and through all possible channels. They are tempted now to substitute expediency for the principles of rectitude. At another time they are tempted to sacrifice the claims of justice or of mercy. They are tempted to-day to give up the interests of the many for the sake of the few ; to-morrow, to sacrifice the interests of the few to the caprices of the many. They are threatened by parties, flattered by individuals, and frequently deceived by all. To act a prominent part in such a scene, and *never err*, is more than can be expected of the best of men ; while even to act with discretion, and with an ordinary share of integrity, must require a large portion of wisdom, firmness and pure moral worth. Pray that your rulers may possess these qualities in a high degree. For, bear it in mind, brethren, that the fall of rulers into certain temptations may cover a nation with disgrace, and may be the cause of wretchedness to millions. Such persons fall not alone ; "when the rulers sin the people suffer."

And, says the Apostle, "pray for them, *that ye may lead quiet and peaceable lives.*" The reflections already thrown out naturally suggest a few remarks on this important truth. It is easy to conceive of a system of government so admirably constructed, that even great folly, or wickedness in the rulers shall not produce an instant derangement in the public affairs, or create any sudden or visible mischief. Things may go on for a time in their usual course; just as you may have seen a piece of machinery when perfectly constructed and fairly put in motion, perform its operations for an hour, although entrusted to the care of persons who neither understood its principles nor regarded its safety. This, however, is a hazardous state of things. To drop the figure—of this be assured, that that land will soon mourn bitterly, the rulers of which are children in wisdom, but veterans in crime. If they are men either of weak intellect or of depraved hearts, their conduct must—it cannot be otherwise—produce among the people confusion, crime and misery. No form of government can prevent wicked men in power from doing mischief. Even in our own Government, spite of its admirable system of checks, it is easy to see how wicked men may originate, and, if sufficiently powerful, may carry through measures, the ruinous effects of which may soon be felt in the remotest parts of the body politic. If you would enjoy the blessings of good government, and wish to lead quiet and peaceable lives, pray to God that your rulers may be men who possess much wisdom—"men who fear God and hate covetousness."

And, may I be allowed to remark for once—from this place it shall but be for once—that when you are called upon at any time to choose persons to represent you in Parliament, you should do so with candour and wisdom. Banish all party animosities and all low selfish considerations. Let your suffrage be given—honestly and fearlessly given—for men of talent; men sound in their political views, of genuine moral worth, lovers of liberty, but haters of licentiousness; for men who will neither fear to oppose what is bad, nor shrink from the defence of what is good —who will neither cringe to the great, nor pander to the passions of the multitude.

But, in fine, while you strive to act wisely in this matter, never lose sight of the important duty which I have been urging on your attention. The man who never prays for himself is mad—is utterly forgetful of God. He that prays for himself and will not pray for others—for rulers—neither understands the principles of our holy religion, nor have his feelings been purified or warmed by its graces. Happy is that Prince who rules over a praying people. Nor is it possible for a Sovereign to contemplate a more sublime and cheering spectacle than that of a nation of families as they approach their Heavenly Father to supplicate blessings for themselves, at the same time imploring the Divine Benefactor to protect by His omnipotent hand, and with all His good graces to bless their Sovereign. Around such hearths as these, a good Prince has no reason to fear that sedition will ever be hatched; while the hands thus lifted up to supplicate blessings on the throne will be the first to be lifted up to defend a righteous throne when assailed by violence. Would to God that rulers but understood how much their honour, safety and happiness depend on the virtue and piety of the people. But I remark,

II.—*That it is the duty of subjects to pay taxes, that the Government under which they live, and by which they are protected, may be supported.*

This duty is also enjoined by Divine authority. "Render tribute to whom tribute is due, custom to whom custom," Rom. xiii. 7. In the context the reason for this is in substance stated to be that Governments may be supported, and subjects preserved in their rights by an efficient magistracy. As to the obligatory nature of this duty, the Saviour's example will be held to be decisive by all who bow to His authority. Indeed, this, when viewed in the abstract, hardly admits of two opinions. All men are agreed on the principle. Yet, on this very matter, more than any other, have differences arisen which, in the end, have shaken constitutions to pieces, and more than once changed the whole face of society in a country. It is not my intention to go fully into the subject. At the same time its importance very plainly warrants, or rather demands, a few passing remarks.

Taxes are, in a sense, the sinews of Government. For, except in the rudest conditions of savage life, Government cannot be supported, save at considerable expense; while, from the peculiar circumstances in which a people may be placed, the means required for its support may, for a time at least, be very great. On the relative merits of different Governments, from their comparative expense, it were improper in this place to enter. The subject is one, indeed, which admits of declamation to any extent; but on which wise men will find it difficult, if not impossible, to come to any definite or practical conclusions. Suffice it to say, that the least expensive in appearance is often the most so in reality; while the cheapest is often, in every sense, the worst, because to the people the least efficient. The parsimony that enfeebles a Government is not a whit less mischievous than the profusion that corrupts it; while, on the simple principle of calculation, the saving is often a loss. Nothing were easier than to fix on cases in which the ill-timed economy of a certain class of politicians has frustrated the most beneficial and best concerted measures, and in the end led to the most ruinous waste of national resources. It is, however, a maxim as sound in politics as in morals, that a Government ought to deal as *carefully* and *prudently* with the public money as a wise man will deal with his own personal property.

But, alas! who will say that this has always been the case? The truth is, rulers have often been guilty of wanton profusion and gross dishonesty, in handling the public money. Men who thus act are foul stains on Government, and their conduct, more than anything else, makes authority cheap and despicable in the eyes of the people. And God forbid that I should say aught to screen the peculating courtier, or the minister prodigal of his country's wealth. The wickedness of apologizing for such men were, if possible, even greater than their crimes. When we think that a large portion of the taxes is drawn from the earnings of the hard-toiling labourer, we cannot fail but look with horror at men, who, instead of laying out the money thus obtained for the public benefit, expend it on the gratification of their own lusts, and in the accomplishment of their own selfish ends. Such criminals stand among ordinary sinners, as Saul stood among the people. The crimes of such men partake at once of the most loathsome meanness, and the most appalling guilt. He that plunders his country, let him do it *in what way* soever he may, ought to be held up to reprobation, and, if possible, brought to condign punishment.

Yet, you must not suppose that all that is said on the prodigality of rulers is true, or is said from a generous sympathy for those who bear the burdens. The public money may be expended to a vast amount, yet there may be no waste. Nothing more may be laid out than the exigencies of the time may absolutely require. Hence the *opposition in power* have oftener than once been compelled to own that retrenchment could be carried no further. This was candid. But, then, what are we to think of past professions and past appeals? The truth is—and it ought not to be concealed, the people need to know it—that much of the outcry against profuse expenditure is often nothing more than a *low fetch* of ambitious and unprincipled men, by which they at once embarrass those in authority, and minister to the basest passions of the most ignorant portion of the people. The tax, or finance, argument is, indeed, the patent argument of the demagogue. Without it, it is extremely difficult to see how he could at all get on. This argument he can at all times employ without *any expense* of thought, and with the certainty of a considerable share of applause, such as it is. For who so generous, honest and patriotic, as the man who labours incessantly to save the people's money!

All that is necessary, indeed, to render such men the first of patriots, and entitle them in all justice to profound gratitude and the highest applause, is merely *honesty* of motives, accompanied with *mature wisdom* in their plans, and a *rigorous consistency* betwixt their professions and their practice. Did they possess these qualities, it were almost impossible to admire or praise their labours too highly. But, alas! for poor human nature, the history of not a few of these disinterested patriots is the bitterest satire which their bitterest enemy can utter. Their professions when struggling to gain public favour, and their conduct after they have got hold of the public purse, and the patronage of the Government—what a contrast!

But, admit that all uttered on this matter by the political economist is uttered in perfect sincerity, and still it may be good for nothing: yea, may turn out ruinous folly. Suppose that his savings are made at the loss of national honour, or that they endanger the existence of the state, by weakening its means of defence—cramp internal improvement—derange, or, it may be, utterly destroy some great branch of commerce; his folly, not his wisdom, his waste, not his saving, would soon be made apparent in the most calamitous results. The truth is, that with men of wisdom the question is not, how much is expended? but, can it be spared—is it well laid out—will it contribute to increase the wealth, honour and security of the people—will it enlarge their means for moral and intellectual improvement—will it tend, on principles of equity, to advance the political influence of the country? These are obviously the questions that will engage the attention of every statesman of sagacity and true patriotism; and by these questions will the wise financier be guided. But these are questions which the man of fractions has neither the will nor the ability to investigate.

Let it not be supposed, however, that these remarks are intended to encourage a profuse, far less a reckless, expenditure of the public money, or to cast odium on an honest, wise, and temperate *opposition*. For such an *opposition* the genius of the Constitution makes ample provision; while history furnishes abundant proofs that this is the best and most natural protection of liberty, as well as an admirable security against executive extravagance. Yet, who can see the public mind abused by hollow professions, and the interests of a people sacrificed, under a fair show of generosity and patriotism, by fools who understand not one *sound principle* in politics ; or by hypocrites who only seek their *own ends*, and not be filled with indignation, to which it is difficult to give utterance in decent terms? He that robs the public mind of truth is surely not less wicked than the man who robs the public purse. What shall we think of him that would do both?

No one entertains a higher respect for the good sense of the people than I do. But this very respect, while it warrants plain speaking, forbids flattery. I must, then, tell you there are two points in this matter on which the greater part of men must ever be very imperfect judges. *First*, the amount necessary for the support of Government. *Second*, the best methods of laying out a revenue. Any man, it is true, may, by a little reading and reflection, acquire some knowledge of the outlines of national finance; but to understand this subject thoroughly demands means for obtaining information, as well as talents for making a proper use of that information, which few, indeed, possess. Now, let us suppose—a thing that has often assumed more than the form of a supposition—that whenever the people are taxed beyond what they think is necessary for the support of the Government, or when the revenue is not expended in perfect accordance with their preconceived notions of *utility* and *frugality*, although the whole may be done by their own representatives, they shall refuse to pay the taxes. Who can conceive the mischiefs and general anarchy to which this conduct must give rise? Nor will the evil be much mitigated, should the popular branch of the Legislature withhold the supplies whenever it feels checked by the one above it. I am not to be told that the Constitution has made provision for this, and, therefore, it may at any time be done. The Constitution allows the Sovereign to withhold the royal assent and thus prevent any bill from becoming a law. Yet in a hundred years this right has not been exercised by the *crown;* the power in both cases is similar. It is a sacred reserved power on which *either* party may fall back, and at a desperate crisis—never but then—employ it. There is hardly anything that shows a man more clearly to be a fool, than when he is seen drawing the most remote exceptions, and the most delicate principles, into general rules and common practice. Such an order, or rather disorder, of things would overturn the whole social system in a day. Matters have come to a frightful pass, when the popular branch of the Legislature can only cause its power to be felt by stopping the supplies. Depend upon it, this cannot be often done without dissolving the Government, and bringing matters to an issue in another place than a Legislative Hall, and with other weapons than those of argument and votes. Men should understand this. Still the principle in the Constitution to which we refer is admirable as a reserve principle. But it must only be employed on *extraordinary* occasions. To use it otherwise is matchless folly and great wickedness.

In short, without taxes no Government can be supported, unless it possesses great hereditary revenues. In modern times, revenues of this sort are not possessed to any great extent in the more powerful and civilized nations. Nor is it desirable that this source of supply should be increased. Hereditary revenues, held by the Crown, and, in a great measure, under the influence of the Executive —and, theories apart, this must ever, to a great extent, be the case—it is easy to see how an ambitious Prince, aided by a set of unprincipled Ministers, might enslave a people, or at least prevent them from enlarging the foundations of liberty by safe and constitutional means. Had certain of the Princes of the House of Stuart not been under the necessity of calling the Parliament together to obtain the supplies, the liberties of England might yet have been to achieve.

Hence, the tax which the Government requires, and which the people, through their representatives, grant, though when viewed abstractedly it may be regarded as an evil, yet as a part of the system it becomes an efficient security against the usurpations of the Crown, and gives the people a right in the Government and a power over its measures which they otherwise could not possess. If men are to be free, they must submit to taxation—they must support their own Government. Nor, unless it is well supported, can it ever be efficient for good. If you realize these truths as you ought, you will pay taxes, "not of constraint, but willingly."

And is it not true, my friends, that the taxes paid hitherto in this country amounted to nothing more than a *mere peppercorn tribute?* Had our taxes been less, we had absolutely forgotten that we had a Government to support. I know of no country, that has anything like a regular form of Government, in which the people are so lightly taxed as they have been in Upper Canada. Nor is it difficult to account for this. We enjoy the protection of the mightiest and most efficient Government on earth, without contributing anything to its support. Truth and common sense have often been outraged, but scarcely ever to the same extent, as by the outcry raised in this Province about oppressive burdens. There is an insolent impudence about the whole thing, which makes one for a moment forget the monstrous falsehood, in the insult offered to his understanding. That persons could be found who would utter this cry of oppression to *answer an end*, is not surprising; but that thousands should have been found so credulously mad as to assent to it, is really fitted quite as much to excite a smile of pity at their weakness, as the conduct of their deceivers is fitted to provoke the frown of indignation. He were a magician, indeed, who could as easily and completely persuade suffering men that they are happy, as certain persons have persuaded happy men that they were wretched. And wretched they have made them. Long did they amuse, or, if you will, torture their victims with fancied ills: at last, they have plunged them into real calamities. And, had it not been for the generosity of that Government which they had so shamefully maligned, these calamities would have proved disastrously ruinous. There are others, verily, besides Satan that perplex the mind with gloomy phantoms, that they may drive their victims to despair—to utter ruin. But I remark,

III. *That subjects ought to honour their rulers.*

Respect, or a well tempered and enlightened veneration for those clothed with authority, whether they be parents, princes or subordinate magistrates, is a dictate of nature. On this the word of God is full and explicit: while the Divine injunctions to honour superiors are enforced by numerous promises and threatenings. "Honour thy father and thy mother, that thy days may be long upon the land which the Lord thy God giveth thee." "Fear God. Honour the King." Render "fear to whom fear" is due, and "honour to whom honour" is due. And, at the same time, men are warned against using language by which this respect for superiors may be weakened. Hence, says another inspired writer, "thou shalt not speak evil of the ruler of thy people." These are but a few of many passages in which this duty is brought before us in the Scriptures. Nor will the frequency and the force with which it is urged on our attention appear surprising, if it be borne in mind that unless the principles of subordination are thoroughly instilled into men, society cannot be held together without a constant course of miracles. God never works miracles to set aside or overthrow the great principles of morals. Government rests on these. On these it must stand, or go down. It is true that Government may exist, after a sort, although some of its elements are wanting, or possessed but in a small degree; but subordination, and what this implies —lost, whether in the family or in the state, and all order and morals will quickly perish. Now mark it, my friends, all subordination must turn either on *fear* or *respect* for those who are clothed with authority. Respect is the basis of subordination in the minds of enlightened freemen, living under a righteous Government. Plain it is, that all subjects ought to honour wise and virtuous rulers. If they do not, to me it is very clear that their neglect, or, which is not uncommon, their ignorant insolence, which some mistake for independency of mind, will, in the end, lead to anarchy, that will quickly bring them under an iron despotism that will compel subjection without either caring for or seeking respect. Making it, for a moment, a matter of mere selfish calculation, I aver that every man who does not wish to see the Government overthrown and is not fully prepared for all the consequences of such an overthrow, must feel sacredly bound to honour the rulers of the country in which he lives. Many who neglect this, and treat their rulers with scorn, are only vain men or more vulgar fools. They are not malignant haters. Yet this sort of folly, or vanity, is assuredly far more entitled to severe censure than pity. The man who refuses respect to rulers fails quite as much in his duty as he who refuses to pay tribute. For just the freer and the more excellent any form of Government is, so is there just the more need that rulers be sincerely honoured. And let it be written down in your minds, that such a Government as ours cannot stand if the rulers are despised; and never deceive yourselves by thinking that you can honour the Government in the abstract, while at the same time you treat with silent contempt, or assail with open abuse, the persons entrusted with its administration. This sort of abstract respect is like abstract charity; each must have its object—its living object—or it is mere deception.

But, if respect for rulers be so essential to the existence and efficiency of Government, what must we think of those who labour to root out of the human mind this sentiment, or class of sentiments? They are—profess what they may —the bitter, the deadly, enemies of all Government, and, by consequence, of human happiness. True, their aim is not exactly to destroy the sentiments of respect. They wish rather to transfer its fruits to themselves, or to others equally worthless. But are they so ignorant as not to know that, even were they entitled to respect, the course they pursue will much sooner entirely destroy the principle than transfer its fruits? Hence, the reason why those who thus abuse and madden the mind of the multitude may be borne to-day on their shoulders into power, and to-morrow trampled under their feet. Natural and just retribution, this.

But do not suppose that I wish to encourage a blind devotion to those in authority, or would have you to present them with a gross and obsequious homage. This is the incense which slaves may offer to tyrants. But this, if offered to high-minded British rulers, would, I doubt not, be as loathsome to them, in our day, as it would be intolerable to their high-minded subjects, if it were demanded. Than this, nothing can be more at variance with the genius of our free institutions, and the manly character of the people. Our rulers are not to be regarded as the Grand Llamas of Thibet—sacred personages whom few shall see, and of whom none shall speak but in terms of adulation. Those, who exclaimed, "it is the voice of a god, and not of a man," beheld their idol the next hour a lifeless corpse. And he that would flatter, or teach others to flatter rulers, in the present state of the world, is the most dangerous enemy to those in high places. But are men to be doomed perpetually to the mischiefs of extremes? When they cease to flatter, must they abuse? and when they do not abuse, must they flatter? Alas, so it is! And, just because sycophants and traitors find their account by it, enlightened friends of their country—men who revere those in authority from proper motives—will do neither. They will cherish a sincere respect for those who, under God, rule over the destinies of men, and are sent "for the punishment of evil-doers and for the praise of them that do well." Hence the respect of such men is truly valuable. It springs from pure principles—it depends not for its existence on the smiles of the great, the splendours of a throne, or the trappings of office. It is as far removed from cringing as it is from insolence; it is the product of the higher and severer virtues. In a word, my brethren, let us honour our rulers for the place which, under God, they have been called to occupy. If they are wise men, let us admire them; if they are just men, let us revere them; if they are benevolent men, let us esteem them.

But, then, it will be asked, what shall be done in case rulers are weak, vacillating, or wicked? The man who acts from right motives, and cherishes for good rulers the most profound regard, will feel no difficulty here. If they are weak, he cannot admire them; if they are vacillating, he cannot esteem them; if they are wicked and tyrannical, he must oppose them. Yet, even in his opposition, the respect due to authority will never, for a moment, be lost sight of. His obedience to the law will not be weakened in the slightest degree; although, for a time, *it* may be under the direction of persons whom he can neither esteem nor love. He will never confound the man and the magistrate; and while he strives, by all constitutional means, to reform the erring or displace the guilty statesman, he will never do so by trampling on his office, or by holding up to scorn the duties of his high station. Of worthless men in power he will speak with regret, and what is said will be said with the strictest regard to truth —with moderation and charity. He will make all possible allowance for the circumstances amidst which the faulty ruler has been placed—the peculiar difficulties that may be found in the situation—the temptations to which the individual has been exposed, as well as the explanations which the objectionable measures may admit of. And does he who acts thus manifest a want of either courage, or wisdom, or love of order? We think not.

But the character of public men, it is said, is public property, and therefore ought to be carefully scrutinized. Granted. And, if it is candidly and temperately gone about, the scrutiny may be of real advantage to rulers as well as subjects. The man who is able and faithful fears no investigation. But, surely, the character of public men is not public property, *to be abused.* One would suppose that what is so valuable to a nation ought to be carefully preserved. That country is deplorably forgetful of its best interests that permits the character of its rulers to be destroyed by insidious villains, or torn to pieces by a furious mob. Yet what is more common? Hence it is that the character of rulers of the highest worth is constantly assailed by every weapon which ingenuity can devise, and the most reckless malice employ. Dark surmises, sly insinuations, insolent jests and gross falsehoods, are the weapons employed. And the wretches that employ them are frequently as cowardly, and not less wicked, than those savages that pierce the traveller with poisoned arrows from their thickets. It were bad enough if such attacks were made merely against the individual. But, almost universally, in the individual, the authority with which he is clothed—the law—the Government with which he stands connected, are all, if the assailant has wit, turned into contempt, and if he has only dull malignity, trodden down with a coarse and vulgar joy. Now, whether this be done through the Press, or in conversation, it is alike to be condemned. It is wicked in design and most hurtful in its effects.

Nor will it do to reply, that, if what is said be slanderous, the ruler has ample means for vindicating—for indemnifying himself. The law is open. There is a deception in this. To see it clearly two things must be taken into account. (1) The liberty of speech and of the press is completely secured by our precious Constitution. This liberty, one of its most invaluable and fundamental principles is dear to the heart of every British subject, and is guarded by each with the most jealous care. God forbid it should ever be otherwise. Yet who can look at the way in which this liberty is abused when turned into licentiousness, and not be greatly shocked? Yea, this capital principle in the Constitution is sometimes so viciously employed as to threaten its entire overthrow. Things not less strange have happened than that this liberty—licentiousness of the Press—should, in the end, lead to slavery. Because the Constitution has made the law of libel rigorously difficult and narrow for the prosecutor, and because men are patriotically delicate in giving a verdict for a slandered statesman, shall every low scribbler take advantage of these things to spread abroad base surmises, and, by all possible means, blacken the character of rulers? Thus, alas! it is, that the most precious rights are abused. But (2) rulers, in many cases, cannot so easily prosecute the slanderer as some persons seem to think. Every contemptible defamer is not entitled to the distinction which such a prosecution gives. An infamous notoriety is valuable to such wretches. It secures bread as well as *fame* to them. Now, they are not to be thus fed or honoured. Prosecute them, and you give power to vice, and dignity to folly. Thus, at least, it is in many cases. Neglect is at once their punishment and their desert. Let the community thus treat them and great good will follow. But further, a mind of true greatness and conscious rectitude is apt to treat slander, in many cases with silent scorn and *calmly leave its own worth* to find proofs, or, if need be' vindication, from time and events. Nor will escape the' notice of persons who reflect, that the dignity of office may forbid its possessor hastily to descend and meet some miserable calumniator either through the Press or in Court. Under these means *of protection*—for such they really are—the official and extempore slanderer pursues his vocation—disseminates the poison of calumny, until the public mind is, in the end, deeply and fatally affected by it. You are aware, that a falsehood may be so often repeated, and repeated under such a variety of forms, that it shall come at length to be credited by the simple-minded as if it were really a self-evident truth. In this way the credulity of men is scandalously abused by those who speak evil of dignities—who malign Government. The most excellent institutions are thus shamefully misrepresented; the most elevated and worthy characters most vilely belied; faults are imputed; excellences concealed; doubts started; crimes hinted at. And whether all this be declared aloud, or merely whispered—declared in affected solemnity, or low jest—with many the thing takes; the calumny sticks in the mind, and entirely destroys the honour and respect due to rulers. Fatal effect —but not more fatal to the ruler than, in the end, it must prove to the subject.

Let me earnestly caution you, my brethren, to beware of men who labour to destroy in the minds of others all respect for those who are clothed with authority. Their end accomplished, and one main-stay of order and Government is removed—and men are just so far prepared for anarchy, and exposed to all its horrors. Pretend to what they may, they are low inhuman miscreants. We say, they are in the worst sense low. For no man that uses the language which these persons employ, has any better claims to the manners of a gentleman, than he has to the wisdom of a philosopher, or the morals of a Christian. It is painful to think to what an extent *writers* of this sort have succeeded in perverting the views, and souring the minds, of honest and simple-hearted men. These men have been wrought upon, year after year, until many of them have come at length to regard their rulers as little better than a set of monsters whom it is a *virtue to despise*, and whom it would be a greater virtue to drive from the face of the earth. The person who can produce such an impression as this on the public mind regarding wise and virtuous rulers is no imperfect exemplification of the Spirit of Evil—is no mean representative of the Father of Lies.

And here I cannot but notice what some of the best men in our times have marked with extreme pain—I mean a general decay of respect for authority in all relations of life. Persons of reflection will not consider this as a groundless complaint, or the evils which it involves as of trivial consequence.

Where the honour due is not altogether withheld, it is often rather reluctantly conceded, than frankly given. Indeed, a restlessness under restraint—a desire to get clear of all superior influence—an utter dislike to all subordination, and a strong wish to see an end put to all distinctions—are prominent and alarming features of the present age. This state of things prevails, to a less or greater extent, in all the relationships of life, from the family circle to the community made up of millions. This bodes no good, my brethren. For whether we think of the cause that gives rise to this spirit, or of its effects, if we either love our fellow-men, or fear God, we cannot fail but think of the whole with much uneasiness. Do you tell me this is mere peevishness, or a wish to see arbitrary power established, and men and children curtailed of their natural rights and just liberties? Well—well, be it so. If I am to be thus judged, be it so; but hear me —listen—remember I tell you that this spirit, if not checked, will produce a licentiousness of *intellect* and of *heart* that will ere long spurn all just restraints, substitute will for law, fit men for every folly and every crime, and endanger the very existence of society. But lest anyone should say that now, or formerly, when I have spoken plainly on this matter, I plead merely for the authorities in civil Government being honoured, I answer no—not merely do I plead that all civil authority may be respected, but that all in authority may be honoured. And can I not appeal to yourselves to say, if I have not often and earnestly urged this thing home to the conscience of your children? And is there a parent so mad as to trifle with the respect, with the sacred honour, which is his due?

If he does, he perils the peace, virtue and happiness of his family. Let subjects refuse all honour and respect to rulers—treat them with all the contumely they can muster, and dare manifest—and what is often witnessed in a family will be seen on a wider scale, and with the most dreadful results in a state. And never, oh! never forget that in the family circle only, can the principles of submission and respect for authority be produced, matured and first exemplified. Family authority universally neglected, and the honour and reverence due to parents universally withheld, and will magistrates be revered and obeyed? Vain thought. In any country where such domestic dissoluteness prevails, the throne of the Prince and the Judge's bench will soon become things "for the slow-moving finger of scorn to point at." But,

IV.—*It is the duty of subjects, in all cases, to aid their rulers; and, if assailed by violence, to defend them.*

This may be looked at under two aspects. *First*, it is the duty of all subjects to aid their rulers in carrying the laws into effect. It really matters nothing how excellent soever the laws may be, unless the people generally are ready to lend their assistance in detecting offenders, and in bringing the guilty to punishment. Without such aid from the people, the magistrate will be impotent, and the law become a dead letter. And this truth and its consequences are just the more apparent the freer the civil institutions of a country are. Where disregard to the laws begins, all safety ends. Nor can there be a more dangerous state of things, than when criminals can count on impunity, from the protection thrown around them by the morbid sympathy of a community ignorant or regardless of the high claims of justice. Every man—the meanest not less than the greatest—should feel that he has a deep interest in the laws being fully supported, and the claims of justice being ever held inviolate. Hence, it is his duty to give all the assistance he can to the ministers of justice—the servants of Government.

But, *secondly*, subjects *must defend rulers if they are assailed by violence.* Under ordinary circumstances, the regular force of the state is quite sufficient for the protection of authority. There may, however, be emergencies —you are at no loss to conceive of such—when this force may either not be at hand, or may not be sufficient. The path of duty is then plain; if the Government be unprotected, and assailed by violence, every man who does not wish it overthrown will rush, if he possibly can, to its defence. And when he has done so, and exposed himself to danger, he has done nothing more than what was barely his duty.

But the discharge of this piece of duty rests, of course, on the supposition that defensive war is lawful. This, you are aware, has, of late, in this Province, been frequently called in question. This opinion is not novel, although it has acquired, in our times, rather a novel form, and is found to embrace principles neither wise nor safe, and, in some cases, far from being honourable to those who hold it. I beg that it may be distinctly understood, that it is my sincere conviction that war on any other grounds whatsoever than *those purely defensive,* is the most heinous wickedness. And were it possible to collect all the curses which the prophets of God ever pronounced against sinners, and pour them forth in one deep denouncement, that denouncement ought to fall on the guilty heads of those men who have been the means of originating and carrying on unlawful wars. Aggression in this matter is a sort of wickedness that has hardly any parallel. But does the criminality of this hellish conduct render defensive war unlawful? We think the very reverse. It is just because men will make aggressive wars that defensive war becomes absolutely necessary, and, on the plainest and most sacred principles of justice, clearly lawful. I shall not take up your time by any lengthened argument in support of this. The people whom I address do not need argument on so plain a matter; and they have, I trust, too much honesty and loyalty to pretend perplexity of judgment, where there is merely perversity of will. Those who deny the lawfulness of defensive war, for the sake of consistency, ought to go a step further, and deny the use of all civil Government. For in such a world as ours—and we must just take men as they are, not as we could wish them to be—a Government without force will very quickly be resolved into a number of persons who bear titles, wear certain symbols, play their respective parts in a national pageant, complacently hear, and impotently announce *opinions*. If contending parties choose to listen, good; if not, the matter, as far as the Government is concerned, is at an end. But if force is used by those in authority, in order to carry out their decision, and if violence must be employed in giving effect to law—in defending the innocent, or in bringing the guilty to punishment—whether this shall be the work of five men, or of fifty thousand, the principle is the same.

In a word, a Government without force among depraved creatures, *is will*, in place of *law*. To this it must come; and this, as it appears to me, is just no Government at all. Excellent state of things, this, for the cunning sharper, and the ruffian greedy for rapine: what it might be to the virtuous, peaceable, and simple-minded citizen is quite another matter. But the whole thing is as far wrong in an international point of view, as it is in a municipal. Assuredly, my brethren, the time will come when " nation shall not lift up sword against nation, neither shall they learn war any more." Universal submission to the Prince of Peace will bring all this to pass. But ere this consummation takes place—a consummation for which all Christians are bound to pray and to labour—it will be too soon to beat our swords into ploughshares, and our spears into pruning-hooks. It would be well if persons who speculate on this matter would look a little more carefully into the cause—the true cause of universal peace. The complete triumph of the Redeemer's kingdom alone can bring about this. But to expect universal peace in a world that "lieth in wickedness," is what neither reason nor prophecy warrants. And to suppose a Government to exist without power to enforce all its just claims, in the various relations in which it stands to its own subjects, and to foreign states, is the height of folly. A folly, it is true, quite congruous with the other notions bred in the minds of crazy enthusiasts. But what shall be thought of those who are now clamouring against defensive war, but who neither ask, nor are entitled to, the same apology which, in all fairness, ought to be made for the enthusiast? Who can forbear to smile, when he sees this affected humanity employed to hide principles as different from justice and mercy, as they are from loyalty? Defensive war, murder! Pity it is that John the Baptist did not understand this matter better, so that, instead of telling soldiers "to be content with their wages," he might have told them, in plain terms, that they were murderers. We wonder much what these persons would have said to St. Paul, when he accepted a guard of Roman soldiers to protect him from the daggers of assassins, on his way from Jerusalem to Cæsarea? On more occasions than one did this Apostle find that human law would have been to him a poor protection, had the magistrate borne no sword, or borne it in vain. It is not a little surprising sometimes, to see extremes meet. The upholder of despotic authority cries out: "There must on no account whatever be any defensive war. Lie down and die." The man who is secretly preparing arms to overthrow the Government exclaims: "How horrible to think of men kept on pay to destroy their fellow-creatures—all war is murder." All war, we presume, but his own.

There is something wrong—the intellect or the conscience is diseased, or it is mere hypocrisy in a man to declaim against defensive war. To execrate as murderers all who have drawn the sword in defence of law and human rights, is to execrate some of the noblest for moral worth whose names adorn the page of sacred or profane history. While to condemn the principle in unqualified terms is to shield the guilty—to hold out an inducement for the commission of the most horrid crimes—is to be wiser and more benevolent than Almighty God—is to play the fool or the knave in a manner truly deplorable.— What! are we to see a horde of men—men in nothing but the form—plundering, burning, and murdering around us, and shall we meet them only with opinions and appeals? Is violence, when suffering helpless innocency is flying before its gory weapons, to be met with nothing but cool reasoning? Contemptible madness, cruel mercy were this. And when you see the Government and the Constitution under which you live, and in which you find so large a share of all your earthly happiness treasured up, openly assailed by wicked men, are you to stand coolly by and witness *all, all* torn to pieces, and scattered to the winds, and a whole country filled with confusion, lamentation and woe? This you have not done. This, I venture to affirm, you will not do. All boasting apart, as morally indecorous, I fearlessly aver, that ere that glorious symbol of liberty that waves on a thousand towers, from the banks of the Ganges to those of the St. Lawrence, is torn to the dust in our Western Capital, by the hands of home-bred traitors, or foreign sympathizers, there are many hearts in Upper Canada that will warm to desperate defiance; and if that day of deep desecration and woe comes, that shall see our Constitution and British connection perish, there are many hearts now warm that will be cold ere that day's sun shall go down.

I shall now close this discourse with two general reflections.

First, *I beseech you to think seriously of the civil blessings which you enjoy, and beware of the men who would deprive you of them.*

You may not be profound politicians, and the greater part of you are incapable of estimating, upon rigorous principles, the relative merits of different Governments. With any discussion of this sort I shall not trouble you. There are, however, a few questions to which I must beg your attention. Is not that Government good which protects every man in the full possession of his rights, under which he may employ his powers and resources to the best advantage, and under which the fruits of his industry are secured to him, and which will not allow him to suffer the slightest detriment in person or property, either from the great clothed with power, or from the mob bent on violence? And can that Government be charged with oppression under which every industrious and prudent person has the means of prosperity, and really is prosperous? And were it not as absurd as wicked to talk of tyranny while the poorest inhabitant has the most perfect protection of laws made by men of the people's choice, and administered by Judges of the highest talents and integrity? Now, my hearers, say, are not these things true—substantial y true—of the Government under which you live? In it there may be corruption, from vice or weakness; just as there is, to a less or greater extent, in every Government under heaven. But oppression, where is it? Tyranny, who has felt it? Law prostituted, who has seen it? The industrious and virtuous wretched, where are they? Assuredly there is much misery here, as there is in every country in which sloth, imprudence, intemperance and discontent prevail. But are these vices, and their dreadful consequences, to be charged against the Government? What folly; and yet it is a folly into which thousands of self-ruined persons fall. They accuse the Government of corruption, while the evil is in their own hearts. Hitherto we have been, as you well know, a prosperous community. A winter of sad calamity may set in on us; and, if so, wise men will know where to look for the cause. Cursed sedition—infernal rebellion! This is the cause, if our prosperity is to perish. And I must be permitted to say, that I do not know any part of the world in which honest industry has reaped more substantial fruits than it has reaped in this country. And yet, forsooth, the world must be told that we are a people peeled and oppressed, and, in every sense, wretched; and, in order to improve us, we must be revolutionized, and every thing thrown into hopeless confusion.

But, then, it will be asked, are there no evils that need to be reformed—no corruptions that ought to be rooted out? I have, by implication, admitted both. And, were this stated more explicitly, I am sure no sincere friend to the country could either be offended, or wish to deny it. Every civil institution is liable to corruption; and one or other of its parts will, in course of time, require modification and repair. Consequently, there is room for legitimate reform. And in bringing about this, every honest man will use what influence he may possess. Before, however, he commences in this work let him weigh carefully the following principles :—(1) Let him be sure the thing is an evil, not a political misconception—not the fretting of a discontented mind—not a difficulty which has sprung from his own personal vices or follies : (2) Let him be sure that it is a real abuse, not the watchword of a party : (3) Let him see that what is complained of be not an essential part of the Constitution which may create occasional inconvenience, but the removal of which would produce infinite disorder: (4) Let him ponder well whether the thing really felt to be an evil has originated with the Government, and whether the Government has influence over it: And (5) let it be clearly ascertained that the thing is, in itself and in its consequences, really mischievous. These opinions must be carefully kept in mind by all who wish to reform. How entirely these principles have been disregarded is but too well known. Nor did those persons to whom I refer merely overlook sound principles, but for years past, in the eradication of evils, they have proceeded as an intoxicated surgeon would do, who should commence in a dark room to cut out a cancer, relying solely on his strength of arm, his decision, and the sharpness of his instruments. The figure is only complete when it is borne in mind that our state operators have *thus cut* more frequently at the sound than into the diseased parts.

Beware then *what persons* you follow as leaders in reform.

He that is fully entitled to this character, in its high and proper sense, must be no ordinary man. One capable of detecting defects and abuses, and safely applying the proper remedies, must be possessed of a strong, I had almost said of a capacious, intellect. Cunning, prying, bustling men,—men of mere management—active and really useful among details, are often altogether unfit for dealing with a great plan or system of things. But this the leader in reform must be able to do with very great precision. If he requires a microscopic eye to detect minor abuses, he must also possess a telescopic vision to perceive the more distant objects and relations of things. He must thoroughly understand Government as a science. While the history of his country—all its main relations—the grand sources of its power, both moral and political, as well as the dangers to which it is peculiarly exposed, must be distinctly understood by him, and the whole understood in system. A weak-minded man is incapable of this. He will often mistake excellencies for faults—a partial derangement for a radical defect—the effect for the cause. While in the application of remedies he will employ means which, instead of improving what is faulty, may lead to ruin. A child entrusted with the command of a shattered vessel on a tempestuous ocean is not less fit for the task, than is the imbecile politician, who heads a party and sets about reforming abuses *in a troubled state.* And do not suppose that impudence will ever be a substitute for moral firmness, or presumption an equivalent for high talent. But,

Further, *a leader in reform must be a good man.* No bad

man ever was, or ever will be, an efficient corrector of moral evils. Such a man wants the steadiness of purpose, the ardent philanthropy, the sincere love of truth, the admiration of moral beauty; and, above all, he wants the fear and love of God, without which no man was ever well qualified for dealing with human institutions that required either nice modifications or severe correction. When God intends to reform and to spare a people, He raises up among them wise and good men. But when the same Omnipotent Being is about to destroy a people for their sins, he permits *evil spirits* to arise among them; and they are destroyed. Woe, woe to that land! the leading reformers of which are men without talents, or men of great talents and no principle—men who live by the mob—wield the minds of the rabble, by feeding their insolence and vanity with falsehood and adulation. God's vials of wrath are near to being poured out upon that country that is cursed with such influential Demagogues.

In a word, my brethren, stick to your British connection, cleave with heart and soul to the Constitution. While we have the Constitution and British justice to look to, I will hope for everything that is good. But the former lost, and the Palladium is gone; and if we are abandoned by Great Britain, or crushed by her just indignation, what is to become of us? Then, indeed, shall liberty perish—then, indeed, shall there be oppression, tyranny, and wretchedness to fulfil the predictions, and glut the revenge of our bitterest enemies. Think, then, oh! think seriously of the civil blessings you enjoy, and let no man cajole you out of these, or violently rob you of them. But

Secondly, *let me urge you to cherish a sincere respect for our Constitution, and also for the country with which we stand connected.*

It were easy, as it were vain, to frame ideal systems that might appear even more perfect than the British Constitution. But for all practical purposes, this appears to me incomparably the best system of civil polity for the people who live under it. But then the complaint is, that we have not had the Constitution in its fulness. To this I reply, that we have all which, under present circumstances, can be expected—that we have more of it than many desire, and, may I just add, more than some persons deserve.

Were it asked, Wherein consists the excellence of our Constitution? I should answer briefly, that it consists in the obvious truths—that, *first*, a large portion of its elements are drawn, either directly or indirectly, from revealed religion. That, *secondly*, its fundamental principles are in perfect accordance with the soundest views of human nature. *Thirdly*, the improvement which it has received from a long tract of ages. *Fourthly*, the admirable division of power, by which at once the most perfect liberty is secured, and the most complete responsibility. It is, indeed, take it as a whole, the image of the soul of a great and wise people—a people jealous of their liberty—a people watchful against the encroachments of the Supreme power; yet no less careful that the democratic influence should be kept within proper bounds. And should nothing remain of the Empire, in some distant age, but its Constitution, that would be monument enough—that would stand an intellectual pyramid, to tell the world that a free and a wise people once flourished in Britain.

We are best able to judge of human institutions from their effects. Whatever institutions contribute directly to the virtue, prosperity, and true greatness of a people, must be good. Let us look for a moment at the British Constitution under this light. Not to speak of the military achievements of our country, or to affirm that her armies have at all times fought on the side of right; yet surely truth warrants what patriotism prompts us to declare, that more than once has Britain stood on the Marathon of the world, and fought for the liberties of the human race. Nor ought it to be overlooked, that when she has made conquests, these have, in all cases, been accessions to the domains of intelligence, liberty and virtue. Even in India, where, perhaps, more has happened than in any other part, to humble and grieve us, the people have long since found that, although individuals may, for a time, misdirect and abuse British power, its natural tendency, when it comes forth in the national mind, is not to destroy, but to bless those under it. *There* a hundred dynasties had arisen and fallen, and each had scourged the helpless tribes of Hindostan with reckless oppression. It was reserved for Great Britain—noble distinction—to give repose and protection to the afflicted nations of India. And for the first time for three thousand years *have they found*, that rulers may be just, and conquerors may be merciful. The moral power of Britain at once retains and benefits the whole of Southern Asia. Sublime spectacle; but its full sublimity shall only be seen when Christian Missionaries, through God's help, have broken the chains of superstition that bind the mind of India.

And who can think of what Britain has done, and is still doing, on the shores of Africa for the helpless and much-abused tribes of that continent, and not be filled with admiration? Did she there once, like other nations, sin grievously? Admit it—and say, hath not the reparation been noble, and befitting the case? If atonement can be made, she hath made it. On the shores of Africa she now stands like a guardian angel—one hand, uplifted in pity, she points to the blood-stained coast, and the other she points to the ocean; and the approaching *slaver* sees in it the sword of vengeance. Demon-like man, little cares he what flag appears till the Flag of England is seen in the distance. Then does he tremble—then does his guilty courage fail him, for well does he know that under that flag there are tears of pity for the oppressed, and bolts of just wrath for the oppressor. In this protection of Britain there is surely much of moral grandeur. But more impressive still—more truly grand—was that act by which she made a million of slaves free men in one day—aye, and paid their price, too, from the taxes toiled for by her noble and generous people. What in Grecian story—what in Roman triumphs—can be put in comparison with this?

My brethren, I have aimed at no eulogy on our country. This is as little needed, as I am little able to do justice to it. All the world knows Britain. And where she is not loved, she is feared and envied :—envy often the truest eulogy. But I have thrown out these hints simply for two reasons. *First*, that you may love and revere that country, which has grown to such a pitch of power, and has secured so large a share of prosperity and pure fame under her fostering and protecting Constitution. Now, God forbid that we should forget that this has only been a means. The Lord Omnipotent hath raised her up, and made her a blessing to the world. Nor ought we to forget the moral and religious worth of the people which hath given being, in a sense, to their Constitution, and which hath prepared them for deriving from it all its natural and rich fruits. A people without religion must not think they can possess true liberty. Still, it were improper to overlook the fact that the Constitution has contributed not a little to expand and direct the energies of the national mind.

Next, that you may be upon your guard against those new and untried theories, which are now so often put forth, and never put forth, I am sorry to say it, without some portion of censure levelled at Great Britain and her institutions, and this, too, by men of British birth! Is it not inexpressibly disgusting to see such men labouring to hide the excellencies, searching for the faults, and rejoicing in the anticipated ruin of their country? These be the veriest wretches—the helots of humanity—the most choice miscreants of our race. What! rejoice and glory over the fall—the expected fall—of their country, and such a country! These men do not so much hate their native land as they hate their race. Let the light that now blazes from Britain be quenched, and all nations would feel that a great light had been put out, which the world could ill want. Let the power of Britain be destroyed, and the fulcrum on which the liberty of the world turns would be broken. He that wished that Rome had only one neck was hardly a wretch more hateful than is that man who calls himself a British subject, and yet would rejoice to see his country covered with confusion, and all her glory pass away. Of such men I will say—"O my soul, come not into their secret; unto their assembly, mine honour, be not thou united!" And of our country I will say, "If I forget thee, let my right hand forget her cunning. If I do not remember thee, let my tongue cleave to the roof of my mouth."

CHAPTER XV.

THE SOLEMNITY PROPER TO THE HOUSE OF GOD.*

"How dreadful is this place! this is none other but the House of God."—Genesis xxviii. 17.

F the names of those who are mentioned by the Saviour as being in heaven Jacob's is one. Hence, we cannot entertain any doubt that, while on earth, he was a true child of God. But, although Jacob was possibly from early life a man of piety, yet he was far from being a perfect man. There is a wonderful candour in scriptural biography. The sins and faults of the best are stated without any disguise or apology. If the excellences of Jacob are mentioned to his honour, so are his sins frankly recorded to his dishonour, and as a warning to us. In supplanting his brother Esau, and depriving him of his birthright, Jacob had, at the instigation of his mother, employed a piece of base deception on his father. That Esau was a worthless man was no reason why Jacob should have employed such reprehensible means to gain his end. The rage of the duped and circumvented brother was aroused, not at the moral obliquities of those who had circumvented him, but at the loss which he had sustained. Yet the rage of Esau was such that it was deemed necessary that Jacob should flee to Padan-aram, and seek for refuge in the house of his mother's family. Thus, the sin of Jacob was punished with exile and much suffering for many years. When God's children forsake the path of duty, He will find a

---

* Preached at the opening of St. Andrew's Church, Stratford, Ontario, 10th January, 1869.

rod to correct them. An unjust and deceitful Laban was God's rod to correct Jacob for his sin and deceit to his father. But although he was to be chastised, he was not to be forsaken of his God, who intended that great events in His providence and grace should be connected with him.

Hence, we are told that on his journey, while reposing during the night on the earth, with the open firmament over him, God vouchsafed to him, in a dream, a vision remarkable for the sublimity of its form, and the precious truths which it taught, and with which it was accompanied. While the Patriarch sleeps, the eye of his soul is awake, and the ear of his soul is opened to receive instruction. He sees a ladder, as it were stretching from earth to heaven, God at the top of it, Jacob sleeping at the bottom of it, and on it angels ascending and descending; and God is heard saying, "I am the Lord God of Abraham, thy father, and the God of Isaac: the land whereon thou liest, to thee will I give it, and to thy seed; and thy seed shall be as the dust of the earth, and thou shalt spread abroad to the west, and to the east, and to the north, and to the south; and in thee and in thy seed shall all the families of the earth be blessed. And behold I am with thee, and will keep thee in all places whither thou goest, and will bring thee again into this land; for I will not leave thee, until I have done that which I have spoken to thee of." How sublime the spectacle, and how grand and cheering the Divine utterances! I must, however, dismiss both the vision and the utterances with the briefest possible comment. Plainly, the vision shows that God is ever watching over His people on earth—that there is the most intimate connection and relationship betwixt the children of God in heaven and His children on the earth. The angels are ascending and descending—passing from heaven to earth, where Jacob sleeps, then back to their proper home in the heavens, where the God of men and angels reigns over all. And then, the utterance to Jacob is, in its substance and spirit, applicable to all the people of God in all times. God is their God. He will ever be their covenant-keeping God. He will never leave nor forsake them. But it is not to the whole of this heavenly vision, nor the utterance of God, to which I am to direct your attention, but to one utterance of Jacob. When he awoke, he exclaimed, "How dreadful is this place, this is none other but the House of God!" I have chosen these words as a text suitable for the present occasion.

Waiving all critical disquisition, I shall only make but a few brief remarks on two words in the text, viz. *dreadful*, and *House of God*. The word "dreadful" in this passage conveys the sense of what is morally solemn or awful. By "the House of God" I understand the spot, whether a building or not, where God meets specially with His people. There was, of course, no house where Jacob had this interview with God. But it is no straining of the sense to understand what we call a *Church*, as the House of God. This, you know, is often the designation given to it. The broad sense, then, which I educe from the passage, and which I shall make the basis of my subsequent observations, is this—that a building erected and set apart for the worship of God, and with propriety called God's house, is a very solemn and awful place. In establishing this proposition, I would remark,

I. *That a church is a solemn place, because special business is there done for eternity.* Those who confine all their religion and all their efforts for their souls to the hours of public worship in the church are, I fear, little else but formal and hypocritical worshippers, and really do little business for eternity within the walls of the church. If a man's religion be sincere, he will feel it and manifest it, less or more, in all places, for religion is a spiritual condition of being in which a man lives or moves, be his body where it may. But this fully admitted, and it holds true that the church is the place in which the soul specially does business for eternity. I cannot but think that far more have been awakened to a sense of their danger under sin, and have been savingly converted, and have had all their graces cultivated to a higher sanctification by the public preaching of God's word than by all other means together. Whatever may have been done in private or in secret, yet the whole history of the Church shows that the House of God is the place in which men do most for their souls and for eternity. Now, this should make every church a solemn and awful place.

The human mind is fitted to be moved to high emotions by many objects in nature, as well as by certain objects, the products of genius and human labour. No person who has a taste for the beautiful, or is capable of being moved to sublime emotions, can fail to be touched by a grand and beautiful landscape, or a splendid building. Every person of taste can realize this, and has often experienced from it much refined gratification. You could not help pitying the man who could look at Niagara or gaze on a splendid building, and feel no elation of soul. And yet it is not the sublimest scenery or the grandest buildings that awaken the deepest and loftiest emotions of the soul. Man's deepest emotions of awe or delight are awakened by moral emotions, not by mere combinations of matter. Hence, the spot where a nation's liberty was first secured or bravely defended, such as Runnymede, the field of Bannockburn, or the gates of Derry, will throughout all ages awaken in all well-constituted minds, profounder emotions, and will be looked at with greater awe than a piece of scenery or a building, be it ever so grand. The reason is plain; at these places moral events were transacted that were the springs and fountain-heads of vast results, which will flow on through all time. Nor is it needful to go to history and national events to realize this deep law of our nature, by which certain places move us deeply by their moral associations and memories. Could any one among you visit, after long years have passed away, the humble cottage where a father shook you by the hand for the last time, and said, "God bless you;" or where a mother, through her tears, could only look her blessing, but could not utter it; or the spot where some one first plighted her love to you, but long, long ago sleeps in the dust—the mother of your children, and for many a day the companion of your toils, your joys, and your sorrows. I say, could any one of you, with a soul in him, revisit any one of these spots and not be moved with the purest and deepest emotions? and would he not say, How awful! how solemn is this place! Now, mark it, it is not the place itself that is awful—it is the moral associations connected with it, the hallowed memories it brings up, as the spot where some solemn moral event was transacted that has connected itself with thy moral being, and thy future destiny. The material may be beautiful and grand, or it may not, but it is the moral event that connects itself with the material, that makes the meanest building, or the simplest spot, awful, solemn, and wonderful.

But, assuming this as correct, let us apply it to a church —the House of God. All persons of piety and of taste will admit that the House of God ought not to be a mean and shabby building, if the circumstances of the people admit of something better. Nay, I must express my liking to see the House of God every way a respectable, even an imposing building, if the ability of the congregation warrants it. This is in keeping with good feeling, taste, and piety. Yet it is not the material building, be it as splendid and gorgeous as St. Peter's in Rome, or St. Paul's in London, that gives to the House of God its awful grandeur, or throws around it a solemn awe. If God be not worshipped there, it is but a mass of stone and mortar ingeniously put together; and if truth has ceased to be proclaimed within its walls, *Ichabod* may be written on its door posts. Sanctity is not in stones and mortar, or wood, nor in gold or silver, be it ever so artfully engraved, nor is the sanctity of an enlightened association to be found in these things, but in this—that the church, whether grand or mean, is emphatically a House of God, a place in which business is transacted by the souls of men for eternity. It is this that makes a church, be it ever so plain, ever so mean, a dreadful place—a place of deep and solemn emotion to the heart of man.

That this view may strike its roots deeply among your convictions, let me notice in the briefest possible way, some of the parts of this spiritual business that the soul transacts in the House of God. It is there that the soul oftenest gets its first needful and hallowed fears of its terrible wants—the want of pardon, of the Divine love, the want of holiness, the want of heaven at death. Oh! what a great forward movement that soul has made, that under some pungent sermon has, with clearness of intellectual vision and an awakened conscience, got a plain and an abiding insight into these wants! Man is mad—crazed with self-sufficiency—till he gets a true sense of his wants. Till then he will never cry out, "God be merciful to me a sinner." Till then he will never cry out, "What must I do to be saved?" What a hopeful position has that man gained who sees that he is in himself poor and miserable, and blind, and naked! The House of God is the place where, for the most part, this discovery is made. This is, indeed, the first healthy spiritual act of the soul. But if this were all, it were little. But this is not all. For is it not oftenest in the House of God, under a plain, earnest, and full exhibition of the Gospel, that the soul gets its first views of the sin-pardoning mercy of God through the blood of Christ, and the first hope of acceptance with God, and the first of those joys shed abroad in the heart by the Holy Ghost, and that peace which the world cannot give, nor earth nor hell take away? In a word, it is oftenest in the House of God that the conscience-smitten man is enabled to say, "Lord, I believe," "Lord, save," "Lord, I am thine," "Thou art my God and Saviour," "I shall henceforth be called by thy name." Oh! what a transaction is this for time, for death, for eternity! It is the birth day of the soul! A day to be much remembered. And when the day or the hour cannot be fixed or remembered, yet even the spot where the mighty event took place—the spot where the Divine instruction was got, and the hallowed emotions awakened that led thee to bow at the foot of the cross—can never be regarded as an ordinary place. Can you ever fail to think of it with peculiar awe and delight? When one who is born again visits the place of his spiritual birth, be it the poorest little church in the land, yet he will gaze at it with lowly awe, and say, "this was the House of God to me—here God met with me when a great transaction was gone about for my soul—here was the gate of heaven for my soul."

But the House of God is more than the place of entrance into life for the soul. The soul not only gets its first lessons there, and has its first hallowed emotions awakened there—it is also the place where souls receive a large portion of their spiritual education for the services of the heavenly sanctuary. Sanctification follows upon regeneration, and is not the House of God eminently the place where the prayer of the Saviour, "Sanctify them through thy truth," is often accomplished? Thus it is that a church, in which the truth in all its relations, from the tenderest love, and threatenings from the just wrath of God, are fully, Sabbath after Sabbath, brought home to the understanding, heart and consciences of men—becomes a school in which souls are trained for the high service and pure joys of heaven. If redeemed spirits, as some think, occasionally visit the earth, may they not point to this or that House of God and say, there I got my first schooling for the place I now occnpy? Be that as it may, it cannot be doubted that the people of God on earth, who find that Sabbath after Sabbath their sanctification is advancing, will say of the House of God, where this goes on, "how dreadful, how solemn is this place!"

II. *The House of God is a solemn place, as angels from heaven and devils from hell may be supposed to be present often among those who assemble in it.*

1. First, as to the presence of angels.

That there is an intimate relationship and frequent intercourse betwixt angels and men on earth, especially the people of God, is plainly taught in the Bible. As has been already hinted, the context clearly teaches this. The angels are seen in the vision descending from heaven to earth, where the patriarch sleeps, and again ascending to heaven. Whatever else this implies, it assuredly teaches that there is a constant communication kept up betwixt heaven and earth by these holy creatures. As to the mode of this, as well as to the modes by which they minister to the saints, and the various modes by which they carry into effect the behests of God, we must in our present state be very much in the dark. But although we cannot explain modes of operation here, any more than we can do in many other cases, yet we have many plain and consoling facts on this matter. When Lot was to be rescued from Sodom, two angels were sent to do it. Peter was delivered from prison by an angel. Paul, the night before his shipwreck, was comforted by one, and John in Patmos had frequent visits from them, and communications sent down from heaven by them. These are but a few of the many instances that prove their relationship to the children of God, and the intercourse that goes on betwixt them and the people of God on earth. And what can be more emphatic than these declarations: "He will give His angels charge concerning thee;" and again, "Are they not all ministering spirits sent forth to minister for them who shall be heirs of salvation?" And still more to our purpose, Jesus tells us that "there is joy in the presence of the angels of God over one sinner that repenteth." Without attempting any full exposition of the doctrine I have indicated, yet assuredly the passages quoted clearly warrant the following inferences:—1st.

That angels take the deepest interest in the affairs of God's people on earth. 2ndly. That they are often with them, watching over and ministering to them. 3rdly. That they are especially interested in the conversion of sinners, and feel the deepest joy in that great event. Now, from all this, is it not a fair inference that the House of God is often the place where these pure spirits are found watching and serving with the greatest care? If the House of God be the place where conversion takes its first or final form, can angels fail to be present to mark that grandest moment in the history of an immortal soul? Are they not present to watch the effects of God's truth on sinners, and ready to rejoice when, here in that pew, or another there, one gives up his soul to Jesus, and in the strength of God resolves to forsake his sins and live to God? Oh! how glad must their benevolent hearts be, when they can leave the House of God and carry up the joyous tidings to heaven, that another sinner has repented, another brand has been plucked from the burning, another soul saved! And when they ascend to their compeers, and the spirits of the just gather round them to learn how it goes with the preaching of the gospel in that nation, in that country, in that Church, surely it is no fancy to think that wherever there stands a minister of God to proclaim His message in His house—which must ever be either a savour of life unto life, or of death unto death—the angels of heaven are there, watching the result of every sermon that is preached. *You* may be absent—*they* are not. True, you see them not, yet they are present. It is the House of God, and surely most suitable for being one of the stopping-places, one of the watch-towers of angels on earth, that they may see how the great battle betwixt light and darkness goes. But if so, then well may we say, "how awful a place is the House of God!"

2. But we have said that devils may also be present in the house of God, and they make it a dreadful place. There are some things on the matter in question which,

in addressing a Christian congregation, may be assumed. 1st. That there is a class of fallen and malignant spirits, called devils. 2ndly. That these beings are engaged in a constant warfare against all that is God-like. 3rdly. That they go about with great subtlety seeking whom they may devour. 4thly. That they are capable of being present with men and acting on them by their temptations, although not visible to the senses. Such being the nature and pursuits of these malignant spirits, no one needs wonder that they often make the house of God the scene of their active operations. In addition to the general ground now assumed, I select the following passages, as furnishing direct proofs of the doctrine that the house of God is a dreadful place, for devils come there to seek to destroy souls.

First, we are told that Satan on a very solemn occasion came into Christ's company of the Apostles, and put it into the heart of Judas to betray his Master. And if so, why not into the ordinary assemblies of Christians in the house of God?

Next, we are told that just when the seed of the word is being sown, the devil comes, and at once, ere it has struck its root into the heart, takes it away. This, surely, plainly implies that at the very time when the preacher is communicating Divine truth, the enemy may so work on the minds of the hearers, as utterly to take the truth away, alike from the understanding and the memory.

Lastly, a passage in the Book of Job is a decisive proof of our position. The passage to which I refer is that in which it is said, " The sons of God came to present themselves before the Lord, and Satan came also among them." It has been generally supposed that the sons of God spoken of here are the angels, and heaven the place referred to. This passage has not only given rise to many an infidel sneer, for which there is not the shadow of foundation, except the absurd exposition of theologians. It has been asked, pertinently enough, how can we suppose that

Satan went into heaven, and appeared among the angels before the throne? And the answers given to this are most lame and unsatisfactory. I humbly think that there is an explanation at once simple and consistent, and which removes all the difficulty. The sons of God spoken of are not the angels of heaven, but simply godly men on earth. The assembly spoken of did not meet in heaven, but on earth. In short, it was, as I think, just the congregation of Job's own family and retainers to whom he ministered as patriarch-priest. On some sabbath, when they came together to worship God as His children, Satan came also among them. The omniscient eye saw him, the omnipotence of God laid hold on him, and the King eternal called him to account. This, I think, is the whole; it is all simple, all natural, and clears up all difficulties. With what grows out of the incident we have at present nothing to do. But if this view of the incident be admitted, then it does clearly by inference establish our position—that we may suppose fallen spirits present in the house of God. Nay, is not the house of God, as it were, the grand battle-field where the powers of light and the powers of darkness meet, where angels from heaven watch with delight the triumphs of the gospel, where devils from hell watch with malignity every opportunity to steal away the word, to perplex the mind with the cares of the world, to fill the imagination with vain thoughts and impure desires, to awaken doubts, to darken hope—in a word, to harden sinners and perplex and grieve saints, and so to prevent souls from being comforted and edified in the house of God? But if so, then may we well say, how dreadful is this place, where heaven and hell, under such strange conditions so nearly meet! But,

III.—*The ambassador of Christ stands in the house of God to treat with rebels, and this makes it a solemn place.*

Every true minister of Jesus is an ambassador. Hence, says the Apostle, " we as ambassadors for Christ, beseech you to be reconciled to God." Ambassadors among all nations have been held sacred, and regarded with peculiar respect, inasmuch as they are looked on as representing the sovereign whose commission they bear. But although the office of ambassador is ever one of just honour and responsibility, his duties are not always alike solemn. Yet no one will doubt that when he is sent forth to treat, in the name of his sovereign, with rebellious subjects, and especially to offer terms of mercy to the guilty and helpless, his function is solemn, and every way deeply interesting. But no ambassador from an earthly prince ever bore such a message of mercy to a rebellious people, as the ambassadors of God bring to guilty man. We have all rebelled against God ; we are liable to his wrath both in this life and in that which is to come. We can neither excuse our guilt nor meet our punishment. Under the just government of God, " the wages of sin is death." But ah ! who can tell what that death spiritual, death temporal, and death eternal is ? The tongue of man cannot tell it, for it is the loss of all that is good in God and from God. It is the suffering of all that the physical, intellectual, and moral nature can endure, not for a lifetime on earth, but for an eternity in hell. Devils and lost souls know it, yet know it not fully. For oh ! who can tell to what that misery will grow to the lost, as age after age passes on in that place where hope never comes, but all is misery, and misery ever increasing to them ! on whom God rains fire and brimstone in the furious tempest of His wrath ! Such is the portion of the cup of those who are rebels against God.

And yet, oh ! marvellous, He sends His ambassador to plead with them to be reconciled to Him. Lastly, He sent His Son into the world, not to condemn the world, but to save it. This salvation, procured by the Son of God, a salvation from all the misery of sin, and reinstatement into the friendship of God in all its fulness, is offered by the ambassador that God sends. Every time that a faithful minister of Christ proclaims the gospel from the pulpit in the house of God, he is Christ's ambassador; offers a free pardon to the most guilty; offers the grace of holiness to the most depraved; offers the Divine protection to the feeble pilgrim; offers the consolations of the Divine Spirit to the desponding—beauty for ashes—the oil of joy for mourning; offers support, hope, and peace at death; and, in his Master's name, and as his Master's purchase, offers a heaven of eternal glory to the soul after death. Oh! what a commission is his—what a message is his, who stands as Christ's ambassador, in the house of God, to proclaim all this!

Say, then, is not the house of God a very solemn and awful place, seeing it is the place where the ambassadors sent by God to treat with guilty man, appear to deliver their message? Tell the condemned man that at a certain place there stands one sent to offer him a free pardon, and would he not hasten to that place, and think it then, as he took the pardon, the most sacred spot on earth. The application of this is easy. Oh! make a literal application of it, my hearers. We are all by nature condemned men in the sight of God, and it may be not a few are still in that sad state; for, saith the scripture, "he that believeth not is condemned already." For you who have some hope, that condemnation is cancelled through Christ's blood, what a sacred place is the house of God, in which that gospel is proclaimed that brought peace to thy soul! It may have been in some other place than a church, when the first ray of hope dawned on thy dark and troubled bosom. And yet thou canst never look on a house of God, the appointed place for Heaven's ambassador to proclaim God's mercy to the guilty, without saying: "How solemn, how awful is this place," where Christ's ambassador stands to tell of the great mercy of God to sinful man! No, ye ransomed—ye men of faith in the blood of Jesus, ye men who have got some hope, joy and peace, through that blood, ye cannot look at a house of God, where that precious gospel is preached, and may have been long preached, without saying: "How solemn, how awful is that place!" Nay, are not the very ruins and dust of an old church, as may often be seen in other lands, dear to the soul, and sacred to the feelings, when you think that age after age men went there to hear the gospel, and to transact business for that eternal world into which they have gone. The godly man who is living by faith on the gospel will thus say: "How solemn is the house of God!"

And why should it not also be a solemn place for you who have not yet that faith, nor that hope? Oh! ye children of men, who are even now living without God and hope in the world, what should the house of God be to you? It should be the place where God has promised to meet with you, to pardon you, to accept of you, and to bless you. He is saying in His house, every time the gospel is preached in it, "Turn ye, turn ye, why will ye die?" He is saying, "Look unto me and be ye saved." For it is in the house of God that God pleads with men, that they would not destroy their own mercies; and it is in the house of God where the sacraments, the seals of the covenant, are administered by Christ's ambassadors. In a word, it is there where the rich provisions of the gospel are by special means presented to the souls of men. Now, to those who neglect and despise all the rich provision of the house of God, who either never go there, or go there as mere occasional visitors, or go as mere formalists and hypocrites—to them the house of God will not prove a solemn and delightful place, but in the full sense, a dreadful place. It is fearful to think of a community without the means of grace; for, where no vision is, the people perish: woe and alas to that people who have no sanctuary, no sanctuary-sabbath, and no faithful ambassador of Jesus among them! That people will soon lose all that is refined in feeling, all that is noble in sentiment, all that is pure in morals, and all that can furnish any stable basis for society ; while all lights go out that can guide the soul through death. And yet, is it not more fearful to abuse the means of grace; to grow hardened under these ; to permit *mis*belief to grow into *dis*belief, till the conscience under the means of grace becomes seared?

If the means of grace are to be vouchsafed to you within these walls, and a true man of God is to be sent to proclaim the gospel in all its fulness, oh ! endeavour so to improve these means by earnest preparation for duty, by diligence in waiting on public duty, and a thorough application of truth to conscience, that you shall grow in grace, so that by the increase of your knowledge, the cultivation of your devotional feelings, by the word, sacraments, and prayer, you may at the hour of death find that the house of God here has been instrumental in preparing you for the house of your Heavenly Father above, "where there is fulness of joy and pleasures for evermore."

CHAPTER XVI.

THE TERCENTENARY OF THE REFORMATION IN SCOTLAND.*

"And Moses said unto the people, Remember this day."—Exodus xiii. 3.

FOR a people to celebrate great events in their history, has been customary in all civilized countries. A little reflection will suffice to show, that, from the laws of mind, the commemoration of great national events may, if wisely performed, be instrumental in yielding high social and moral benefits to a people. Hence, we find that divine wisdom employed this laudable custom to preserve truth, strengthen faith, and awaken gratitude in the minds of ancient Israel. For, although the Passover feast was typical and promissory, and hence prospective, yet it had also a grand retrospective significancy which no true Israelite would fail to realize, as it pointed to an extraordinary historical event, in which the power, wisdom, and goodness of God were manifested to his ancient people. If that rite, truly commemorated, led the believer's hope forward to what was to be achieved when the efficacious blood of sprinkling was to be shed, did it not also lead pious souls back to that night, much to be remembered, when the blood was sprinkled on the door-posts, and when the Lord led forth His hosts from the land of Egypt? Hence, through long ages, this national celebration must have awoke, in all the true people of God, many lofty and tender emotions, as well as high and cheering hopes.

---

*Preached in St. Andrew's Church, Kingston, Dec. 16th, 1860.

Now, this day, my brethren, we meet to commemorate another kind of deliverance, wrought by the same God. Three hundred years ago the Lord wrought a mighty deliverance for the people of Scotland, which freed them from a bondage, in some respects more terrible than that of Egypt. It was, indeed, the spiritual emancipation of a people from superstition, and the resurrection of the mind of a nation. It is in the highest sense becoming for Scottish Presbyterians, in what land soever they dwell, to say of the Reformation, it is an event much to be remembered. Patriotism aud Christian piety alike sanction this celebration. It is true, the children of that land, or more properly the children of the Church of that land, cannot meet, as the Israelites met at Jerusalem, in one great convocation. There is no one temple in the courts of which they can assemble. They are scattered over all lands, and have so multiplied that those who hold this occasion sacred, are far more numerous in other countries than in Scotland. But, although they cannot meet in one assembly to celebrate their great deliverance, yet it is grand to think that they will meet in thousands of churches, not only in Scotland, Ireland, and England, but in far-off Australia, and in all the cities and villages of the United States, as well as in these Provinces, to celebrate a day in history dear to every Scottish heart, and sacred to every Presbyterian conscience. When God looks down from His temple on high, may He see in thousands of earthly temples, congregations of devout and humble worshippers thanking Him for the mighty deliverance He wrought in Scotland on that day, which to them is a day much to be remembered. This should be our wish, as to our brethren at home and in other lands. And our desire should be that this celebration may be so gone about that it shall contribute to the glory of God, in an increase of piety in our day. And, that we may derive from it, in this our present meeting, suitable lessons for our understanding and conscience, and an increase of motive to a higher piety as well as lofty emotions, I shall confine your attention to two general views.

I. I shall guard you against cherishing certain sentiments, which, if cherished on this celebration, will be hurtful to piety.

II. I shall direct your thoughts to some of the high advantages the Scottish Reformation has yielded, so that our gratitude to God may be increased, and our sense of obligation deepened.

1. *Then, let us beware, on this occasion, of cherishing mere national pride.* National pride is the arrogant estimate of a people as to their own superior worth, with a foolish and insolent contempt for others. This is every way hurtful. For, although it may not have in it the virulent malignity of personal pride, yet, he has read history to little purpose, who does not know that it has been one of the most fruitful sources of rapine, degradation and misery. But its more obvious evils are, perhaps, not its greatest evils. A strong national pride long cherished, renders a people blind to their deficiencies, scornful of warning and reproof, and ends in that fatal complacency with the worst corruptions and crimes, because the national honour is foolishly supposed to be identified with them. Hence, when national vanity leads a people to say, "We are the men! and wisdom, virtue, and power shall die with us," they are a doomed people. We find from the Prophets, that it was thus with Assyria, Egypt, and Tyre. And where are they? The Lord brought them down, and laid all their glory in the dust. I stop not to show how national pride must lead to national ruin. Philosophical speculations are not needed. He that is infinitely higher than the highest, cannot and will not endure it. Such a people is doomed to ruin. The nobler forms of intellect decay, public morality is paralyzed, and even material greatness and true military prowess in the end perish under this malign spirit. Pride may be the first article in the creed of hell, and there find scope;

but it is the last principle that a people should cherish, who would be either virtuous or great.

But if so, what then of patriotism? My brethren, patriotism does not live by pride. May not a people have a noble and sober high-mindedness, and a keen sense of national honour, without the aid of blind conceit or national arrogancy? The highest forms of national greatness, as they spring from manly humility and sobriety of thought, so do they cherish these qualities in a people. A people ever manifesting a morbid consciousness of their own greatness, either have it not or are in eminent peril of losing it. And what is true of nations, as to this, is eminently so of churches.

But is it not plain that national or church celebrations have been often made the means of nourishing a most unwholesome popular vanity? If the present celebration should have that effect, there would not only be in it pitiable folly, but deep criminality. If the event we celebrate did much to make our country unspeakably lovely and dear to our souls, let us beware of corrupting our hearts by irrational boastings, as if Scotland had made the Reformation, and not the Reformation made Scotland what she is, the dearest and, in some respects, the noblest of all lands. In close connection with this, I would remark:

2. That we should guard, on this occasion, against undue admiration of the men who were merely instruments in bringing about the Reformation.

There were assuredly some great men and many good men engaged in this. *Let these, according to their deserts*, have our admiration and love. It is a debt we owe them; and to refuse to pay it, either to them or like noble souls, gives evidence of a mind not only incapable of reverence and gratitude, but essentially little, and thoroughly base. To withhold the well-merited debt of admiration is the last form of a mean dishonesty. But then, mark it, this admiration which is so beautiful a virtue in moderation, in its excess becomes a frightful folly and vice. For is it not a sad folly to lose sight of the Divine King of the Church, by being so dazzled with the appearance of His humble servants? *It is beautiful to notice how inspired men acted in this.* They never confound the worship due to their Master with the respect and love they cherished to the greatest of their fellow-men. They esteem very highly their fellow-labourers, but they do not adore them; they love them ardently, but it is not the love they felt for Him who redeemed them. It is, "Our beloved brother Paul." "The beloved physician Luke." "The faithful in Christ Jesus." "Beloved fellow-labourers in the gospel, whose praise is in all the churches." This is beautiful; so sincere, so ardent, yet so chastened and guarded. Theirs was indeed the purest and highest brotherly love; but the highest place in the heart is not given to the best of men, but to their precious Lord and Saviour.

This wisdom of Apostolic times decayed with the true piety of the church; hence that confusion of sentiments and emotions which you find in not a few of the early Fathers, when they have to speak of their deceased brethren and their glorified Master. Of Him they speak, but their tone is comparatively cold when contrasted with that which they employ when speaking of the saints and martyrs of the church. In setting forth *their merits*, they exhaust the loftiest epithets which one of the richest of languages could furnish. This was worse than bad taste—it led to bad theology; for those who were thus praised so extravagantly came in the end to be regarded as more than mortal. Hence the idolatry which sprang up in the Church, and which was one of the chief causes that made the Reformation so necessary. Men mould language, but do not always notice how it moulds them. When human beings are praised as Gods, the distinction is first impaired, and finally lost, betwixt God and the creature, and the worship due to Him alone comes to be divided betwixt Him and them. This is fatal alike to piety and morality. In its grosser forms Protestants cannot fall into it, but then, remember, the grossest idolatry began in losing the distinction to which we have referred. Indeed, hyperbolical eulogies uttered on the best of men are mischievous because untrue, and are eminently dangerous, as they confound in the popular mind what is due alone to God, and what should be properly accorded to men.

Yet on such an occasion as the present we are very apt to fall into this criminal folly. Every one competent to form a judgment will readily admit that some of the Scottish reformers were men of high talents, and many of them men of distinguished piety ; yet those best able to do them justice know well that the greatest among them had serious faults, while not a few were cunning and selfish men. In this admission neither the sceptic nor the Papist can find just ground for triumph. Our religion is not of man ; his wisdom could as little devise it, as his folly or selfish wickedness can destroy it. We hold it to be a prerogative of God to use instruments who, by their own voluntary agency, shall accomplish His holy purposes. A Nebuchadnezzar, or Henry the Eighth, or an Earl of Morton may be employed as a besom of destruction to sweep away much error. Men of God only can truly build up. *There is a rhetorical way of writing history*, which, as it lacks discrimination, is exceedingly pernicious to truth. Not seldom have all the Scottish Reformers been spoken of as if they had been men of eminent piety, of great self-denial, and purity of motive. This way of speaking of them is very wrong. Yes, there was much to admire and love in many of these men ; but truth will not warrant the indiscriminate and general eulogy which has been employed. The more thoroughly you sift the history of that period, you see cause to lower, more and more, your estimate of the instruments of the Reformation, and raise your admiration of Him who wrought out such marvellous results with instruments so imperfect. Hence you exclaim, *not unto them*—the Knoxes, the Murrays, or the Melvilles—be the glory of this work, but to Him who moves in the midst of the golden candlesticks, holds the stars in his hands, and makes them shine as He gives grace, or makes men instruments of His will when they are merely seeking their own selfish ends. Let good men have their due meed of praise, but when the work is evidently God's, let Him have the glory of it. It was He who built up our Zion; it was He who repaired our wastes; it was He that was then her true defence, and the glory in the midst of her. If we forget this, our commemoration must be offensive to God and hurtful to ourselves. But,

3. Let not this celebration nourish in us a self-righteous spirit.

The true Christian feels that in no sense can he boast. He cannot boast of a personal or justifying righteousness or holiness. If saved, he feels that it is for the righteousness of Christ. If prepared for heaven, it is through the work of the Spirit. Hence, he is a man of thorough self-abnegation, giving all the glory to God. But how hard is it to reach a position at once so humbling and so elevated! How apt are we to seek for something *in ourselves*, or in our church relationship, by which we shall be able to say we are at least somewhat rich, we are somewhat increased in spiritual goods, we do not just stand in need of simple mercy! It was thus with the Jews. They had Abraham to their father—they were the children of the covenant—they had the law and the testimony, and divinely appointed ordinances; hence they were not poor and needy as other men. Yes, they had these high privileges; but the light in which they looked at them as grounds for boasting, wrought disastrously on their moral and spiritual well-being. Like causes must produce like effects. Are we self-sufficient because we are the descendants of eminent reformers, inherit a pure creed, and a scriptural worship? That cannot justify us. That cannot make us more holy than others; but if we boast of all this, and trust to it for salvation, we fearfully deceive ourselves. High privileges imply high responsibilities, which if not met and improved must deepen guilt and intensify depravity. It were sad if such a celebration as the present should lead us through these false views to think less of the need of a Saviour. As far as this were the result, Satan would gain from the occasion which occupies our thoughts.

II. But now, let us return to a brief contemplation of some of the direct benefits of the Scottish Reformation, so that our gratitude to God may be awakened, and our sense of our responsibility to Him deepened. And,

1. The Reformation imbued the popular mind with correct notions of the character of Popery.

This was of great consequence at the time, and is scarcely of less consequence in our times. Popery may be overthrown, as in France at the close of the last century, and yet the real nature of it as a system of religious error be imperfectly understood. Popular indignation against great practical evils does not necessarily imply either a knowledge of the nature of error, or of the truth. But the Scottish Reformers did far more than expose error and destroy superstitious practices—they taught truth and right practice. In fact they taught the people not to hate Papists, but to hate Popery; and to hate it because of its opposition to Gospel truth. These men saw that it was Popery that had taken away the key of knowledge, made the law of God of none effect by its traditions, put the priest and his offices in the place of the Saviour and His work, the Church's efforts in place of the Spirit's work, and the intercession of Saints in place of the intercession of Jesus. In short, they taught that Popery had given to the world another gospel than that given by the Son of God. This view, however, of the antagonism betwixt Popery and the gospel never could have been given, had the people not been taught fully what the gospel is. It was, indeed, by holding up truth in the face of error that the odiousness of error came to be clearly seen, and a holy hatred awakened against it. It cannot be concealed that in some parts of the world Papists have been, through mere party spirit, intensely hated, while some of the worst elements of Popery have been embraced. For ages there has been hardly any hatred to the Papists in Scotland, but all along an intense hatred to the doctrines of Popery. This hatred has in it something malignant, but very much of high wisdom and pure love.

But the descendants of the Scottish Reformation have not only been taught to abhor Popery as a frightful perversion and caricature of the Gospel, but also to dread it as the enemy of all true civil liberty. They believe it to be the subtle and necessary enemy of this in all parts of the world. Hence, the very general opposition which the Scottish mind made to that great measure by which Papists were intrusted with the functions of Imperial Legislation. It were worse than folly to descant on this measure now. The great political event of 1829 has yet to unfold its fruits. I merely refer to it to show that the opposition to it in Scotland did not arise from any wish to abridge the privileges of civil liberty, but from a dread that liberty might be put in peril if governmental powers were entrusted to men necessarily the slaves of the most despotic priesthood in the world. We may hope much from counteracting influences, yet it will take more time to show whether the views of the popular mind in Scotland were narrow prejudices, or were views that embraced a profounder wisdom on the principles of liberty than were found in the elaborate speculations of many statesmen, and some liberal divines. There are now obviously certain great questions standing ready for solution in Italy, which, as they may be solved, will throw much light on this matter.

And here I cannot but remark that this deep abhorrence of popery in Scottish Presbyterians has led many to accuse them of bigotry. The charge is groundless. A salutary hatred of deadly error, and an enlightened love of divine truth, is not bigotry. Indeed, I do not know any section of the Church freer from bigotry than Scotch Presbyterians; those of them who love the truth as it is in Jesus, love all who hold that truth, in what corner of the Christian world soever they are found. As a proof of this, it is sufficient to say that in no section of the Protestant Church are the great writers of the Church of England, held in more esteem than among the Presbyterians of the Scottish Reformation. Hervey, Bishop Hall, Newton, and Scott, have possibly had more readers among Presbyterians than among Episcopalians. *The Scotch were taught* what popery really is, and they hate it, but they do not hate it either with the malice or blindness of bigots. May it not be truly said that Scottish Presbyterians cherish an enlightened and liberal attachment to all spiritual truth? They know well how to form a sacred circle of union around the ark and the testimony. But their folly and wickedness often break out in shameful conflicts about the hanging of a loop, or the colouring of a badger's skin, in some particular spot of their common Presbyterian Tabernacle. Their wisdom teaches them union on all that is great, but neither logic nor the scorpion whip of honest scorn can drive them out of the folly of ever fighting for what is ineffably little. But,

2. Next, the Reformation produced among the people a high order of thinking.

Men should be careful not to mistake cause for effect, as well as to notice how cause and effect act and react. There can be no doubt that the revival of learning in Europe was one of the causes that aided the progress of the Reformation. This admitted, it should also be noticed, that there was a certain revival of religion which, as an under current, was one chief cause of the revival of learning. It is not, however, with learning in its high and technical sense that we have at present to do, but with a high development of thought in the popular mind. A few great thinkers may flourish, where the mass of the people scarce think at all. Not seldom have these imperial minds pursued their own speculations, with hardly any reference to the popular mind, or without producing on it any practical effects. Thus, learning may advance, while the bulk of the people are left in gross ignorance. It is when the thinking of the few elevates the mass, that great thinkers are true benefactors to their fellow-men. Now, this was done by the Reformers to some extent in all countries, but to an eminent degree in Scotland. It could not be otherwise when they made the Bible the national book; for the Bible assuredly more than all other books, when studied vigorously, humbly, and prayerfully, is fitted to expand and elevate the whole sum of a people's thinking. Its doctrines are so incomparably grand, yet so practical; its moral principles so simple, yet so comprehensive; in a word, its views of God so just and noble, and its theory of nature and of man so philosophically true, that no one can carefully study its principles without having all his intellectual powers wonderfully cultivated, aud his memory stored with the purest and most lofty sentiments.

This is as little abstract theorizing, as it is national boasting. The principle, to which I have referred, has been demonstrated in Scotland. All intelligent foreigners admit that the Scottish people as well as their Presbyterian descendants in other lands, have been distinguished for strong common sense, clear reasoning, and for sound taste in many departments of thought. But, on this I do not enlarge. Let two observations suffice: 1st. There is no reason to suppose that at the time of the Reformation, the natural intellect of the Scotch was equal, and it was certainly not superior to that of many nations of Europe. Next, if we look for a cause sufficient for the effect we witness, we can find no other for this wonderful awakening of thought in the Scottish mind, than the teaching of the Reformation. Without this, the country might have produced men of genius, but without this there would have been no such widely diffused national elements of common sense, vigorous thinking, and correct taste.

That was a gracious promise, "to the poor the Gospel shall be preached;" and it is a grand reflection, that wherever this Gospel is preached in its purity and power, it not only brings healing for the conscience and the heart, but also brings for the poorest of the people a rich intellectual culture. This has been realized to a wonderful extent in the Scottish national mind; and, here, I cannot but remark that when the English mind yielded that harvest of thought to the world, the like of which had never been seen, it was from the virgin soil of the Reformation.

Yet, let me not be mistaken, for, while I hold that the highest forms of national intellect can only be developed from a widely diffused Christianity among a people, yet the intellectual development never can of itself bless any people. It must be sanctified by heavenly motives, and consecrated to sacred ends, in order to be for their honour or their real good. But then, the intellectual force and attainments of a people, that spring from Christian culture, are thus sanctified; hence they are for the glory of God, and for the good of the world. But,

3. Lastly—The Reformation gave to Scottish Presbyterians a high order of domestic religion.

Religion should be with man everywhere. But its proper home is man's proper home—the family. When the religion of a people betakes itself to the church, it may be orthodox in its creed, in all its movements æsthetically correct, and may be able to boast of much learning, and clerical decorum, but it is no longer the religion of Jesus, purifying, directing, and consoling the popular mind. The religion of the home, and the religion of the sanctuary, must respond to each other. Yet the religion of the home must give the tone, and in a sense be the accompaniment of that of the sanctuary. And just for this plain reason, that Christianity is not the religion of priests, not the religion of days and festivals, but the religion of the homes of men, bringing peace and purity to their conscience, and strength, beauty and order to their affections and life. Could we suppose, which we cannot, that the Reformation had cleansed the sanctuary, but had left the firesides of the land without domestic piety, the advantages to the people would have been small indeed. It was the glory of the Scottish Reformation that it carried religion in all the grandeur of its heavenly principles, and with all the force of its divine motives, to the firesides of the poorest of the people. Whatever it might be in other lands, there it found its proper home in Scotland. For just observe, the Bible was by the Reformers made the book not merely of the pulpit, the college and the school, but emphatically the book of the family. Every father was required to read it in his family, and to teach his children from it, or to teach them from summaries of divine truth drawn from the Bible; while all parents were required to pray in their families, so that in a high and holy sense, each father at the head of his family became the instructing and the intercessory priest of his household. This was the theory; a grand theory indeed. Now, it cannot in truth be affirmed that the theory has ever been fully carried into practice. Had this been done, Presbyterians of Scotch extraction would long since have given to the world a most complete exemplification of an enlightened and practical Christianity. Yet, all boasting apart, there has been enough of practice to show how wise the theory of the Scottish Reformers was, as to domestic religion. There may in many cases have been much of formality in it, and also more of the dogmatic, than of the sweet influences of the affections. Yet, oh! when I think of the sound, full, and simple exhibition of divine truth which I have heard from the lips of poor Scottish peasants, addressing their children on a Sabbath evening, and when I think of their earnest, sober, Christian prayers, offered up for all under their roof, and when I think of the beautiful exemplification by these men in their lives of what they taught by their lips, I cannot but exclaim: "Was family religion in any land ever more wisely planned for the godly upbringing of the young, and for the ripening of the graces of the aged?"

Yes; and it has borne much precious fruit. That high domestic theological training made the people familiar with the whole scheme of the gospel doctrine, the whole principles of moral duty, and the high motives by which duty should be performed. This was much, but not all. It enabled the people to detect the aberrations of pulpit teaching from gospel doctrine, while it qualified plain men for appreciating a very high order of Sabbath-day instruction. Let no man doubt it: the firesides of such a people furnish a surer protection for sound doctrine from the pulpit, and clerical consistency of conduct, than either imperial statutes or the decrees of church courts; and, moreover, do not such a people give strength as well as scope to a pious minister's efforts, which he can well understand, but cannot easily express? The law of action and reaction is beautifully seen when the pulpit is seen blessing houses and homes; and they in their way bringing down rich blessings on the pulpit. And oh! was it not also beautiful to see that while the minister in that land made many homes virtuous, pious, and happy, no man was more loved and revered than he, in these homes. The love and respect for their minister among Scottish Presbyterians was cherished for ages with singular ardour, wisdom, and sobriety. This sentiment sprung from the domestic piety of the people, and did much not only to strengthen the piety, but to mould the whole character of the people. I appeal to the patriotic and pious Scotchmen to say, if among all the institutions of his native land, he knows one which, if transported into all other lands, where Scotch Presbyterians dwell, would be a greater blessing than the institution of the domestic piety of these simple but godly homes. These are but a few of the benefits. Time prevents me mentioning more. Nor will time allow of the suitable application which this celebration demands. There are two views which must at least be slightly touched on.

1st. This celebration ought to awaken ardent gratitude. The benefits we see which God conferred on us through the Scottish Reformation, are many and precious. Well may we exclaim, "hath God dealt so with any other people?" To some others He has given much; but I think to none so much as to us. Truly "the lines have fallen to us in pleasant places, and we have a goodly heritage." For three hundred years there has been open vision in Scotland. Possibly in no other land, or to no other people, save to Scotch Presbyterians, has the finished work of a Saviour been preached more fully or more truly. And in the olden times, when wicked men arose to quench gospel light, what noble martyrs have started up within our Church, ready to die for Christ, rather than deny Him as their Saviour and their King. If the truth was not always preserved in purity in the pulpits, and if the heroism of these men was sometimes wasted on false theories, yet there was much of grand, simple truth, in these old times, and much of true moral heroism in these noble men and women who sealed their testimony with their blood, that the land might have a pure gospel, and the Church have Christ for her sole King. Now, mark it, we have got from these men, and from others that came after them, an open Bible, a gospel pulpit, a scriptural school education, an admirable system of domestic piety, and their moral and godly heroism as ensamples. Now, my brethren, all this and more God has given us, and that unspeakable boon, civil and religious liberty; and for all this, ought not our hearts to burn with gratitude to God on this day?

2ndly. But next, let us on this day try to realize the responsibility which these Reformation benefits involve.

THE REFORMATION IN SCOTLAND.

"To whom much is given, of them shall much be required." To boast of privileges without realizing responsibilities, is a folly that must lead to the saddest consequences. There is not a man whose mind has been nurtured by these Reformation principles who has not received the five talents. But if *he* was justly condemned, who buried the one talent, what must be their condemnation who pervert the *five?* Woe unto thee, Capernaum; thou hast been exalted to heaven in privileges, and for their abuse thou shalt be cast down to hell; and it shall be more tolerable for Sodom and Gomorrah than for thee. Ah! my countrymen;—ah! my fellow Presbyterians, may not this terrible doom hang over us? Think of it; exalted to heaven in privileges, are these realized? are these rightly employed? If not, woe and alas! for God is just. Well, then, let us this day rejoice with trembling, and ask with humility, "Lord, what wouldst thou have us to do?" Yes, there is work for all Christian men in this land. There are yet living, men who can remember when there were in Upper Canada but a few scattered settlements, with a few thousand inhabitants. There is now in the same region a greater population than was in all Scotland at the time of the Union. There will be children in the Sabbath school to-day that will live to see possibly a population of ten millions to the west of the Ottawa. What a thought! But this is the solemn part of it for us. What are we doing to give to these millions, who are to live after us, a high-toned piety, and a pure and high-toned morality? For be assured that what we are now thinking, speaking, and doing in our homes—in our Sabbath schools and in our churches, will, when our bodies are dissolved into dust, be found moulding into spiritual life, and heavenly beauty, those generations of men and women, or will be found shedding through their souls a deadening and demoralizing influence, which shall lead them down to perdition. Ah! my brethren, if from these homes and churches, in our native land, there hath come with us a hallowed influence into this land, let us see to it, that we send it down to our children's children, so that at the next celebration they may rise up and call us blessed, and thank God that the doctrines of the Scottish Reformation were brought to this country by their ancestors, and taught with some measure of truthfulness and zeal.—Amen, Amen, and Amen. One word more. The next celebration, 1960. Children of men, there will not be one of us here. When the bells ring on that Sabbath morning, not one of us will hear them. Where then, if not here? As thou sowest now, oh! man, thou shalt then be reaping. It will not be to us 1960; it will be eternity.

www.ingramcontent.com/pod-product-compliance
Lightning Source LLC
Chambersburg PA
CBHW031952230426
43672CB00010B/2131